NELSON • MORA • CASSATA

HEXED™

THE HARLOT & THE THIEF VOLUME THREE

BOOM! STUDIOS

BOOM! STUDIOS

HEXED: THE HARLOT & THE THIEF Volume Three, August 2016. Published by BOOM! Studios, a division of Boom Entertainment, Inc. Hexed: The Harlot & The Thief is ™ & © 2016 Michael Alan Nelson and Boom Entertainment, Inc. Originally published in single magazine form as HEXED ONGOING No. 9-12. ™ & © 2015 Michael Alan Nelson and Boom Entertainment, Inc. All rights reserved. BOOM! Studios™ and the BOOM! Studios logo are trademarks of Boom Entertainment, Inc., registered in various countries and categories. All characters, events, and institutions depicted herein are fictional. Any similarity between any of the names, characters, persons, events, and/ or institutions in this publication to actual names, characters, and persons, whether living or dead, events, and/or institutions is unintended and purely coincidental. BOOM! Studios does not read or accept unsolicited submissions of ideas, stories, or artwork.

A catalog record of this book is available from OCLC and from the BOOM! Studios website, www.boom-studios. com, on the Librarians Page.

BOOM! Studios, 5670 Wilshire Boulevard, Suite 450, Los Angeles, CA 90036-5679. Printed in China. First Printing.

ISBN: 978-1-60886-853-7, eISBN: 978-1-61398-524-3

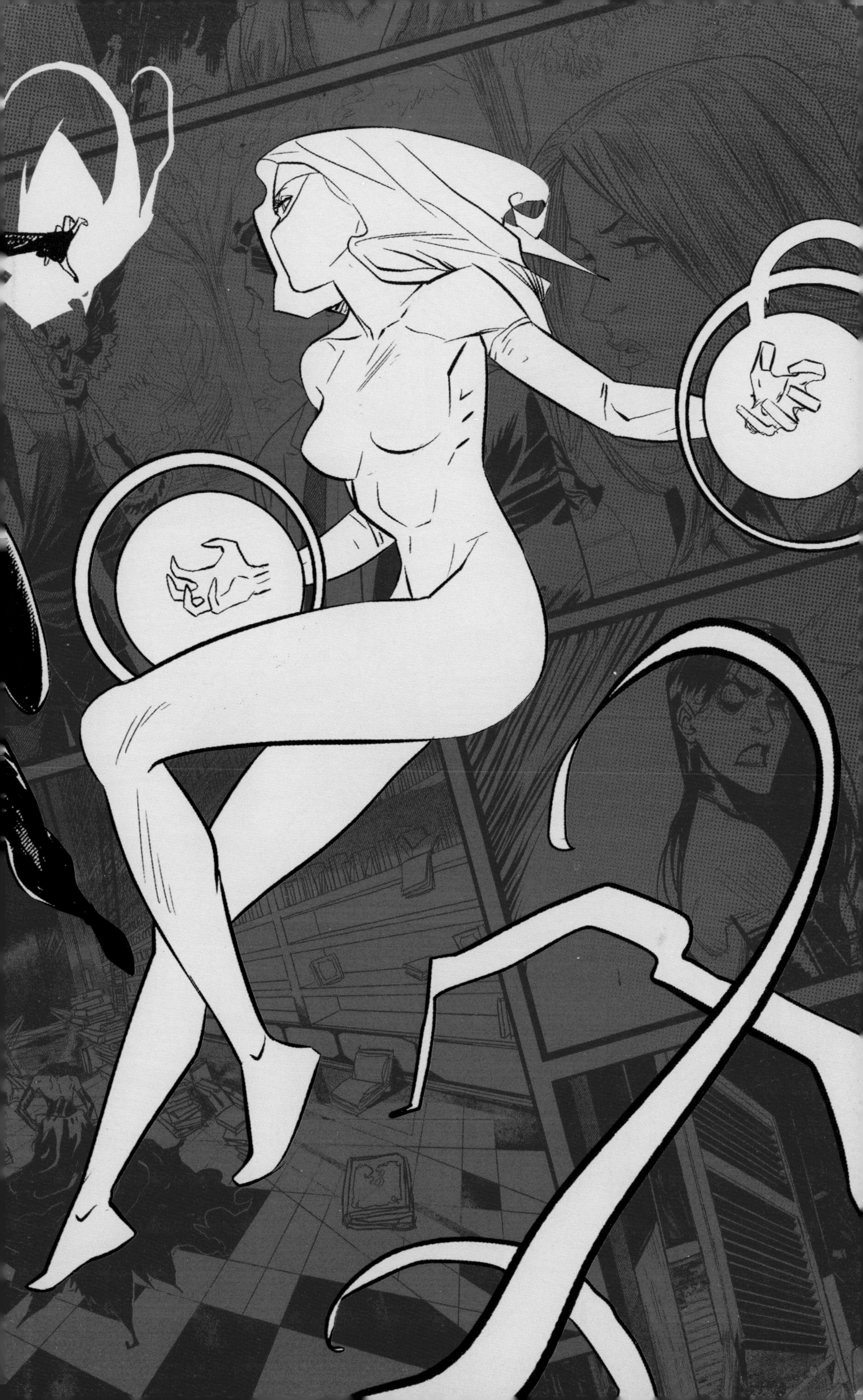

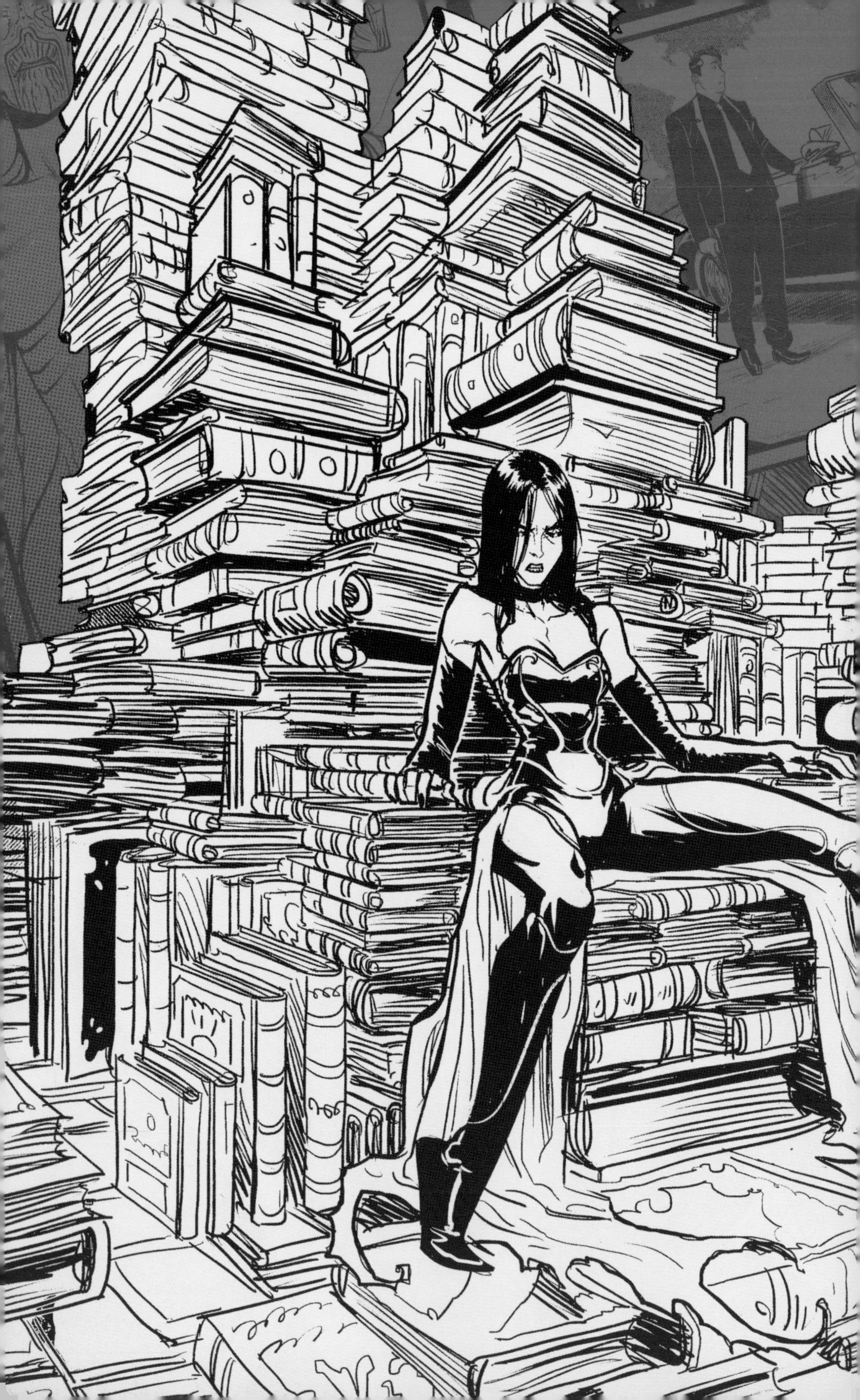

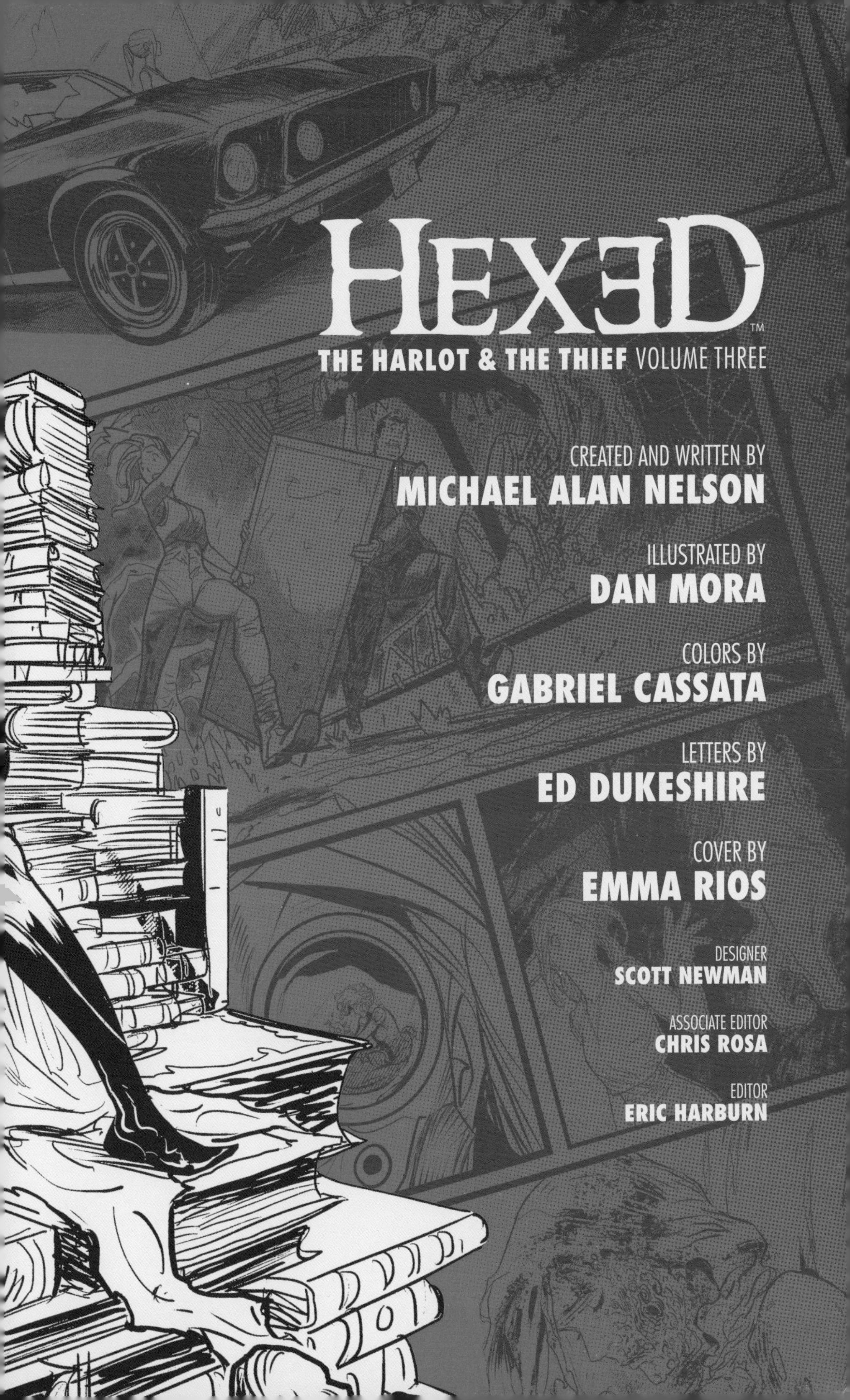

HEXED™

THE HARLOT & THE THIEF VOLUME THREE

CREATED AND WRITTEN BY
MICHAEL ALAN NELSON

ILLUSTRATED BY
DAN MORA

COLORS BY
GABRIEL CASSATA

LETTERS BY
ED DUKESHIRE

COVER BY
EMMA RIOS

DESIGNER
SCOTT NEWMAN

ASSOCIATE EDITOR
CHRIS ROSA

EDITOR
ERIC HARBURN

CHAPTER 9

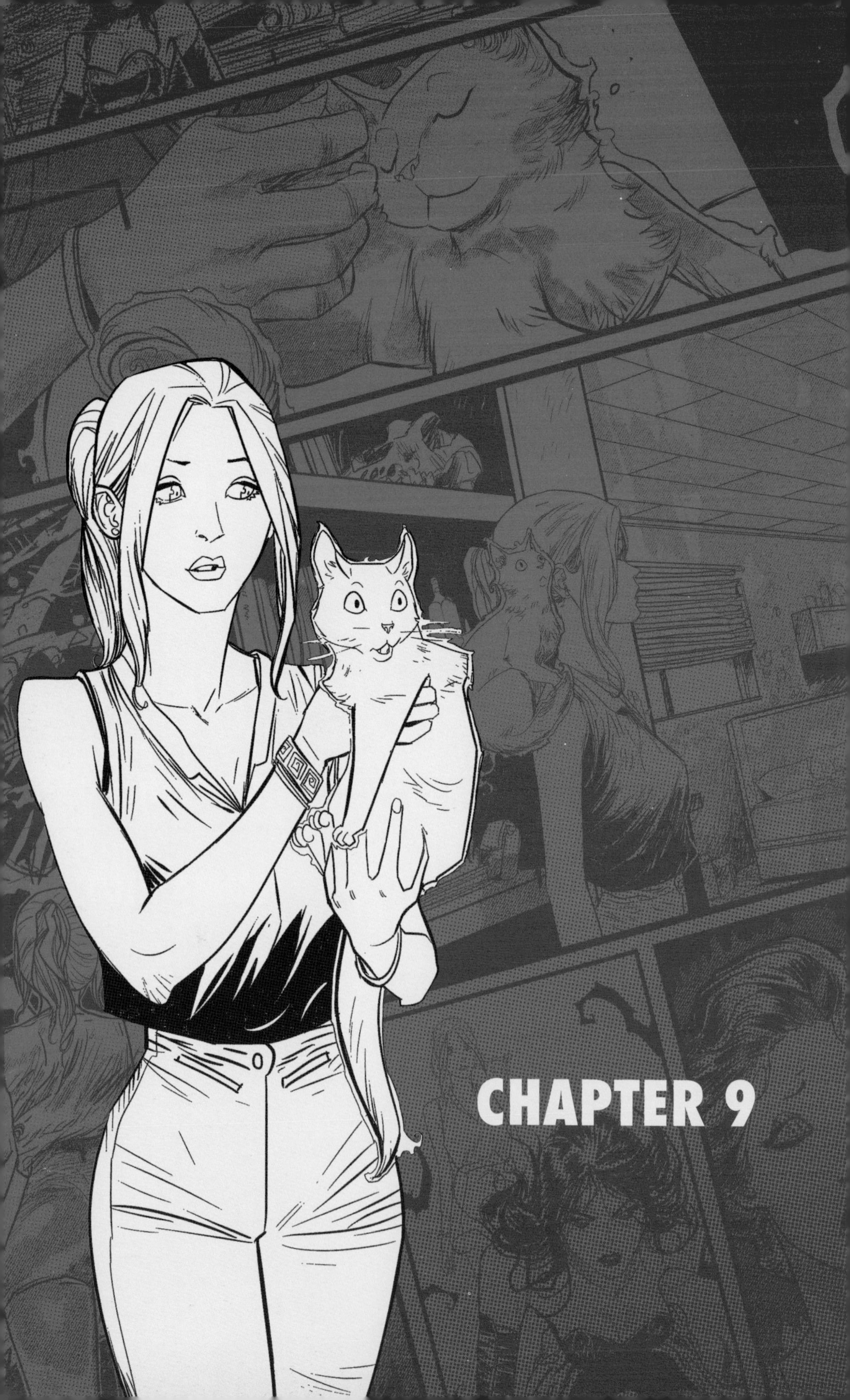

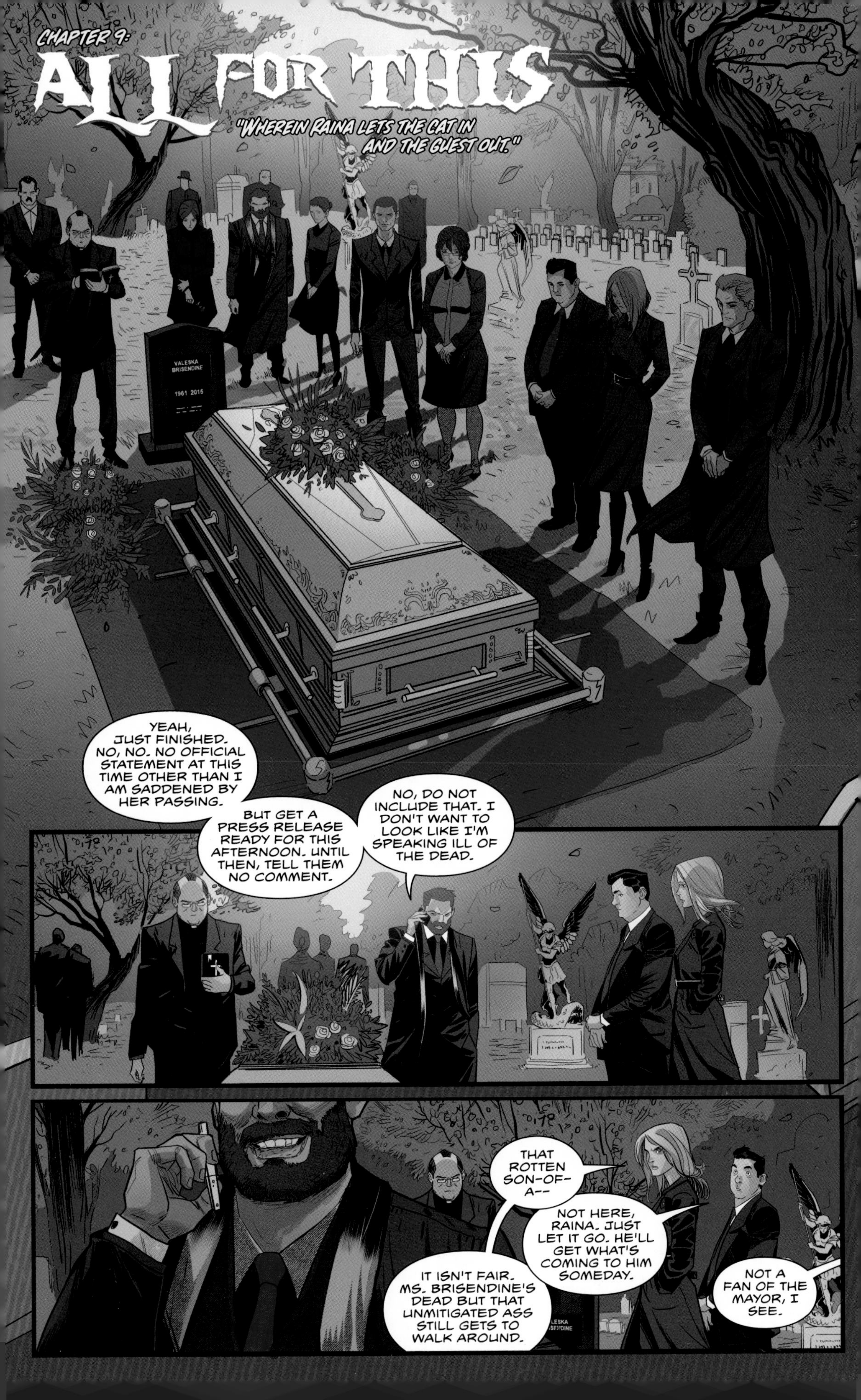
CHAPTER 9:
ALL FOR THIS
"WHEREIN RAINA LETS THE CAT IN AND THE GUEST OUT."
VALESKA BRISENDINE
1961 2015
YEAH, JUST FINISHED. NO, NO. NO OFFICIAL STATEMENT AT THIS TIME OTHER THAN I AM SADDENED BY HER PASSING.
BUT GET A PRESS RELEASE READY FOR THIS AFTERNOON. UNTIL THEN, TELL THEM NO COMMENT.
NO, DO NOT INCLUDE THAT. I DON'T WANT TO LOOK LIKE I'M SPEAKING ILL OF THE DEAD.
THAT ROTTEN SON-OF-A--
IT ISN'T FAIR. MS. BRISENDINE'S DEAD BUT THAT UNMITIGATED ASS STILL GETS TO WALK AROUND.
NOT HERE, RAINA. JUST LET IT GO. HE'LL GET WHAT'S COMING TO HIM SOMEDAY.
NOT A FAN OF THE MAYOR, I SEE.

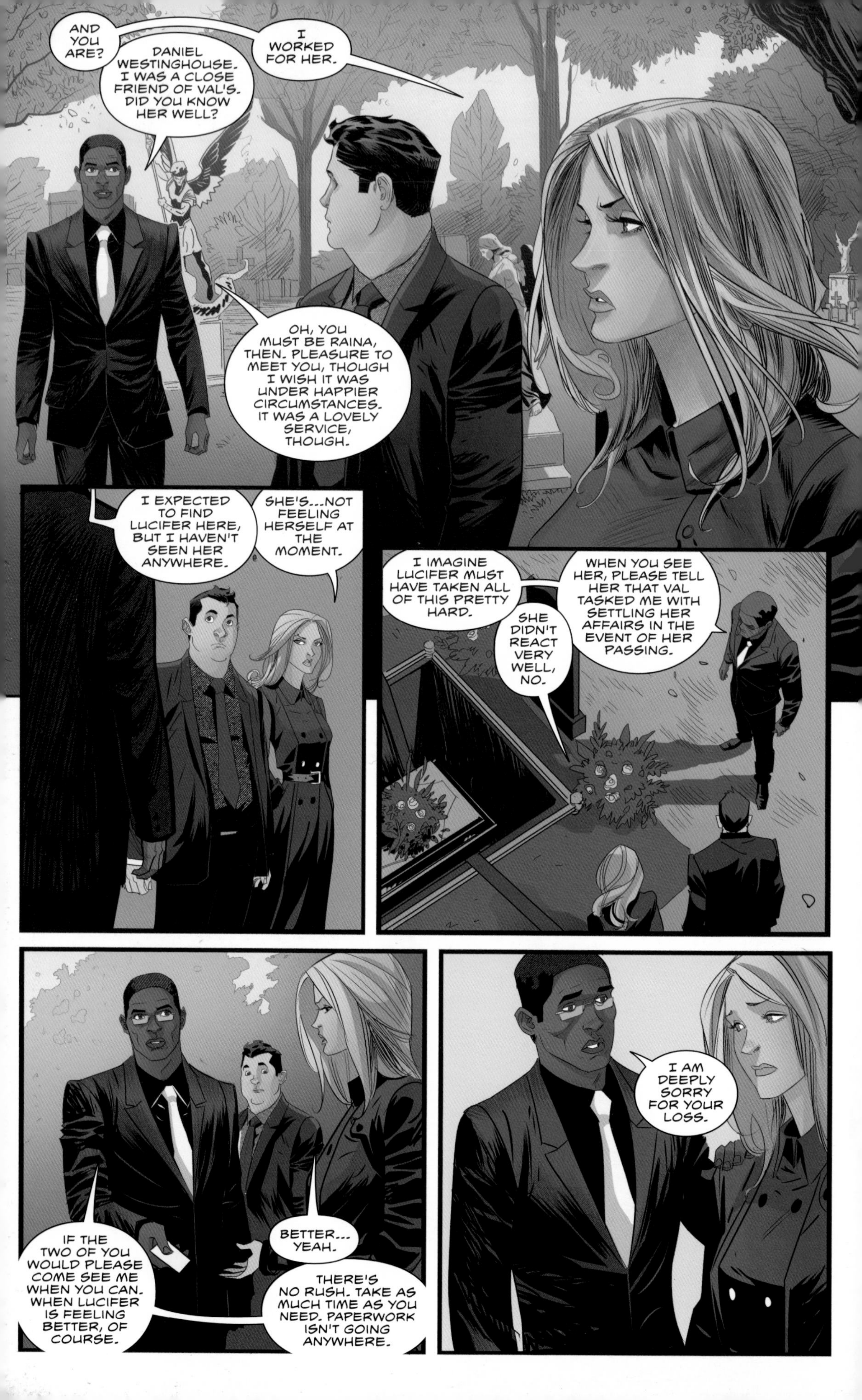
AND YOU ARE?
I WORKED FOR HER.
DANIEL WESTINGHOUSE. I WAS A CLOSE FRIEND OF VAL'S. DID YOU KNOW HER WELL?
OH, YOU MUST BE RAINA, THEN. PLEASURE TO MEET YOU, THOUGH I WISH IT WAS UNDER HAPPIER CIRCUMSTANCES. IT WAS A LOVELY SERVICE, THOUGH.
I EXPECTED TO FIND LUCIFER HERE, BUT I HAVEN'T SEEN HER ANYWHERE.
SHE'S...NOT FEELING HERSELF AT THE MOMENT.
I IMAGINE LUCIFER MUST HAVE TAKEN ALL OF THIS PRETTY HARD.
SHE DIDN'T REACT VERY WELL, NO.
WHEN YOU SEE HER, PLEASE TELL HER THAT VAL TASKED ME WITH SETTLING HER AFFAIRS IN THE EVENT OF HER PASSING.
IF THE TWO OF YOU WOULD PLEASE COME SEE ME WHEN YOU CAN. WHEN LUCIFER IS FEELING BETTER, OF COURSE.
BETTER... YEAH.
THERE'S NO RUSH. TAKE AS MUCH TIME AS YOU NEED. PAPERWORK ISN'T GOING ANYWHERE.
I AM DEEPLY SORRY FOR YOUR LOSS.

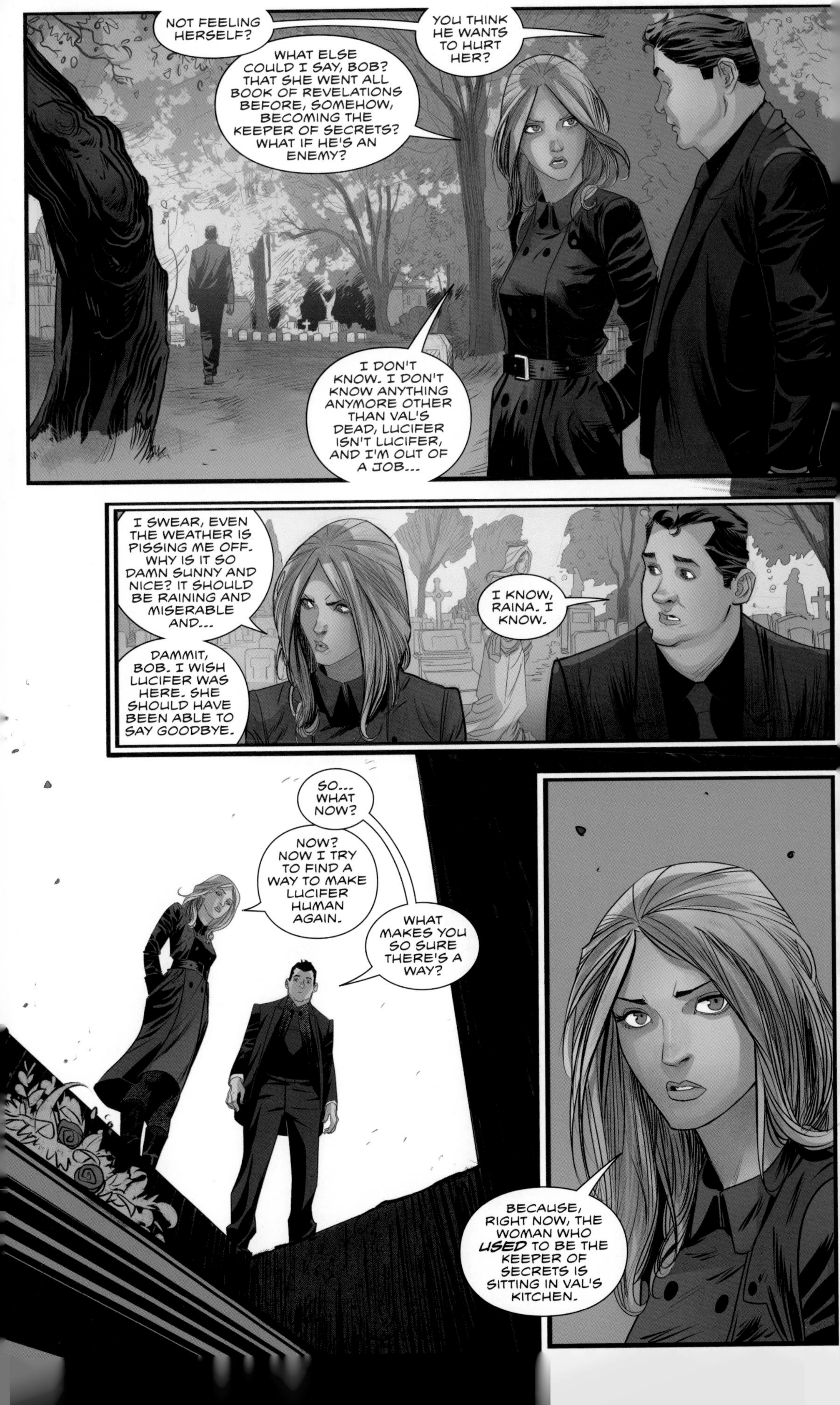
NOT FEELING HERSELF?
YOU THINK HE WANTS TO HURT HER?
WHAT ELSE COULD I SAY, BOB? THAT SHE WENT ALL BOOK OF REVELATIONS BEFORE, SOMEHOW, BECOMING THE KEEPER OF SECRETS? WHAT IF HE'S AN ENEMY?
I DON'T KNOW. I DON'T KNOW ANYTHING ANYMORE OTHER THAN VAL'S DEAD, LUCIFER ISN'T LUCIFER, AND I'M OUT OF A JOB...
I SWEAR, EVEN THE WEATHER IS PISSING ME OFF. WHY IS IT SO DAMN SUNNY AND NICE? IT SHOULD BE RAINING AND MISERABLE AND...
I KNOW, RAINA. I KNOW.
DAMMIT, BOB. I WISH LUCIFER WAS HERE. SHE SHOULD HAVE BEEN ABLE TO SAY GOODBYE.
SO... WHAT NOW?
NOW? NOW I TRY TO FIND A WAY TO MAKE LUCIFER HUMAN AGAIN.
WHAT MAKES YOU SO SURE THERE'S A WAY?
BECAUSE, RIGHT NOW, THE WOMAN WHO USED TO BE THE KEEPER OF SECRETS IS SITTING IN VAL'S KITCHEN.

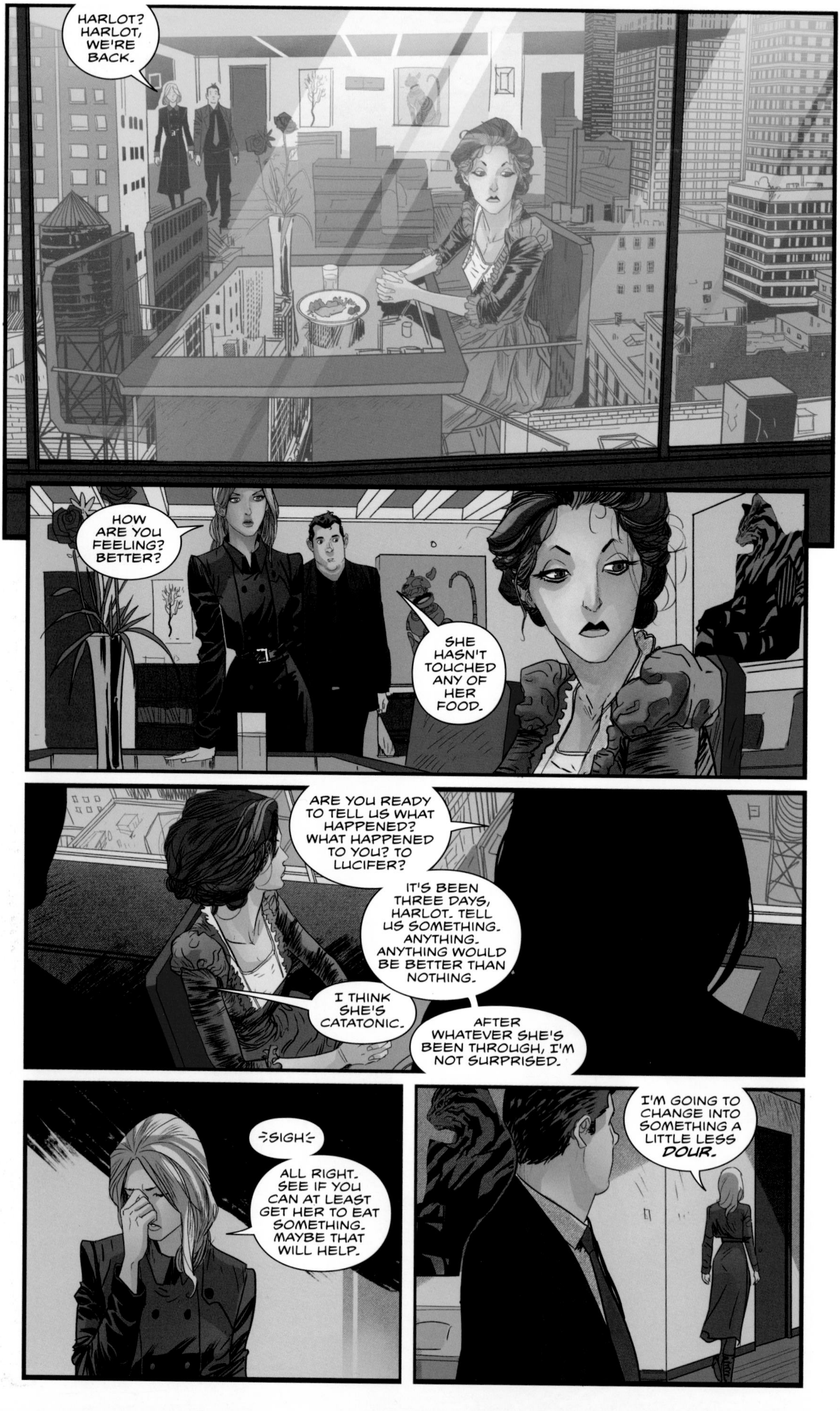

HARLOT? HARLOT, WE'RE BACK.
HOW ARE YOU FEELING? BETTER?
SHE HASN'T TOUCHED ANY OF HER FOOD.
ARE YOU READY TO TELL US WHAT HAPPENED? WHAT HAPPENED TO YOU? TO LUCIFER?
IT'S BEEN THREE DAYS, HARLOT. TELL US SOMETHING. ANYTHING. ANYTHING WOULD BE BETTER THAN NOTHING.
I THINK SHE'S CATATONIC.
AFTER WHATEVER SHE'S BEEN THROUGH, I'M NOT SURPRISED.
=SIGH=
ALL RIGHT. SEE IF YOU CAN AT LEAST GET HER TO EAT SOMETHING. MAYBE THAT WILL HELP.
I'M GOING TO CHANGE INTO SOMETHING A LITTLE LESS DOUR.

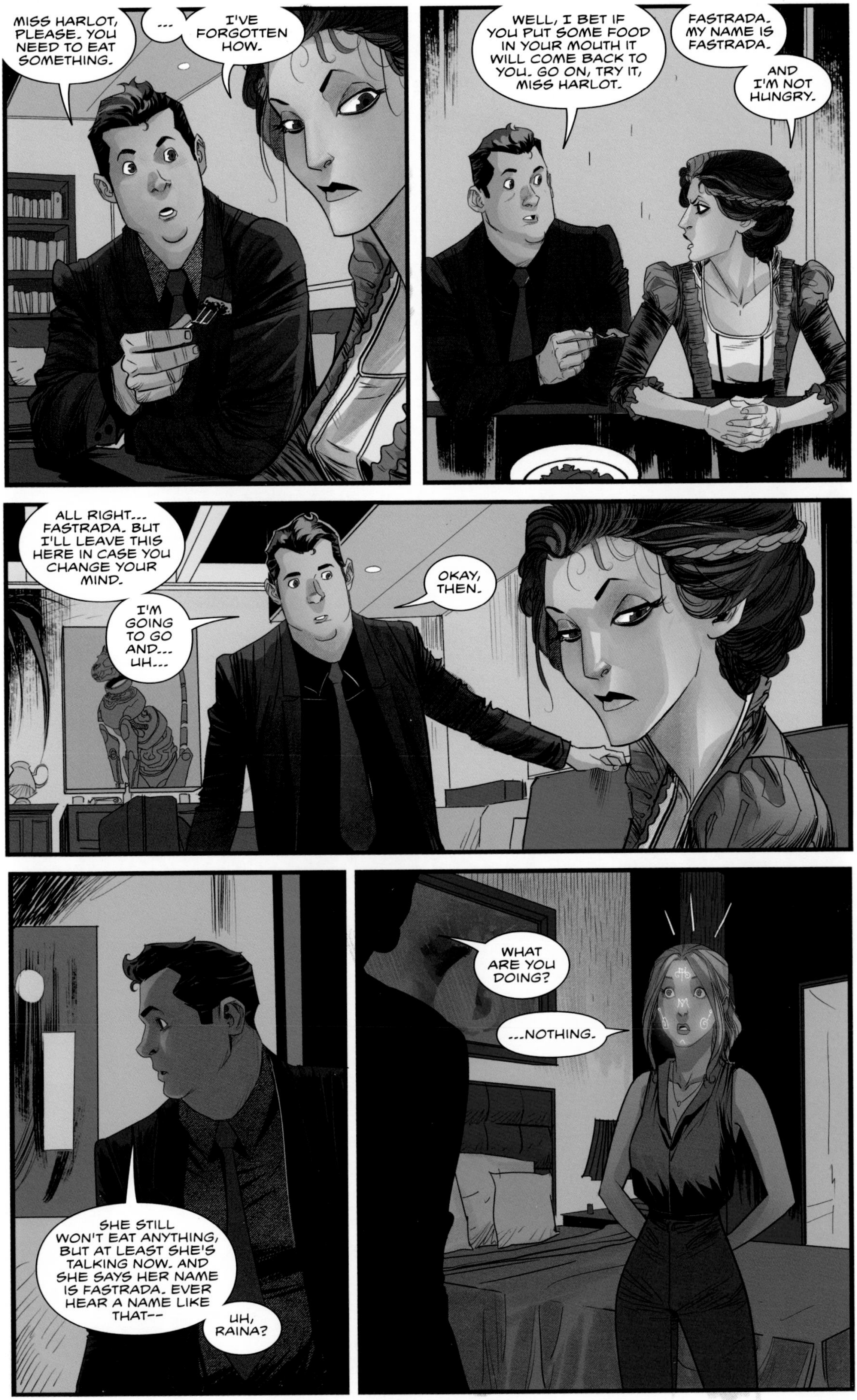
MISS HARLOT, PLEASE. YOU NEED TO EAT SOMETHING.
...
I'VE FORGOTTEN HOW.
WELL, I BET IF YOU PUT SOME FOOD IN YOUR MOUTH IT WILL COME BACK TO YOU. GO ON, TRY IT, MISS HARLOT.
FASTRADA. MY NAME IS FASTRADA.
AND I'M NOT HUNGRY.
ALL RIGHT... FASTRADA. BUT I'LL LEAVE THIS HERE IN CASE YOU CHANGE YOUR MIND.
I'M GOING TO GO AND... UH...
OKAY, THEN.
SHE STILL WON'T EAT ANYTHING, BUT AT LEAST SHE'S TALKING NOW. AND SHE SAYS HER NAME IS FASTRADA. EVER HEAR A NAME LIKE THAT--
UH, RAINA?
WHAT ARE YOU DOING?
...NOTHING.

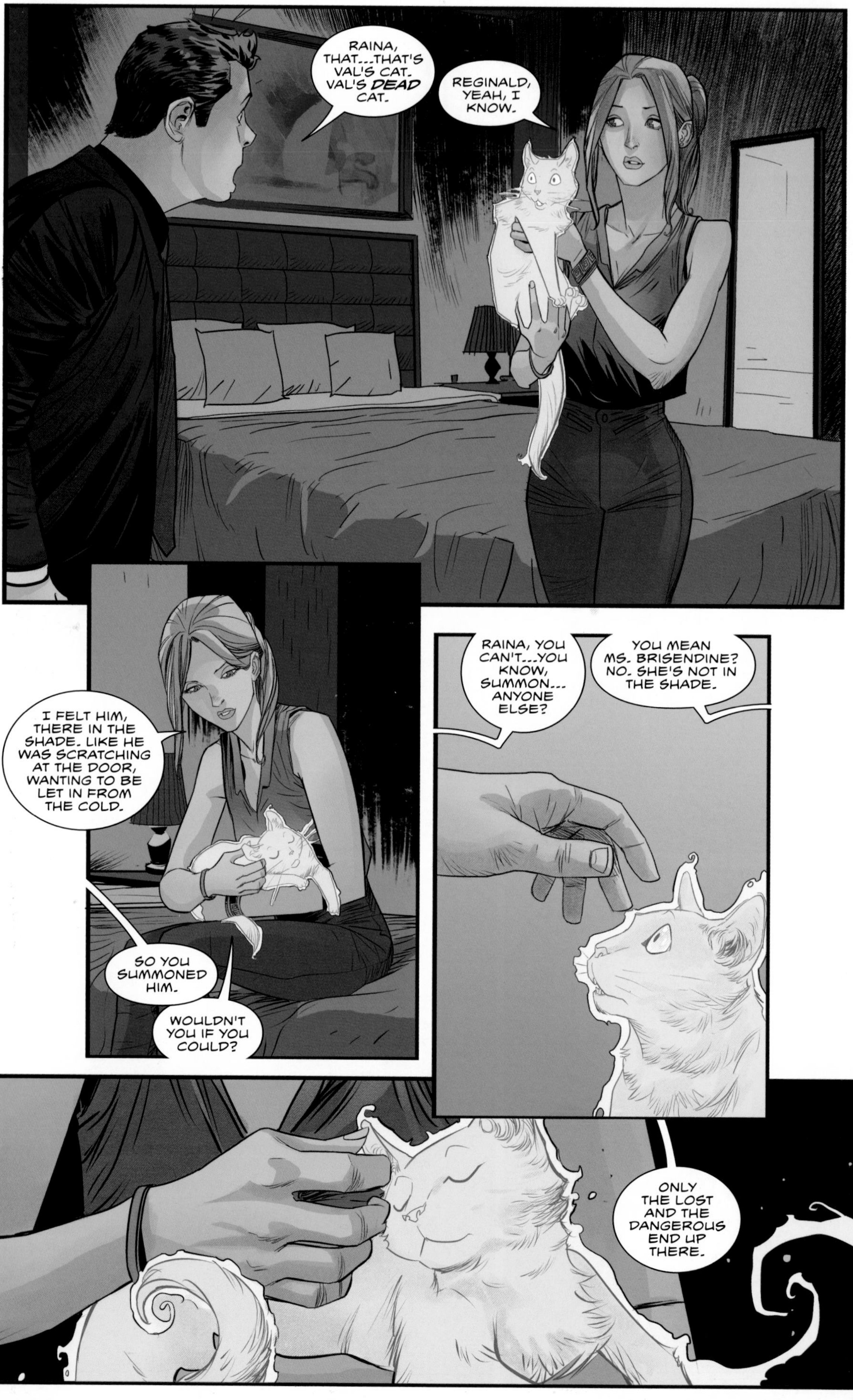
RAINA, THAT...THAT'S VAL'S CAT. VAL'S DEAD CAT.
REGINALD, YEAH, I KNOW.
I FELT HIM, THERE IN THE SHADE. LIKE HE WAS SCRATCHING AT THE DOOR, WANTING TO BE LET IN FROM THE COLD.
SO YOU SUMMONED HIM.
WOULDN'T YOU IF YOU COULD?
RAINA, YOU CAN'T...YOU KNOW, SUMMON... ANYONE ELSE?
YOU MEAN MS. BRISENDINE? NO. SHE'S NOT IN THE SHADE.
ONLY THE LOST AND THE DANGEROUS END UP THERE.

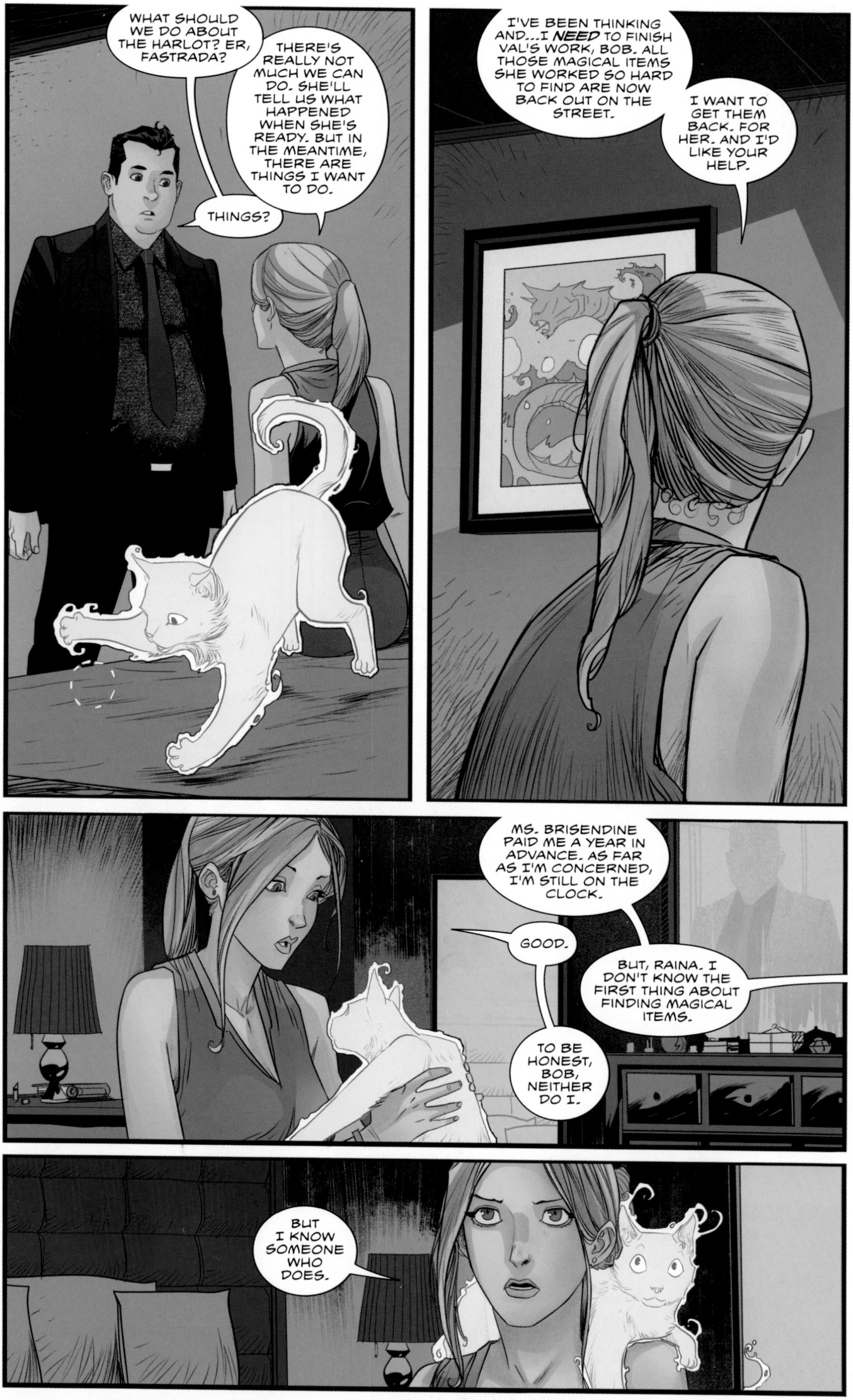
WHAT SHOULD WE DO ABOUT THE HARLOT? ER, FASTRADA?
THERE'S REALLY NOT MUCH WE CAN DO. SHE'LL TELL US WHAT HAPPENED WHEN SHE'S READY. BUT IN THE MEANTIME, THERE ARE THINGS I WANT TO DO.
THINGS?
I'VE BEEN THINKING AND...I NEED TO FINISH VAL'S WORK, BOB. ALL THOSE MAGICAL ITEMS SHE WORKED SO HARD TO FIND ARE NOW BACK OUT ON THE STREET.
I WANT TO GET THEM BACK. FOR HER. AND I'D LIKE YOUR HELP.
MS. BRISENDINE PAID ME A YEAR IN ADVANCE. AS FAR AS I'M CONCERNED, I'M STILL ON THE CLOCK.
GOOD.
BUT, RAINA. I DON'T KNOW THE FIRST THING ABOUT FINDING MAGICAL ITEMS.
TO BE HONEST, BOB, NEITHER DO I.
BUT I KNOW SOMEONE WHO DOES.

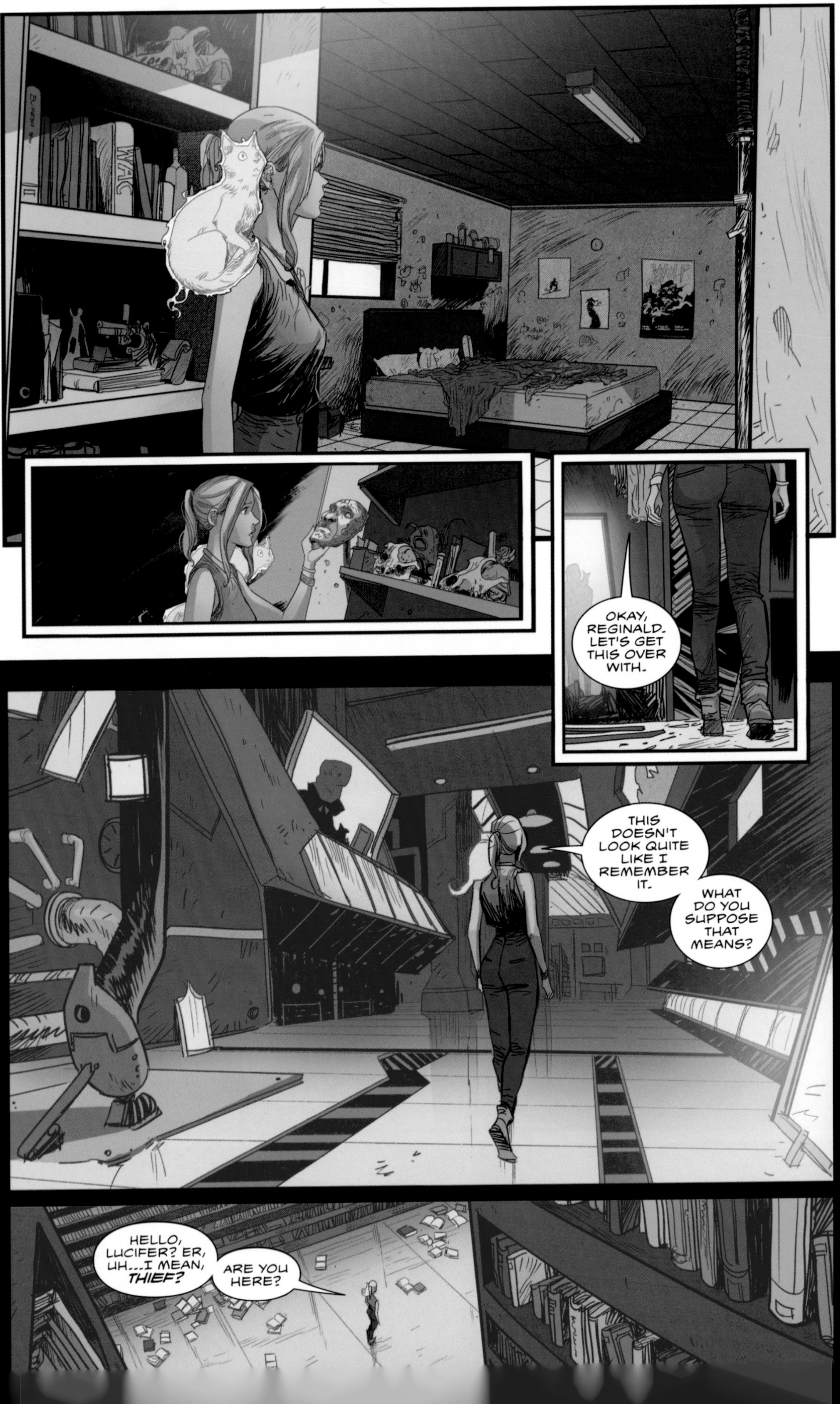
OKAY, REGINALD. LET'S GET THIS OVER WITH.
THIS DOESN'T LOOK QUITE LIKE I REMEMBER IT.
WHAT DO YOU SUPPOSE THAT MEANS?
HELLO, LUCIFER? ER, UH... I MEAN, THIEF?
ARE YOU HERE?

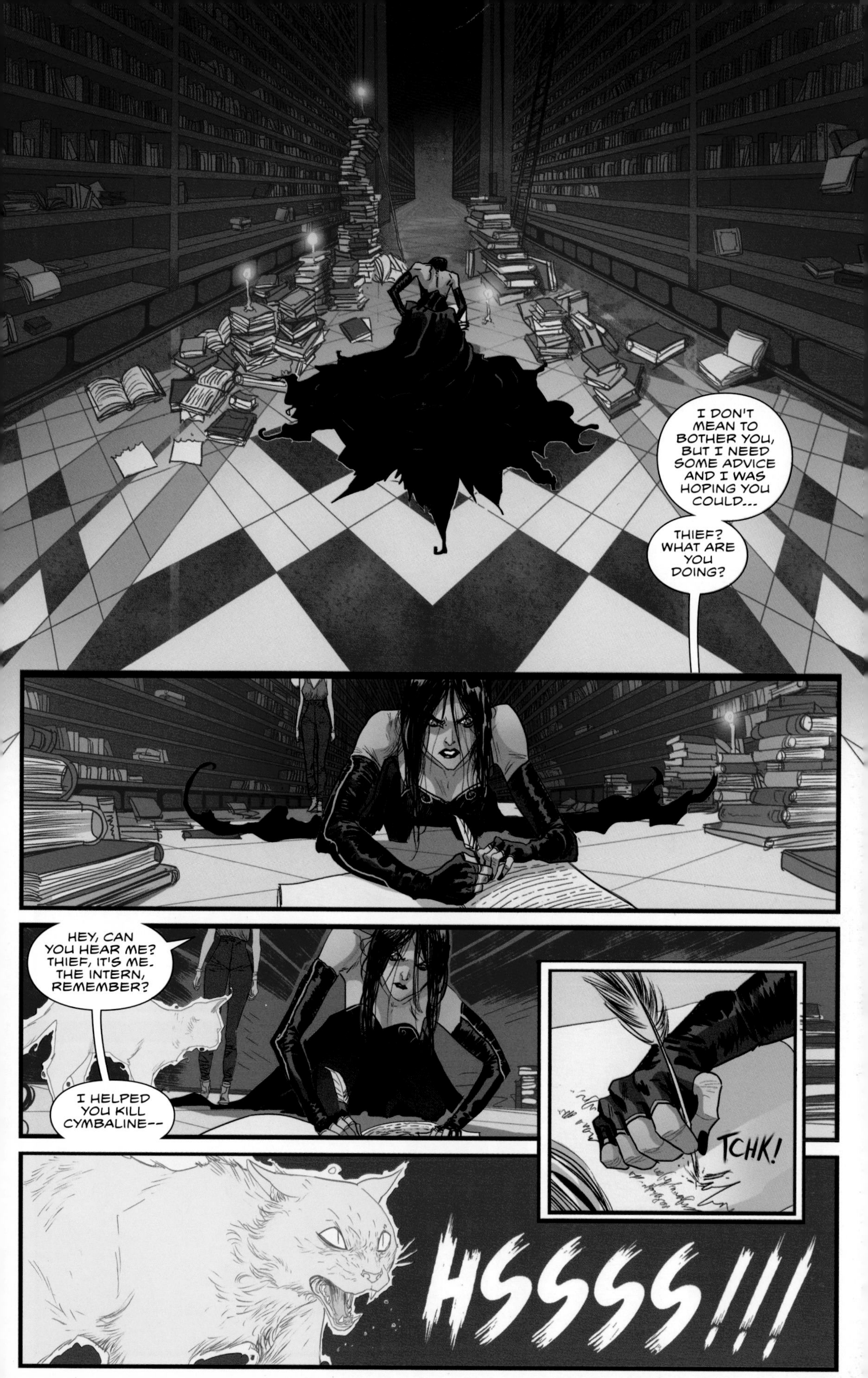
I DON'T MEAN TO BOTHER YOU, BUT I NEED SOME ADVICE AND I WAS HOPING YOU COULD...
THIEF? WHAT ARE YOU DOING?
HEY, CAN YOU HEAR ME? THIEF, IT'S ME. THE INTERN, REMEMBER?
I HELPED YOU KILL CYMBALINE--
TCHK!
HSSSS!!!

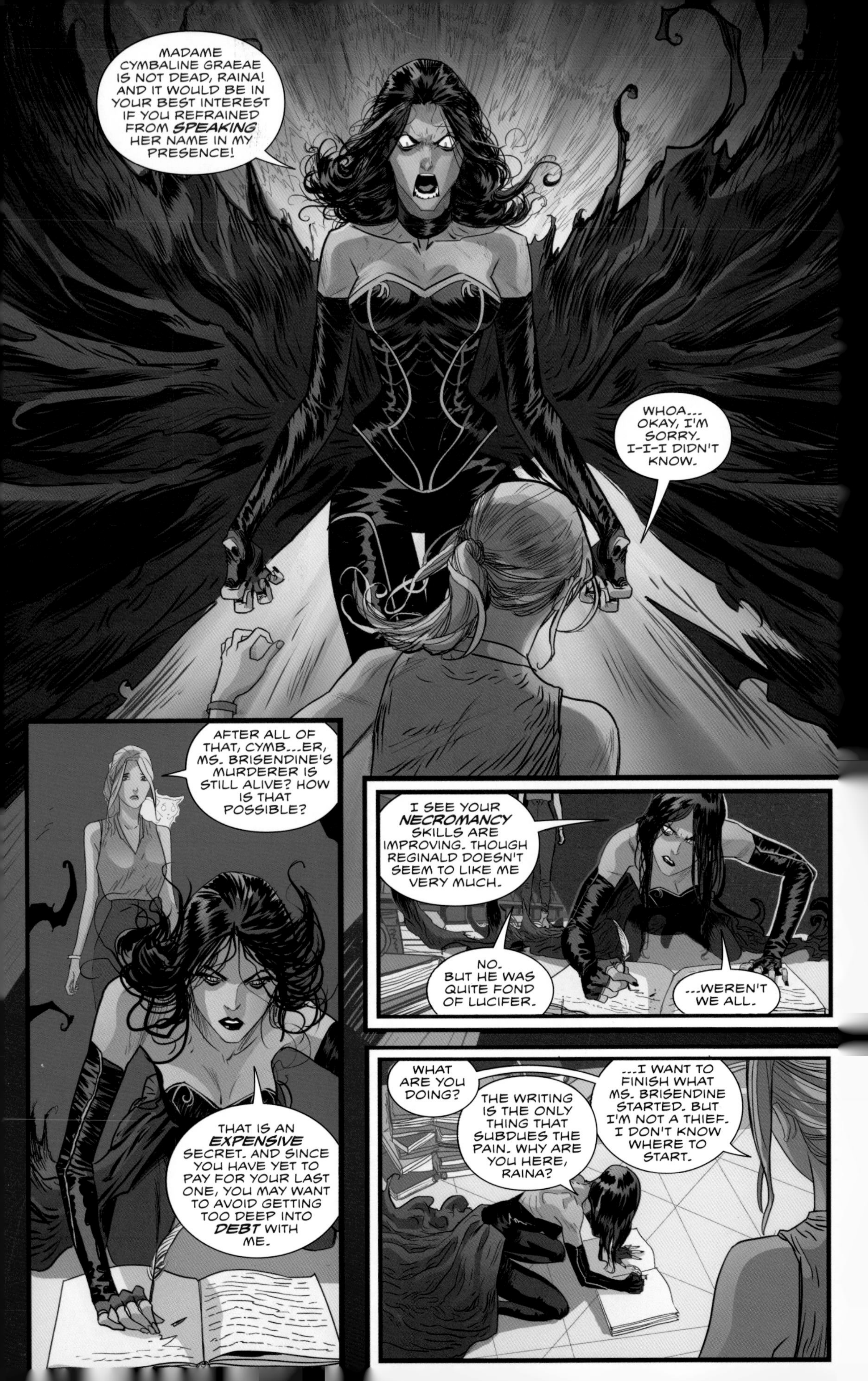
MADAME CYMBALINE GRAEAE IS NOT DEAD, RAINA! AND IT WOULD BE IN YOUR BEST INTEREST IF YOU REFRAINED FROM SPEAKING HER NAME IN MY PRESENCE!
WHOA... OKAY, I'M SORRY. I-I-I DIDN'T KNOW.
AFTER ALL OF THAT, CYMB...ER, MS. BRISENDINE'S MURDERER IS STILL ALIVE? HOW IS THAT POSSIBLE?
THAT IS AN EXPENSIVE SECRET. AND SINCE YOU HAVE YET TO PAY FOR YOUR LAST ONE, YOU MAY WANT TO AVOID GETTING TOO DEEP INTO DEBT WITH ME.
I SEE YOUR NECROMANCY SKILLS ARE IMPROVING. THOUGH REGINALD DOESN'T SEEM TO LIKE ME VERY MUCH.
NO. BUT HE WAS QUITE FOND OF LUCIFER.
...WEREN'T WE ALL.
WHAT ARE YOU DOING?
THE WRITING IS THE ONLY THING THAT SUBDUES THE PAIN. WHY ARE YOU HERE, RAINA?
...I WANT TO FINISH WHAT MS. BRISENDINE STARTED. BUT I'M NOT A THIEF. I DON'T KNOW WHERE TO START.

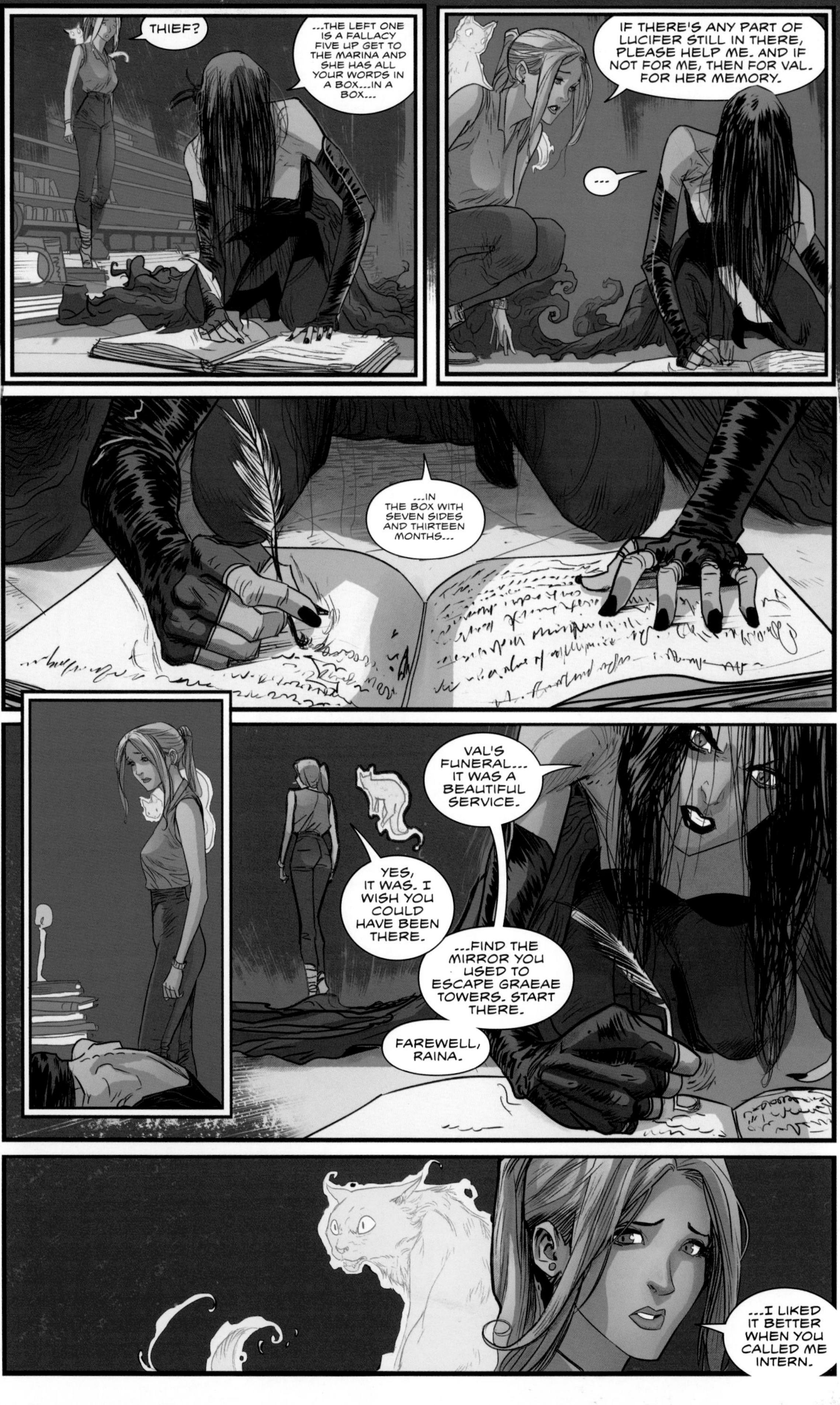
THIEF?
...THE LEFT ONE IS A FALLACY FIVE UP GET TO THE MARINA AND SHE HAS ALL YOUR WORDS IN A BOX...IN A BOX...
IF THERE'S ANY PART OF LUCIFER STILL IN THERE, PLEASE HELP ME. AND IF NOT FOR ME, THEN FOR VAL. FOR HER MEMORY.
...
...IN THE BOX WITH SEVEN SIDES AND THIRTEEN MONTHS...
VAL'S FUNERAL... IT WAS A BEAUTIFUL SERVICE.
YES, IT WAS. I WISH YOU COULD HAVE BEEN THERE.
...FIND THE MIRROR YOU USED TO ESCAPE GRAEAE TOWERS. START THERE.
FAREWELL, RAINA.
...I LIKED IT BETTER WHEN YOU CALLED ME INTERN.

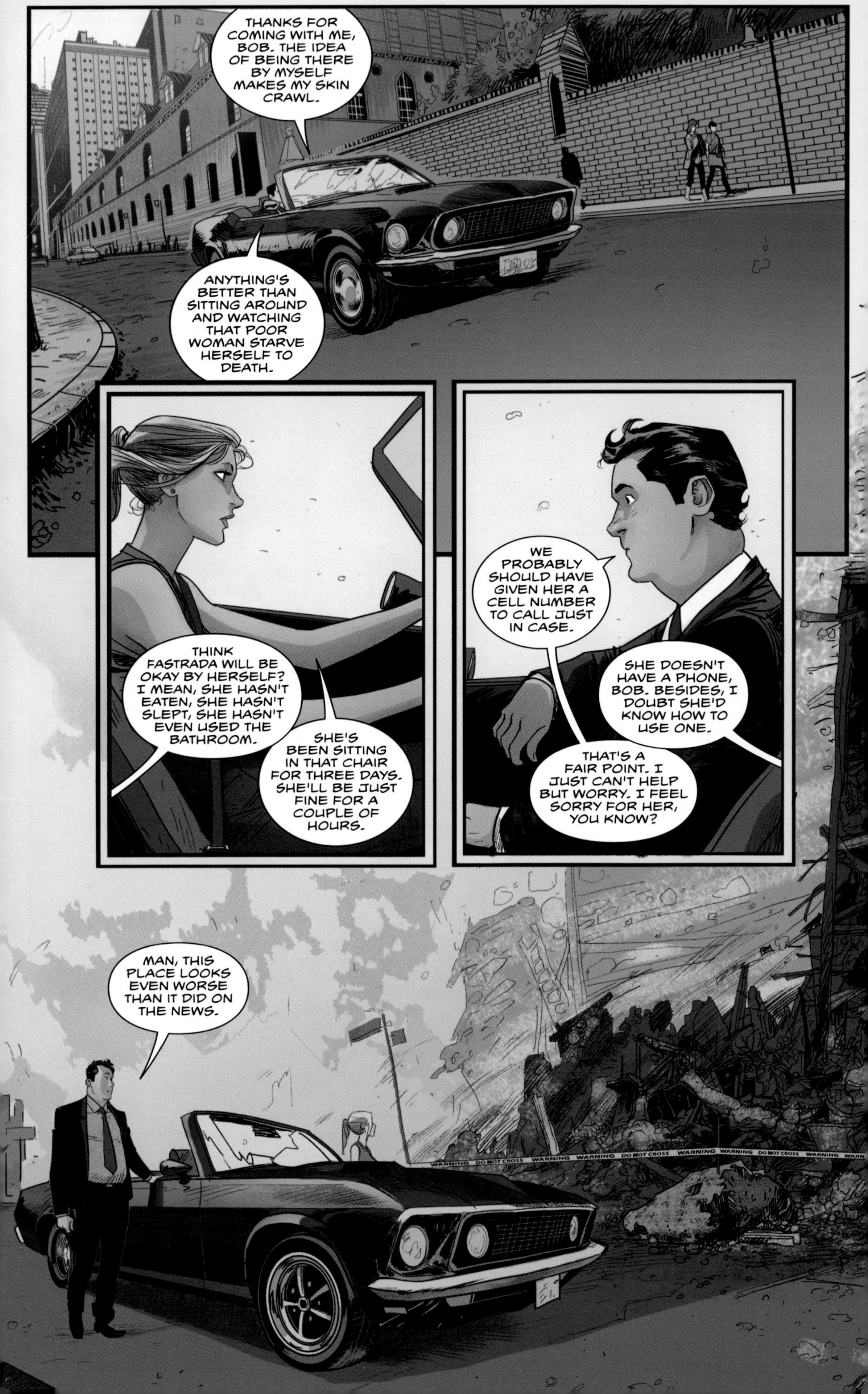
THANKS FOR COMING WITH ME, BOB. THE IDEA OF BEING THERE BY MYSELF MAKES MY SKIN CRAWL.
ANYTHING'S BETTER THAN SITTING AROUND AND WATCHING THAT POOR WOMAN STARVE HERSELF TO DEATH.
THINK FASTRADA WILL BE OKAY BY HERSELF? I MEAN, SHE HASN'T EATEN, SHE HASN'T SLEPT, SHE HASN'T EVEN USED THE BATHROOM.
SHE'S BEEN SITTING IN THAT CHAIR FOR THREE DAYS. SHE'LL BE JUST FINE FOR A COUPLE OF HOURS.
WE PROBABLY SHOULD HAVE GIVEN HER A CELL NUMBER TO CALL JUST IN CASE.
SHE DOESN'T HAVE A PHONE, BOB. BESIDES, I DOUBT SHE'D KNOW HOW TO USE ONE.
THAT'S A FAIR POINT. I JUST CAN'T HELP BUT WORRY. I FEEL SORRY FOR HER, YOU KNOW?
MAN, THIS PLACE LOOKS EVEN WORSE THAN IT DID ON THE NEWS.
WARNING DO NOT CROSS WARNING WARNING DO NOT CROSS WARNING WARNING DO NOT CROSS WARNING

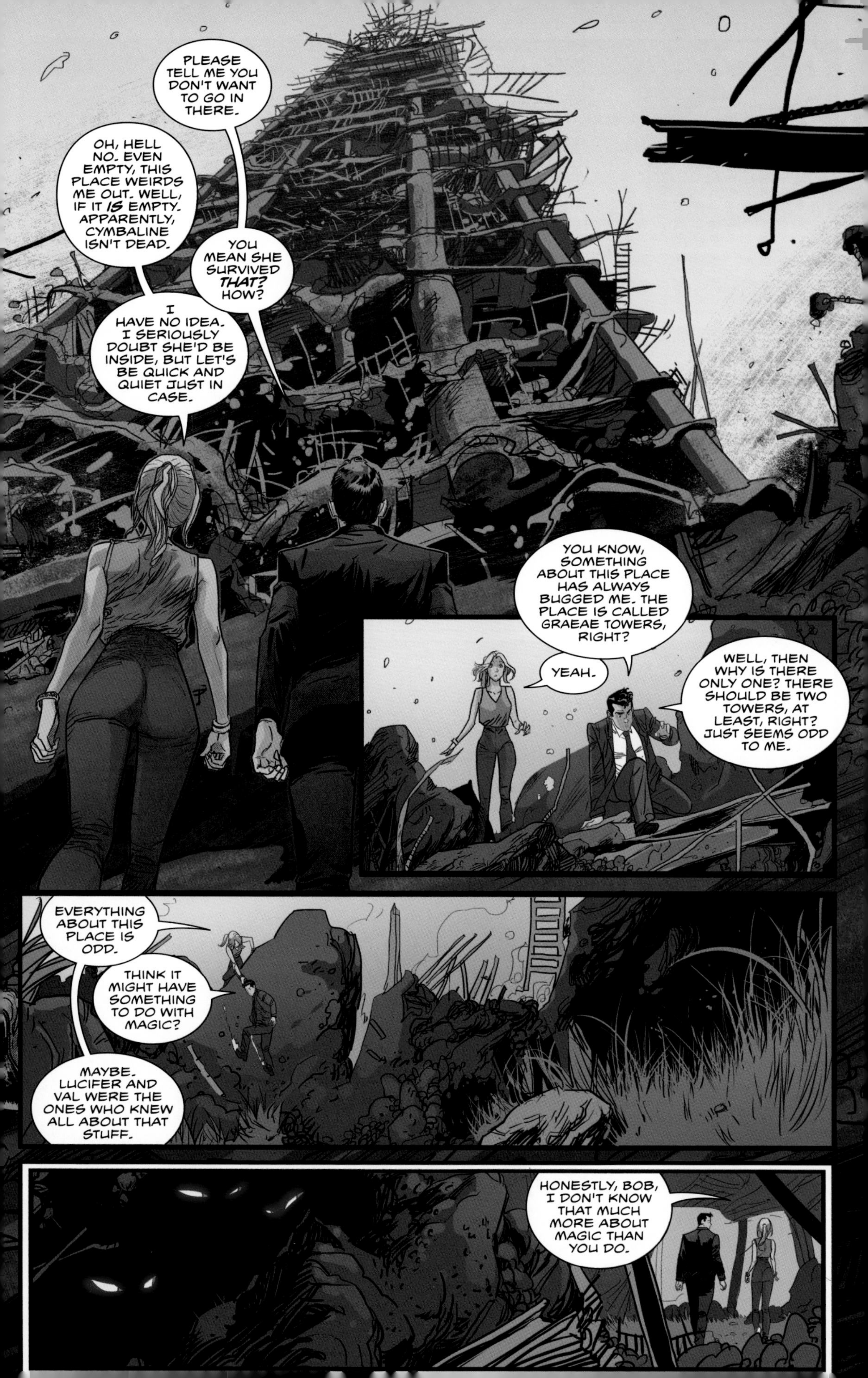
PLEASE TELL ME YOU DON'T WANT TO GO IN THERE.
OH, HELL NO. EVEN EMPTY, THIS PLACE WEIRDS ME OUT. WELL, IF IT *IS* EMPTY. APPARENTLY, CYMBALINE ISN'T DEAD.
YOU MEAN SHE SURVIVED ***THAT?*** HOW?
I HAVE NO IDEA. I SERIOUSLY DOUBT SHE'D BE INSIDE, BUT LET'S BE QUICK AND QUIET JUST IN CASE.
YOU KNOW, SOMETHING ABOUT THIS PLACE HAS ALWAYS BUGGED ME. THE PLACE IS CALLED GRAEAE TOWERS, RIGHT?
YEAH.
WELL, THEN WHY IS THERE ONLY ONE? THERE SHOULD BE TWO TOWERS, AT LEAST, RIGHT? JUST SEEMS ODD TO ME.
EVERYTHING ABOUT THIS PLACE IS ODD.
THINK IT MIGHT HAVE SOMETHING TO DO WITH MAGIC?
MAYBE. LUCIFER AND VAL WERE THE ONES WHO KNEW ALL ABOUT THAT STUFF.
HONESTLY, BOB, I DON'T KNOW THAT MUCH MORE ABOUT MAGIC THAN YOU DO.

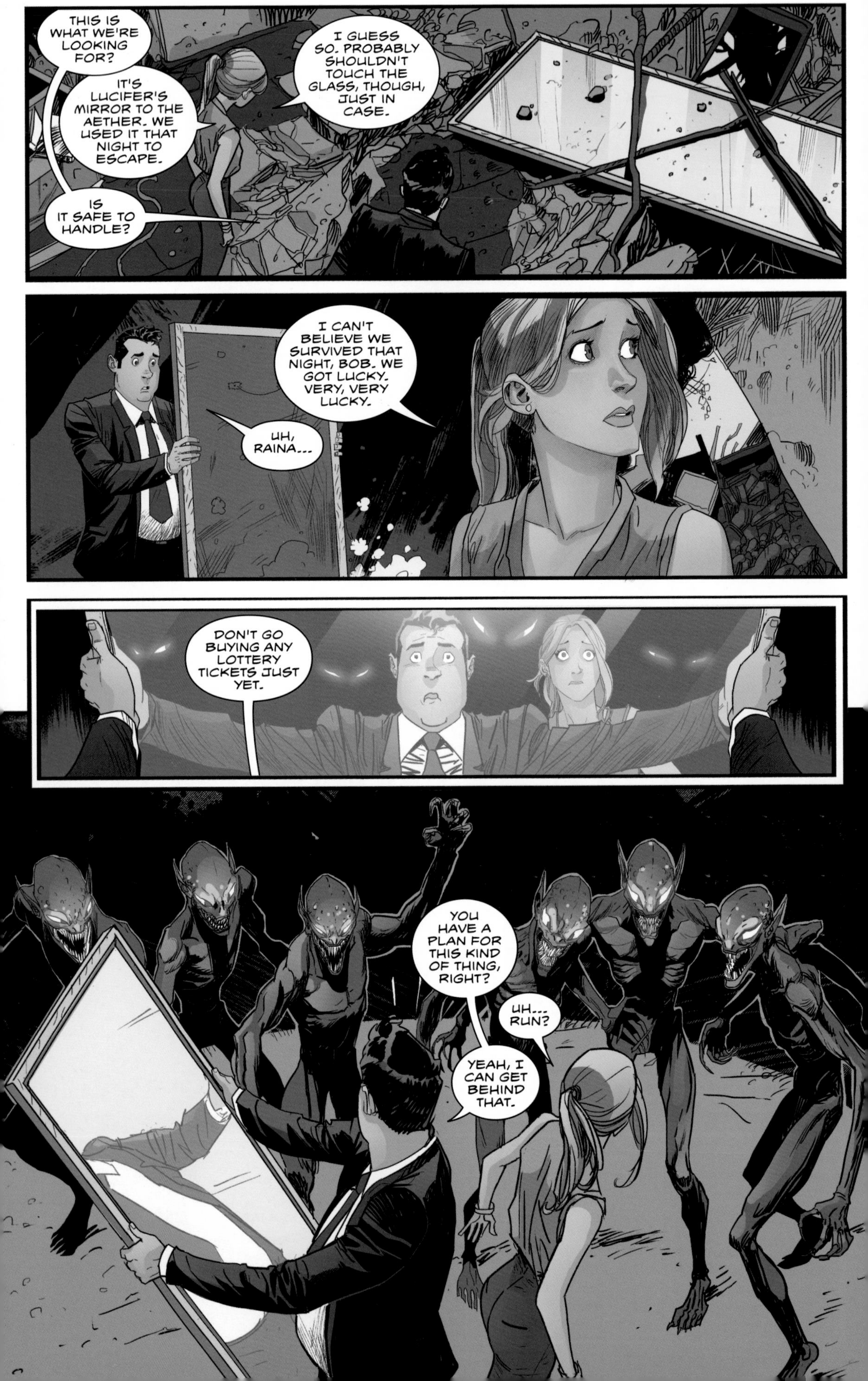
THIS IS WHAT WE'RE LOOKING FOR?
IT'S LUCIFER'S MIRROR TO THE AETHER. WE USED IT THAT NIGHT TO ESCAPE.
IS IT SAFE TO HANDLE?
I GUESS SO. PROBABLY SHOULDN'T TOUCH THE GLASS, THOUGH, JUST IN CASE.
I CAN'T BELIEVE WE SURVIVED THAT NIGHT, BOB. WE GOT LUCKY. VERY, VERY LUCKY.
UH, RAINA...
DON'T GO BUYING ANY LOTTERY TICKETS JUST YET.
YOU HAVE A PLAN FOR THIS KIND OF THING, RIGHT?
UH... RUN?
YEAH, I CAN GET BEHIND THAT.

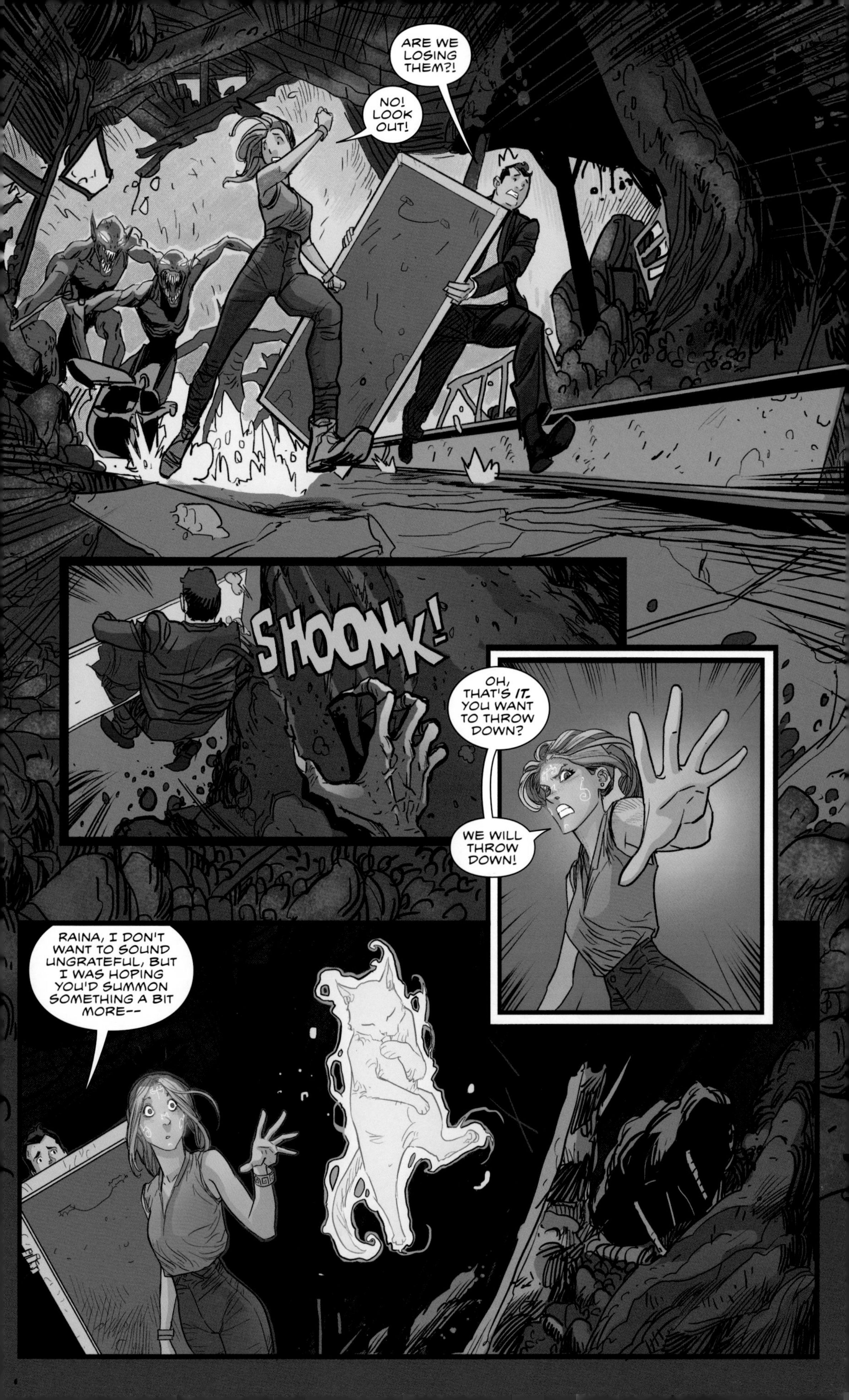
ARE WE LOSING THEM?!
NO! LOOK OUT!
SHOONK!
OH, THAT'S IT. YOU WANT TO THROW DOWN?
WE WILL THROW DOWN!
RAINA, I DON'T WANT TO SOUND UNGRATEFUL, BUT I WAS HOPING YOU'D SUMMON SOMETHING A BIT MORE--

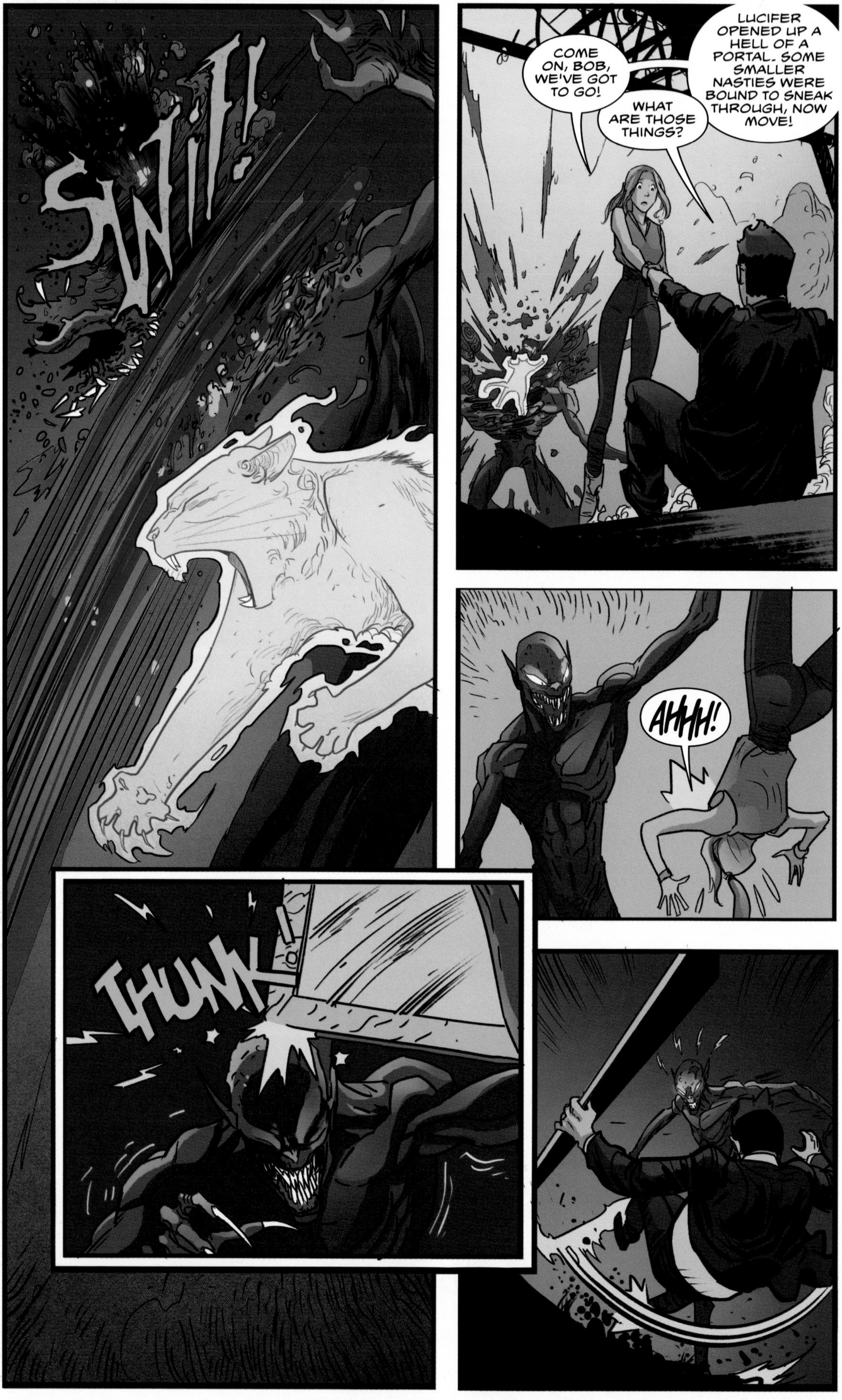
SWIIII!
COME ON, BOB, WE'VE GOT TO GO!
WHAT ARE THOSE THINGS?
LUCIFER OPENED UP A HELL OF A PORTAL. SOME SMALLER NASTIES WERE BOUND TO SNEAK THROUGH, NOW MOVE!
AHHH!
THUNK

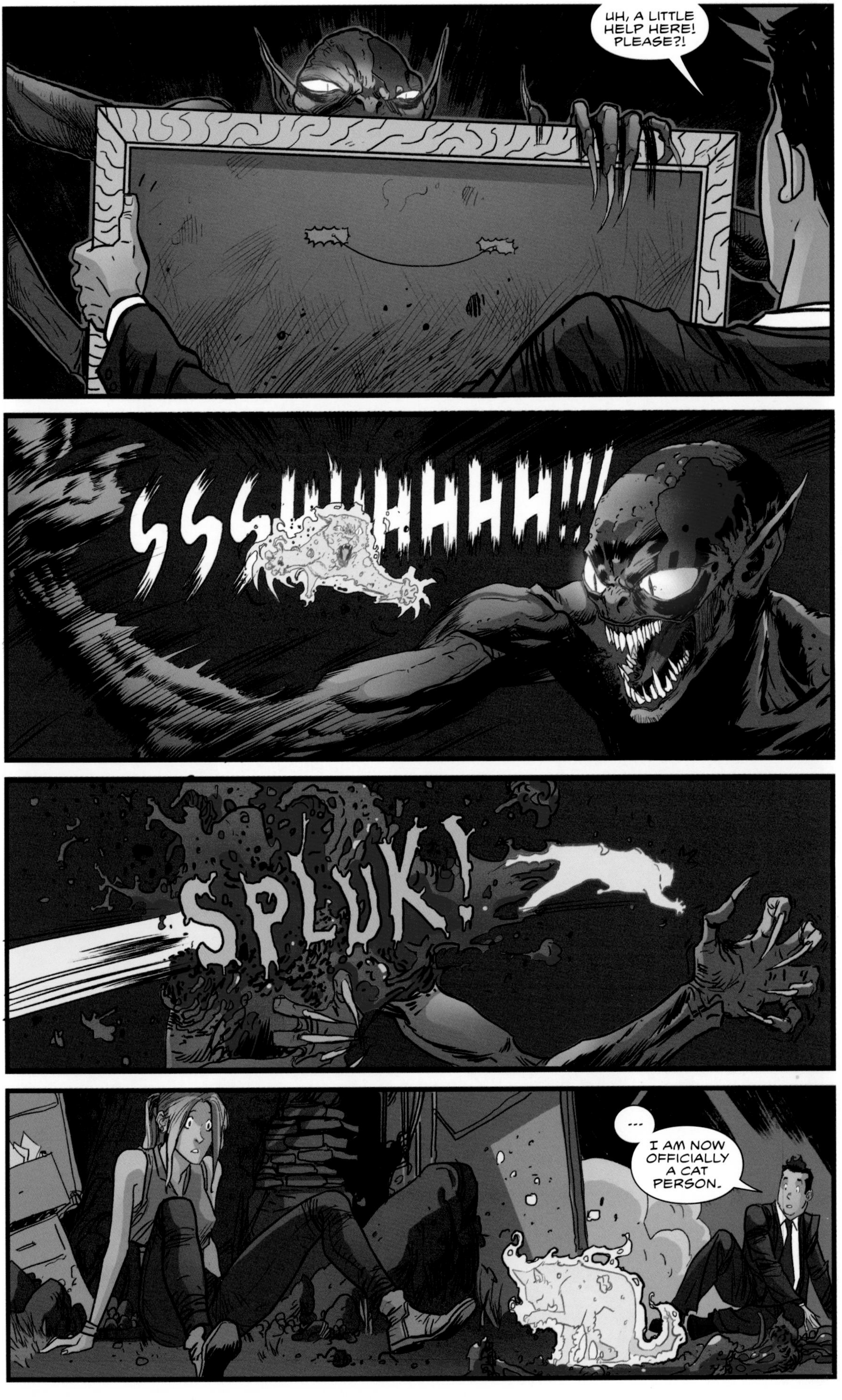

UH, A LITTLE HELP HERE! PLEASE?!
SSSHHHHHH!!!
SPLUK!
...
I AM NOW OFFICIALLY A CAT PERSON.

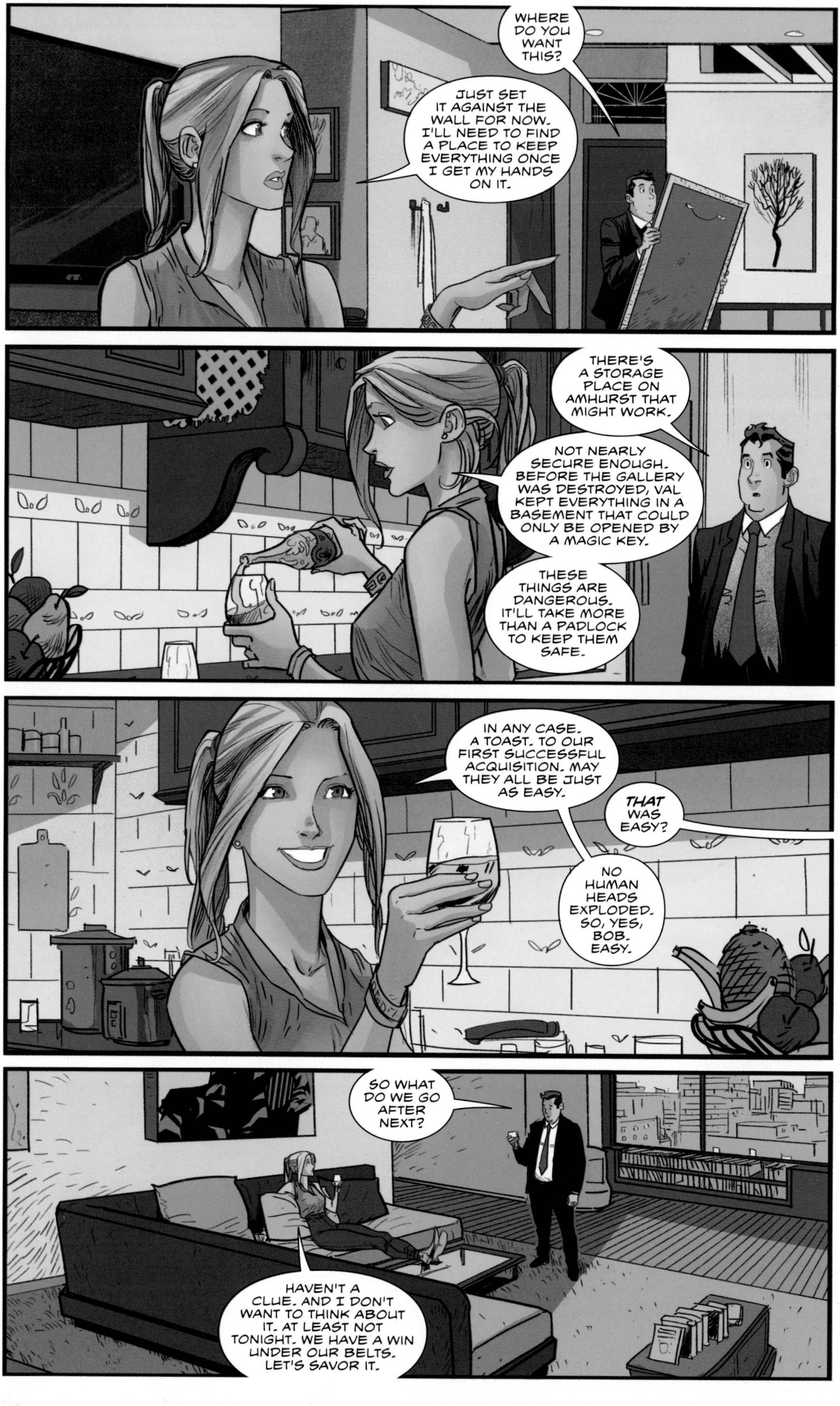
WHERE DO YOU WANT THIS?
JUST SET IT AGAINST THE WALL FOR NOW. I'LL NEED TO FIND A PLACE TO KEEP EVERYTHING ONCE I GET MY HANDS ON IT.
THERE'S A STORAGE PLACE ON AMHURST THAT MIGHT WORK.
NOT NEARLY SECURE ENOUGH. BEFORE THE GALLERY WAS DESTROYED, VAL KEPT EVERYTHING IN A BASEMENT THAT COULD ONLY BE OPENED BY A MAGIC KEY.
THESE THINGS ARE DANGEROUS. IT'LL TAKE MORE THAN A PADLOCK TO KEEP THEM SAFE.
IN ANY CASE. A TOAST. TO OUR FIRST SUCCESSFUL ACQUISITION. MAY THEY ALL BE JUST AS EASY.
THAT WAS EASY?
NO HUMAN HEADS EXPLODED. SO, YES, BOB. EASY.
SO WHAT DO WE GO AFTER NEXT?
HAVEN'T A CLUE. AND I DON'T WANT TO THINK ABOUT IT. AT LEAST NOT TONIGHT. WE HAVE A WIN UNDER OUR BELTS. LET'S SAVOR IT.

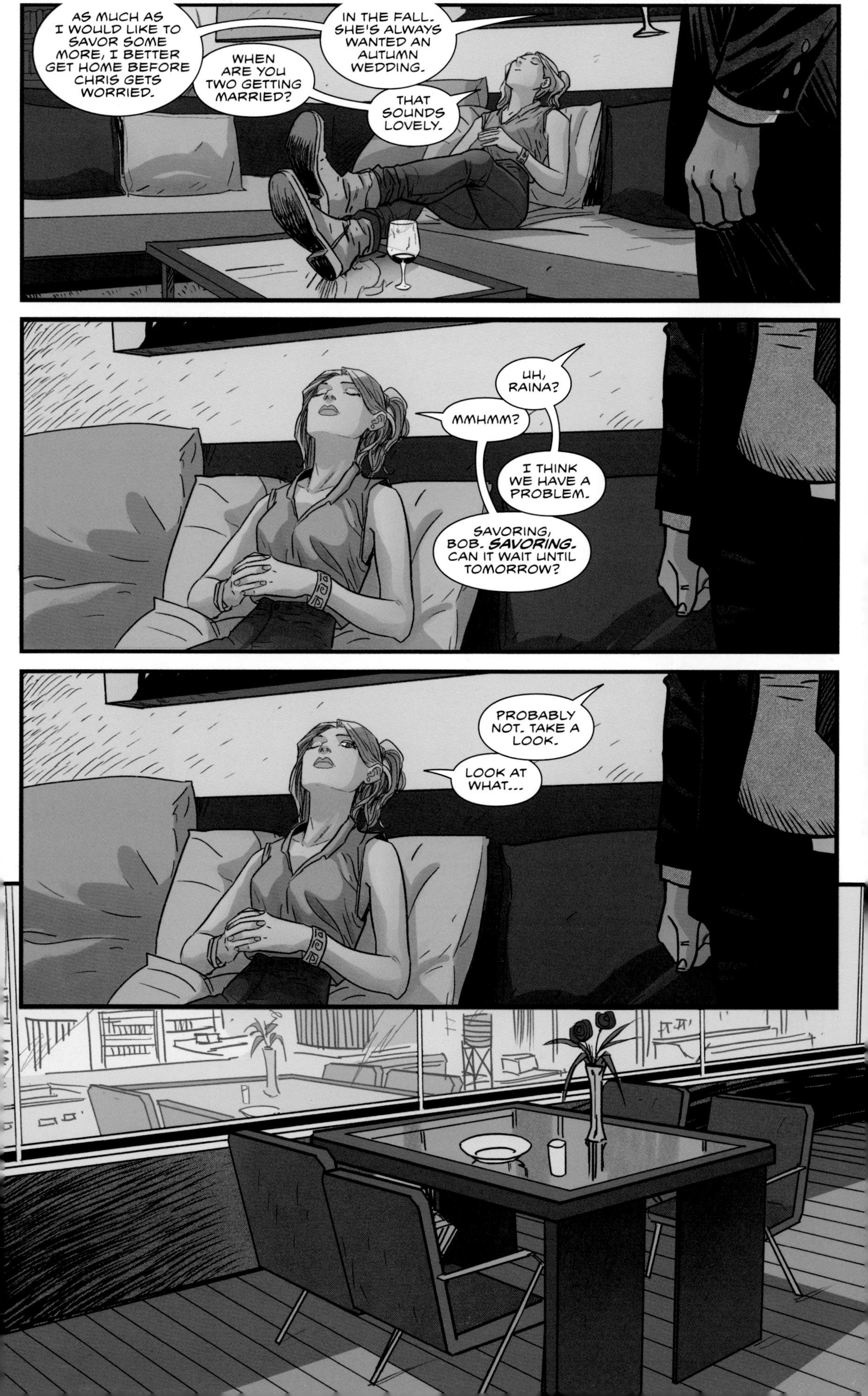
AS MUCH AS I WOULD LIKE TO SAVOR SOME MORE, I BETTER GET HOME BEFORE CHRIS GETS WORRIED.
WHEN ARE YOU TWO GETTING MARRIED?
IN THE FALL. SHE'S ALWAYS WANTED AN AUTUMN WEDDING.
THAT SOUNDS LOVELY.
UH, RAINA?
MMHMM?
I THINK WE HAVE A PROBLEM.
SAVORING, BOB. SAVORING. CAN IT WAIT UNTIL TOMORROW?
PROBABLY NOT. TAKE A LOOK.
LOOK AT WHAT...

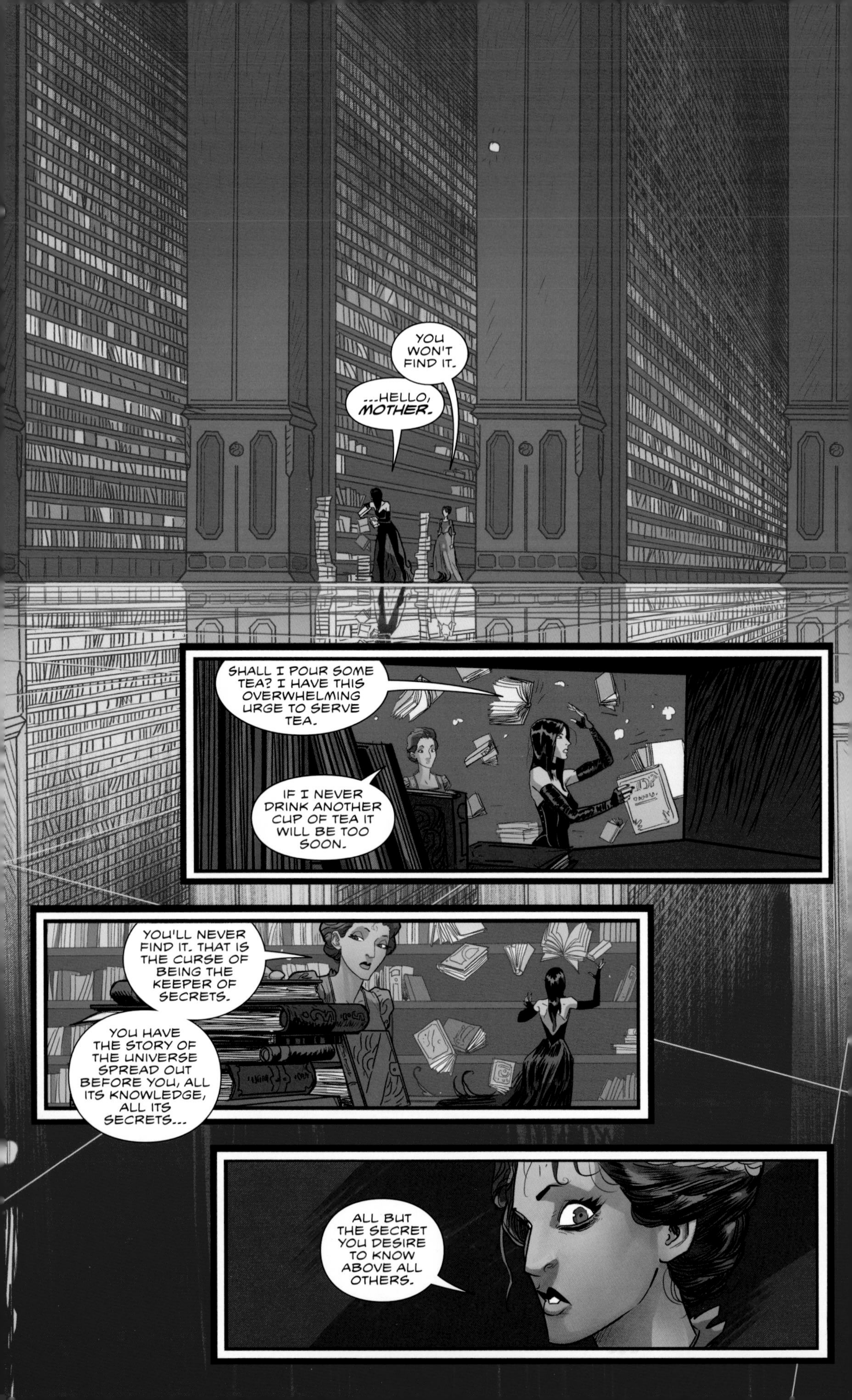
...HELLO, MOTHER.
YOU WON'T FIND IT.
SHALL I POUR SOME TEA? I HAVE THIS OVERWHELMING URGE TO SERVE TEA.
IF I NEVER DRINK ANOTHER CUP OF TEA IT WILL BE TOO SOON.
YOU'LL NEVER FIND IT. THAT IS THE CURSE OF BEING THE KEEPER OF SECRETS.
YOU HAVE THE STORY OF THE UNIVERSE SPREAD OUT BEFORE YOU, ALL ITS KNOWLEDGE, ALL ITS SECRETS...
ALL BUT THE SECRET YOU DESIRE TO KNOW ABOVE ALL OTHERS.

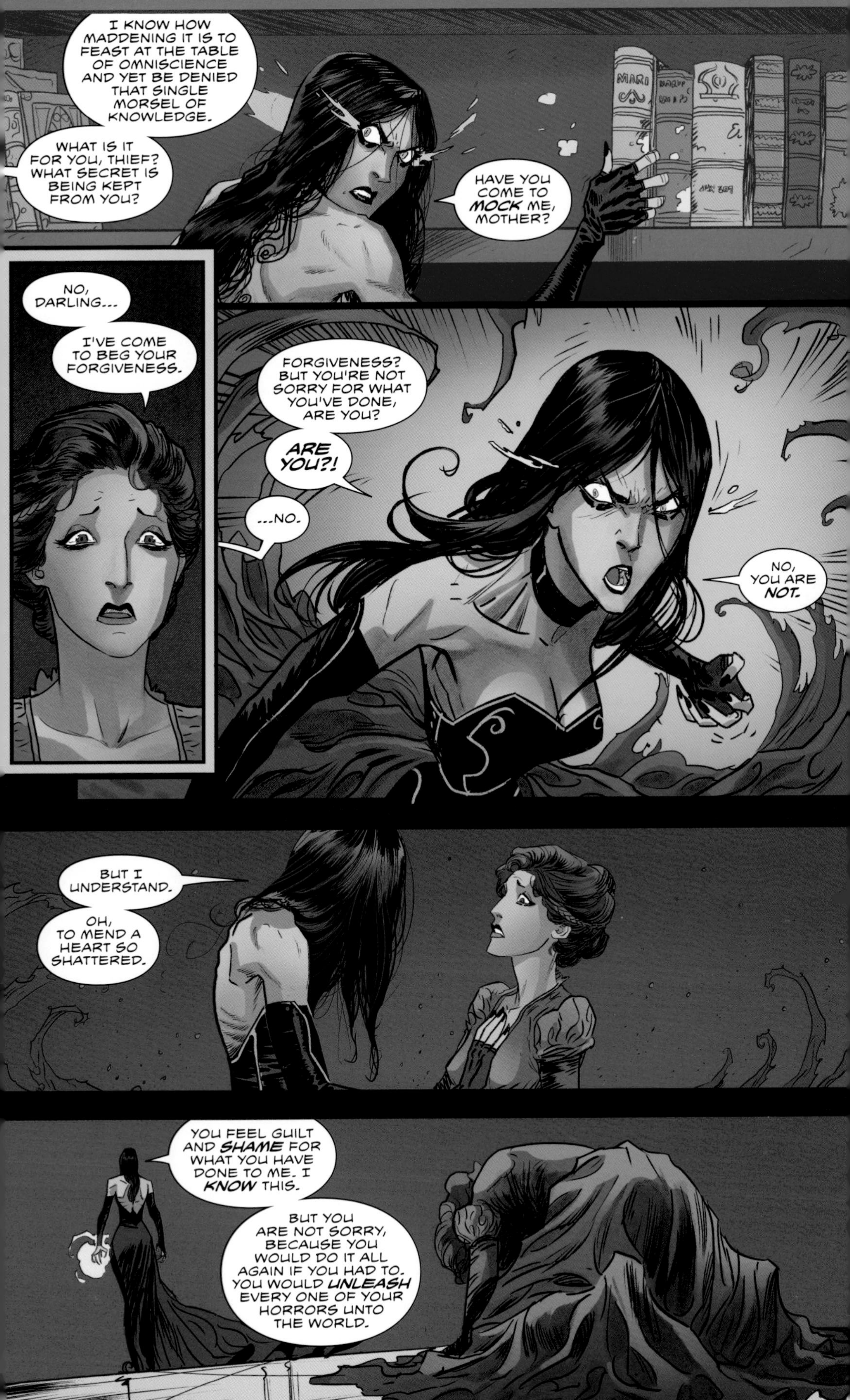
I KNOW HOW MADDENING IT IS TO FEAST AT THE TABLE OF OMNISCIENCE AND YET BE DENIED THAT SINGLE MORSEL OF KNOWLEDGE.
WHAT IS IT FOR YOU, THIEF? WHAT SECRET IS BEING KEPT FROM YOU?
HAVE YOU COME TO MOCK ME, MOTHER?
NO, DARLING...
I'VE COME TO BEG YOUR FORGIVENESS.
FORGIVENESS? BUT YOU'RE NOT SORRY FOR WHAT YOU'VE DONE, ARE YOU?
ARE YOU?!
...NO.
NO, YOU ARE NOT.
BUT I UNDERSTAND.
OH, TO MEND A HEART SO SHATTERED.
YOU FEEL GUILT AND SHAME FOR WHAT YOU HAVE DONE TO ME. I KNOW THIS.
BUT YOU ARE NOT SORRY, BECAUSE YOU WOULD DO IT ALL AGAIN IF YOU HAD TO. YOU WOULD UNLEASH EVERY ONE OF YOUR HORRORS UNTO THE WORLD.

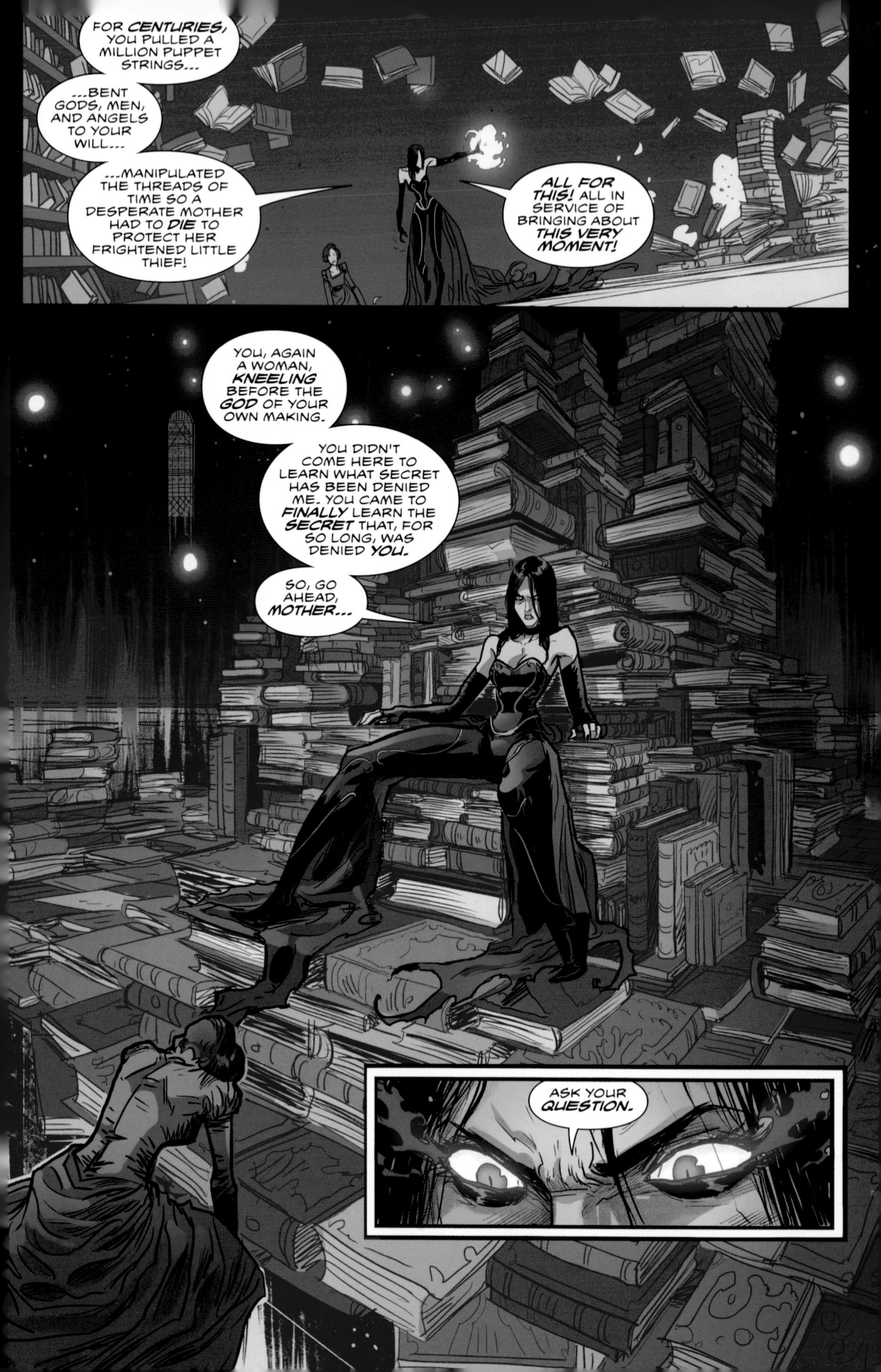
FOR CENTURIES, YOU PULLED A MILLION PUPPET STRINGS...
...BENT GODS, MEN, AND ANGELS TO YOUR WILL...
...MANIPULATED THE THREADS OF TIME SO A DESPERATE MOTHER HAD TO DIE TO PROTECT HER FRIGHTENED LITTLE THIEF!
ALL FOR THIS! ALL IN SERVICE OF BRINGING ABOUT THIS VERY MOMENT!
YOU, AGAIN A WOMAN, KNEELING BEFORE THE GOD OF YOUR OWN MAKING.
YOU DIDN'T COME HERE TO LEARN WHAT SECRET HAS BEEN DENIED ME. YOU CAME TO FINALLY LEARN THE SECRET THAT, FOR SO LONG, WAS DENIED YOU.
SO, GO AHEAD, MOTHER...
ASK YOUR QUESTION.

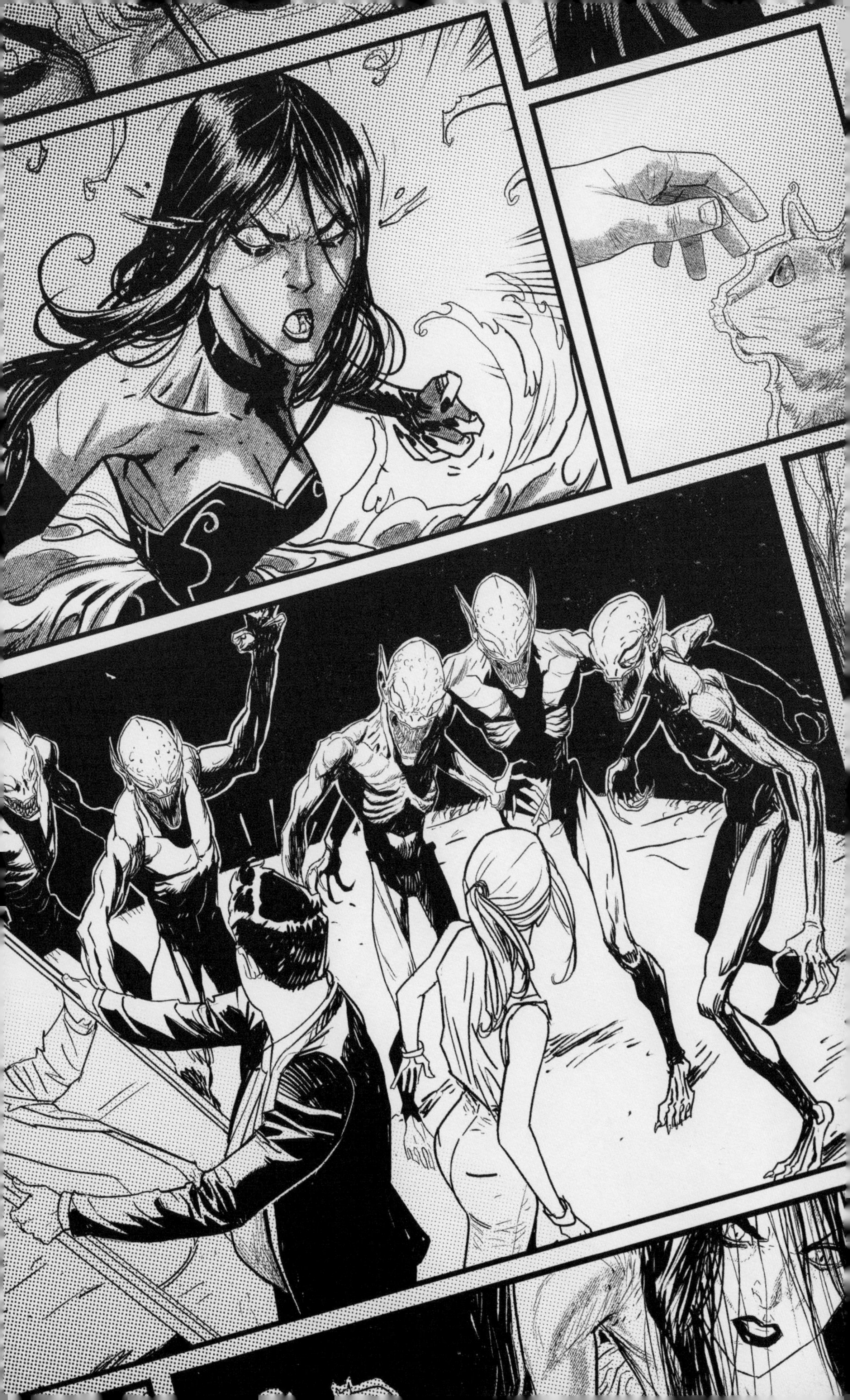

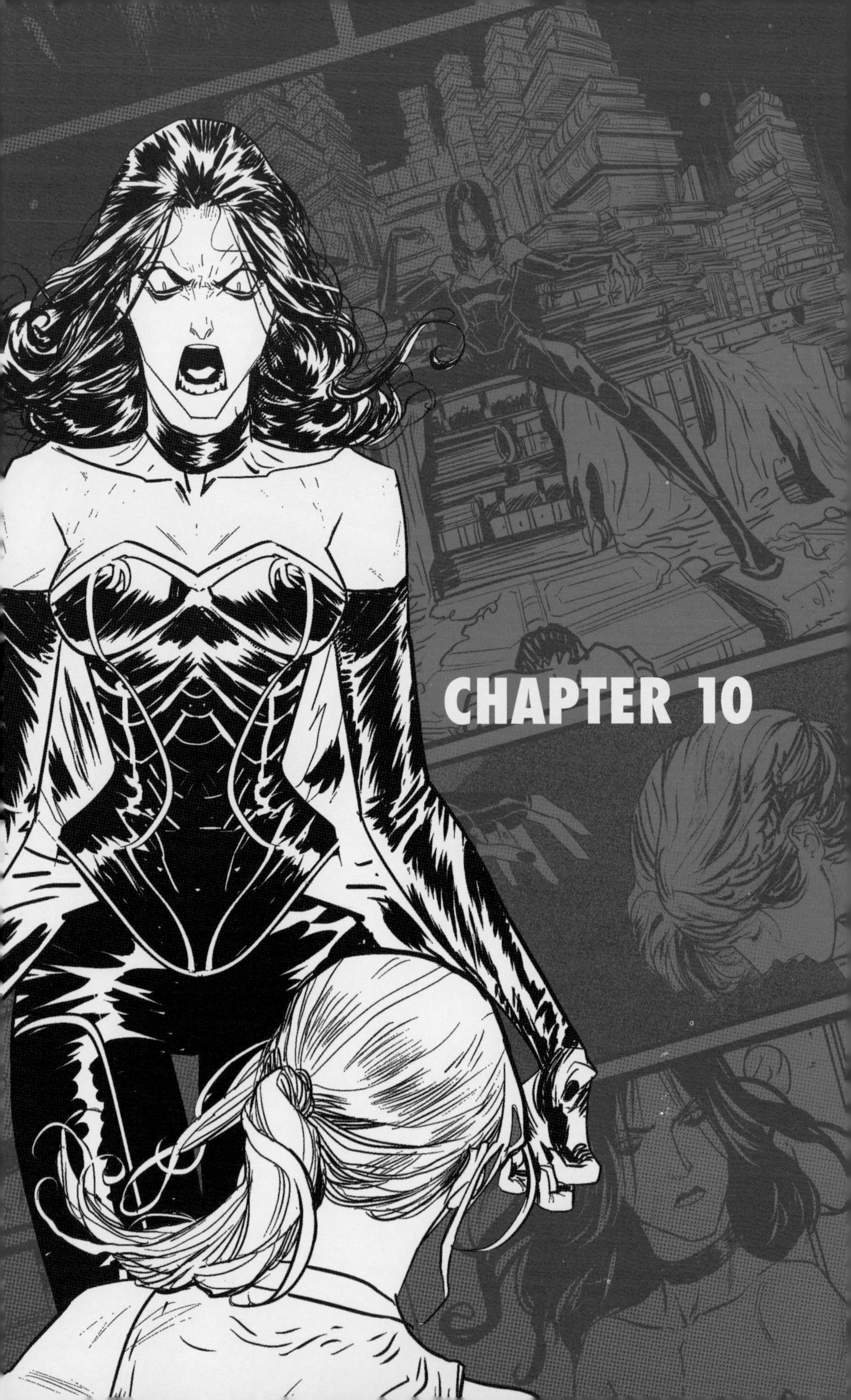
CHAPTER 10

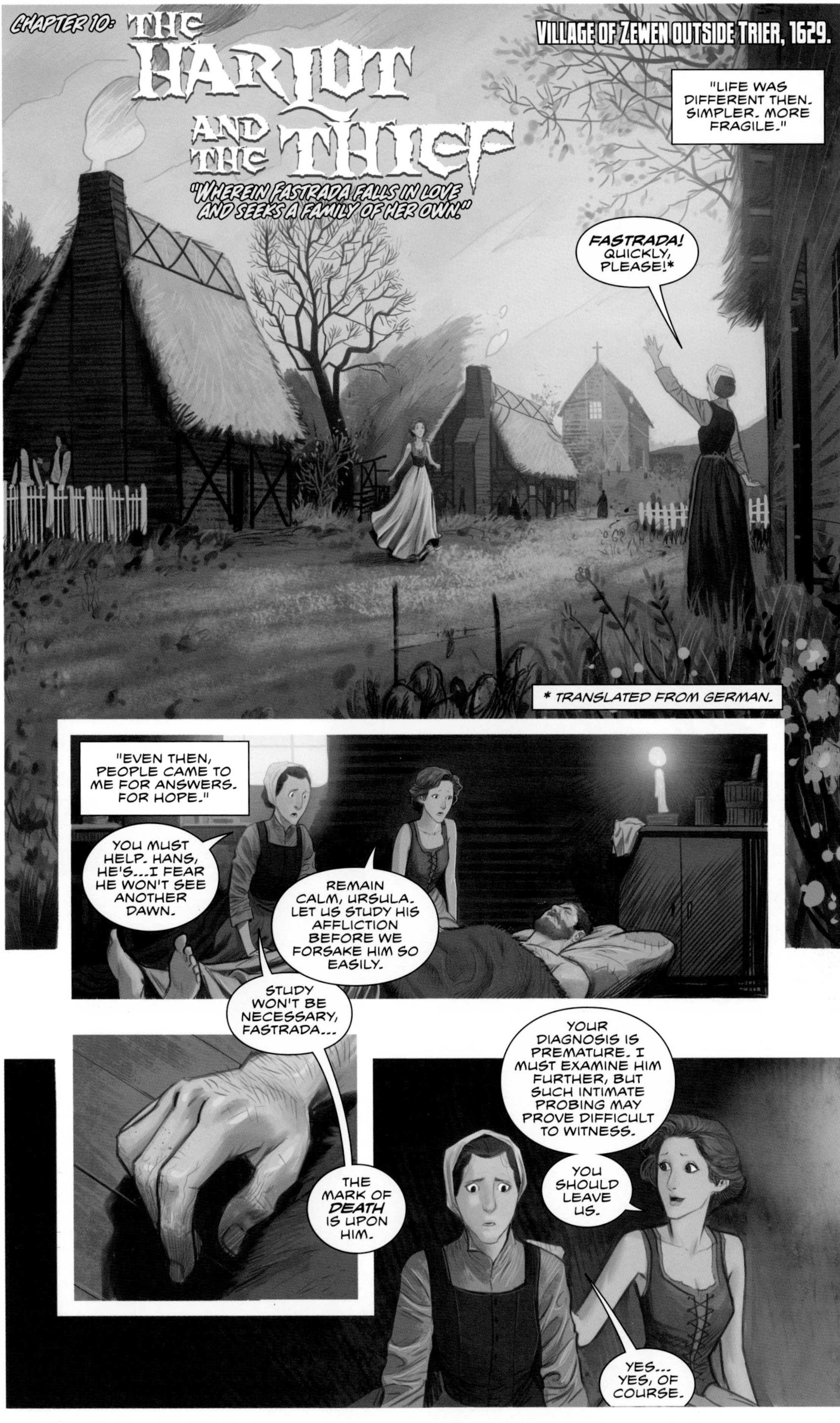
CHAPTER 10: THE HARLOT AND THE THIEF
"WHEREIN FASTRADA FALLS IN LOVE AND SEEKS A FAMILY OF HER OWN."
VILLAGE OF ZEWEN OUTSIDE TRIER, 1629.
"LIFE WAS DIFFERENT THEN. SIMPLER. MORE FRAGILE."
FASTRADA! QUICKLY, PLEASE!*
* TRANSLATED FROM GERMAN.
"EVEN THEN, PEOPLE CAME TO ME FOR ANSWERS. FOR HOPE."
YOU MUST HELP. HANS, HE'S...I FEAR HE WON'T SEE ANOTHER DAWN.
REMAIN CALM, URSULA. LET US STUDY HIS AFFLICTION BEFORE WE FORSAKE HIM SO EASILY.
STUDY WON'T BE NECESSARY, FASTRADA...
THE MARK OF DEATH IS UPON HIM.
YOUR DIAGNOSIS IS PREMATURE. I MUST EXAMINE HIM FURTHER, BUT SUCH INTIMATE PROBING MAY PROVE DIFFICULT TO WITNESS.
YOU SHOULD LEAVE US.
YES... YES, OF COURSE.

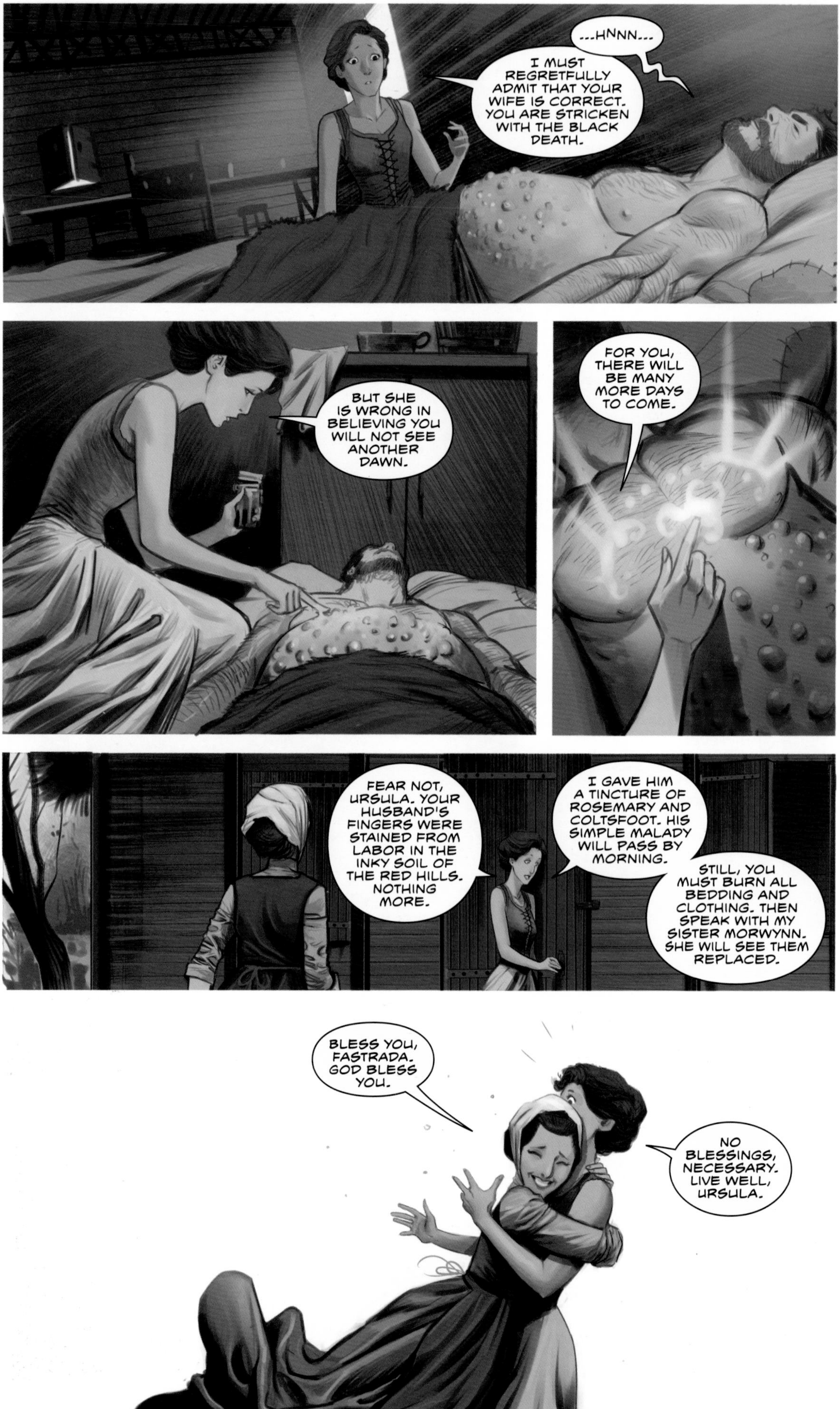
I MUST REGRETFULLY ADMIT THAT YOUR WIFE IS CORRECT. YOU ARE STRICKEN WITH THE BLACK DEATH.
...HNNN...
BUT SHE IS WRONG IN BELIEVING YOU WILL NOT SEE ANOTHER DAWN.
FOR YOU, THERE WILL BE MANY MORE DAYS TO COME.
FEAR NOT, URSULA. YOUR HUSBAND'S FINGERS WERE STAINED FROM LABOR IN THE INKY SOIL OF THE RED HILLS. NOTHING MORE.
I GAVE HIM A TINCTURE OF ROSEMARY AND COLTSFOOT. HIS SIMPLE MALADY WILL PASS BY MORNING.
STILL, YOU MUST BURN ALL BEDDING AND CLOTHING. THEN SPEAK WITH MY SISTER MORWYNN. SHE WILL SEE THEM REPLACED.
BLESS YOU, FASTRADA. GOD BLESS YOU.
NO BLESSINGS, NECESSARY. LIVE WELL, URSULA.

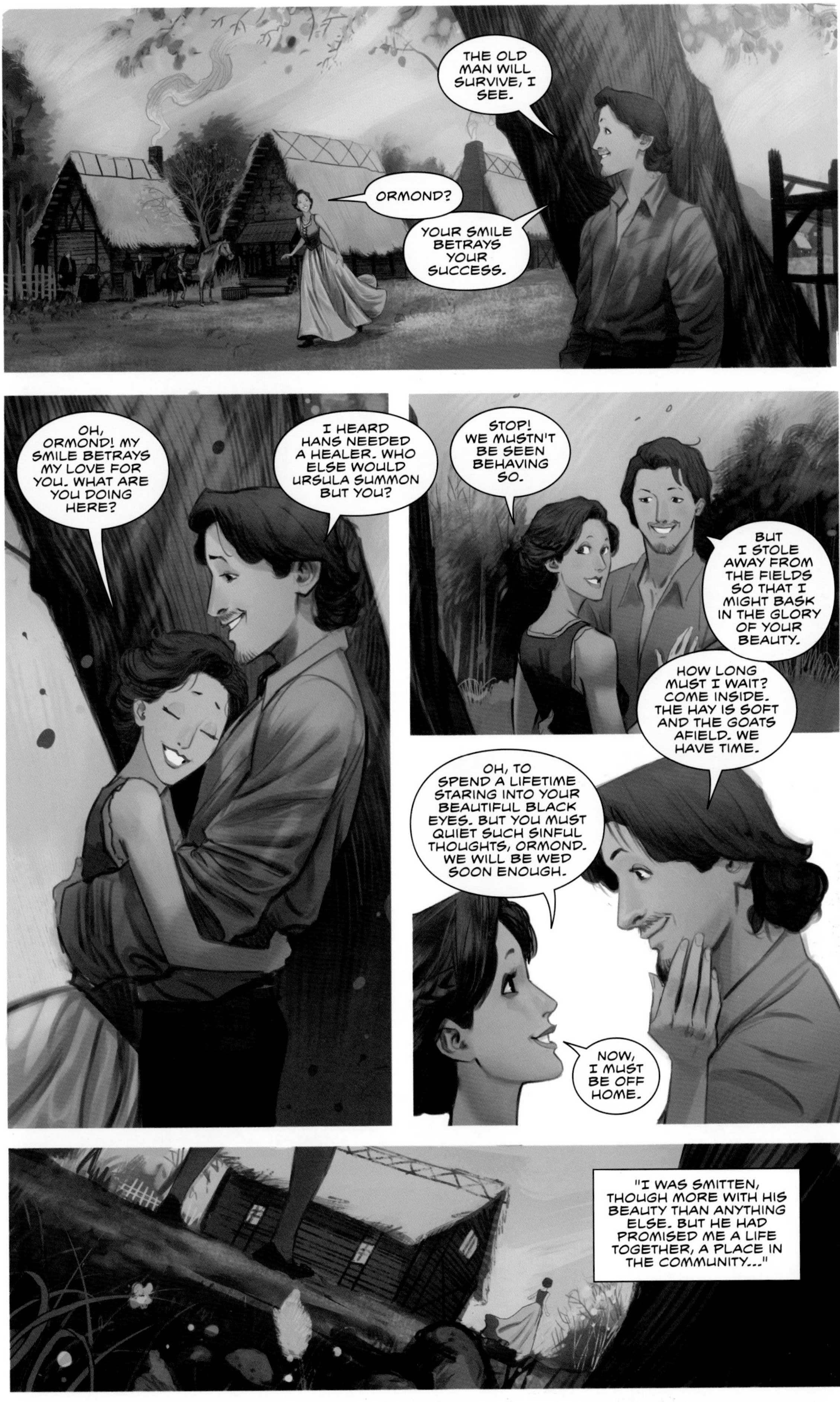
THE OLD MAN WILL SURVIVE, I SEE.
ORMOND?
YOUR SMILE BETRAYS YOUR SUCCESS.
OH, ORMOND! MY SMILE BETRAYS MY LOVE FOR YOU. WHAT ARE YOU DOING HERE?
I HEARD HANS NEEDED A HEALER. WHO ELSE WOULD URSULA SUMMON BUT YOU?
STOP! WE MUSTN'T BE SEEN BEHAVING SO.
BUT I STOLE AWAY FROM THE FIELDS SO THAT I MIGHT BASK IN THE GLORY OF YOUR BEAUTY.
HOW LONG MUST I WAIT? COME INSIDE. THE HAY IS SOFT AND THE GOATS AFIELD. WE HAVE TIME.
OH, TO SPEND A LIFETIME STARING INTO YOUR BEAUTIFUL BLACK EYES. BUT YOU MUST QUIET SUCH SINFUL THOUGHTS, ORMOND. WE WILL BE WED SOON ENOUGH.
NOW, I MUST BE OFF HOME.
"I WAS SMITTEN, THOUGH MORE WITH HIS BEAUTY THAN ANYTHING ELSE. BUT HE HAD PROMISED ME A LIFE TOGETHER, A PLACE IN THE COMMUNITY..."

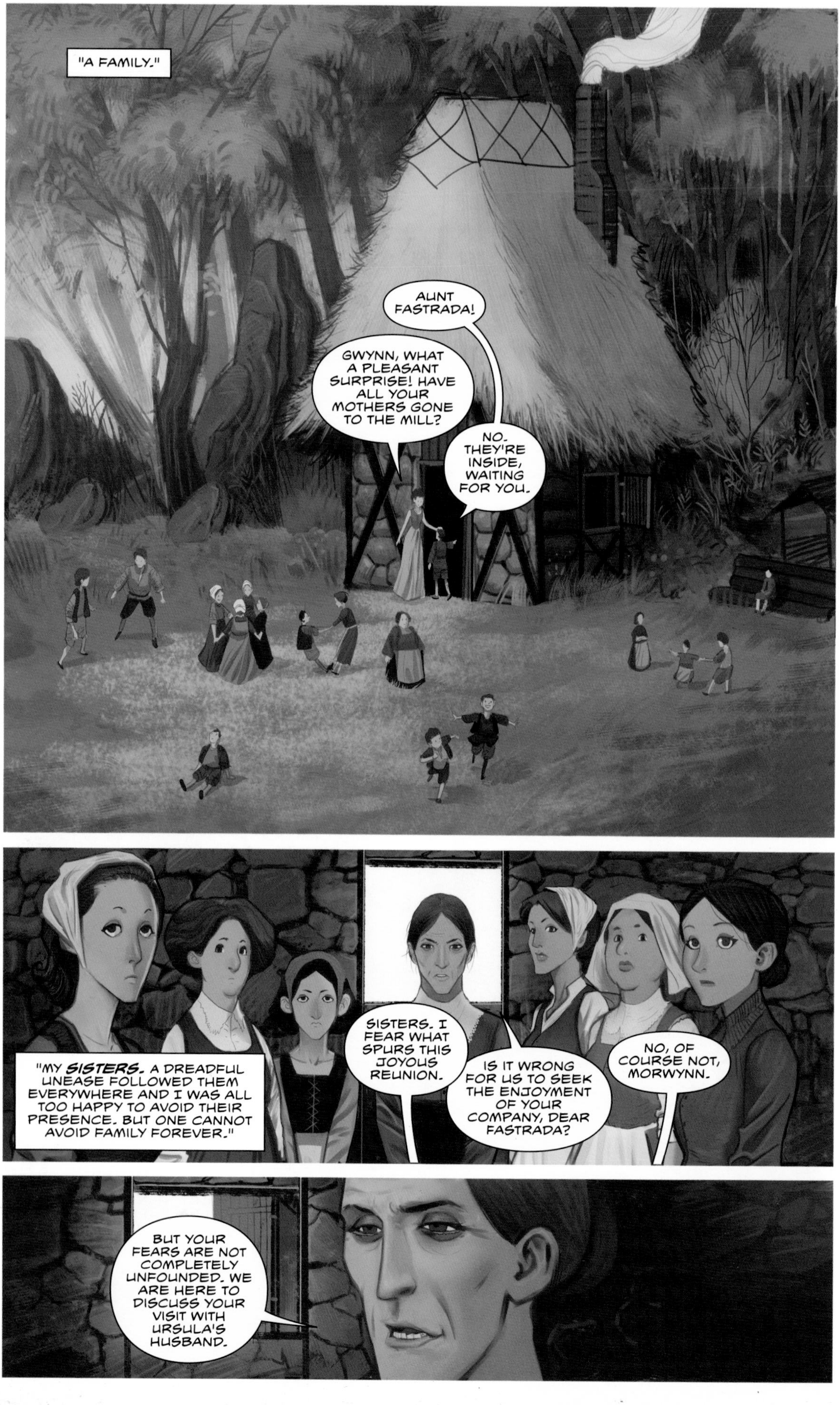
"A FAMILY."
AUNT FASTRADA!
GWYNN, WHAT A PLEASANT SURPRISE! HAVE ALL YOUR MOTHERS GONE TO THE MILL?
NO. THEY'RE INSIDE, WAITING FOR YOU.
"MY SISTERS. A DREADFUL UNEASE FOLLOWED THEM EVERYWHERE AND I WAS ALL TOO HAPPY TO AVOID THEIR PRESENCE. BUT ONE CANNOT AVOID FAMILY FOREVER."
SISTERS. I FEAR WHAT SPURS THIS JOYOUS REUNION.
IS IT WRONG FOR US TO SEEK THE ENJOYMENT OF YOUR COMPANY, DEAR FASTRADA?
NO, OF COURSE NOT, MORWYNN.
BUT YOUR FEARS ARE NOT COMPLETELY UNFOUNDED. WE ARE HERE TO DISCUSS YOUR VISIT WITH URSULA'S HUSBAND.

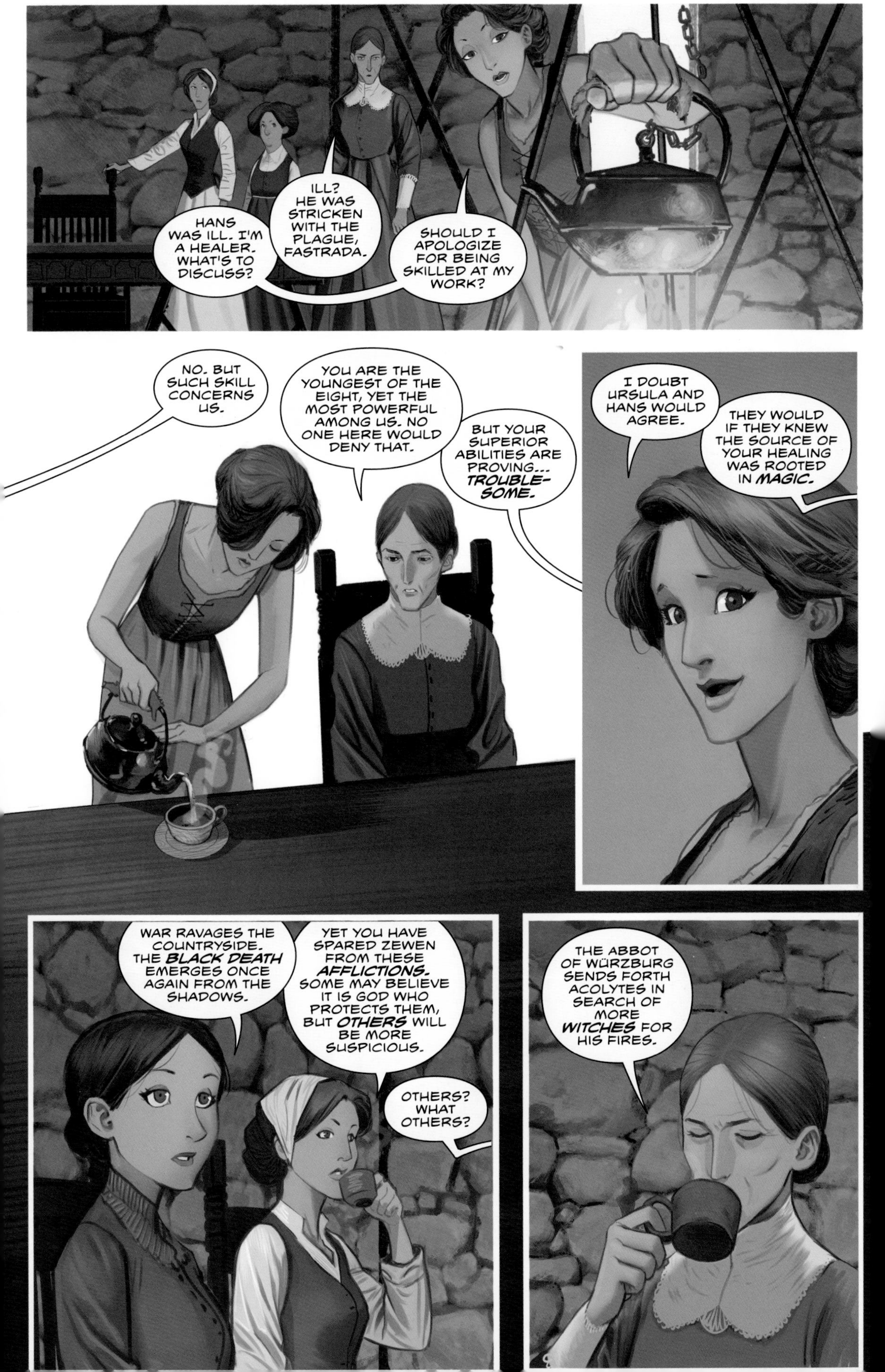
HANS WAS ILL. I'M A HEALER. WHAT'S TO DISCUSS?
ILL? HE WAS STRICKEN WITH THE PLAGUE, FASTRADA.
SHOULD I APOLOGIZE FOR BEING SKILLED AT MY WORK?
NO. BUT SUCH SKILL CONCERNS US.
YOU ARE THE YOUNGEST OF THE EIGHT, YET THE MOST POWERFUL AMONG US. NO ONE HERE WOULD DENY THAT.
BUT YOUR SUPERIOR ABILITIES ARE PROVING... TROUBLE-SOME.
I DOUBT URSULA AND HANS WOULD AGREE.
THEY WOULD IF THEY KNEW THE SOURCE OF YOUR HEALING WAS ROOTED IN MAGIC.
WAR RAVAGES THE COUNTRYSIDE. THE BLACK DEATH EMERGES ONCE AGAIN FROM THE SHADOWS.
YET YOU HAVE SPARED ZEWEN FROM THESE AFFLICTIONS. SOME MAY BELIEVE IT IS GOD WHO PROTECTS THEM, BUT OTHERS WILL BE MORE SUSPICIOUS.
OTHERS? WHAT OTHERS?
THE ABBOT OF WÜRZBURG SENDS FORTH ACOLYTES IN SEARCH OF MORE WITCHES FOR HIS FIRES.

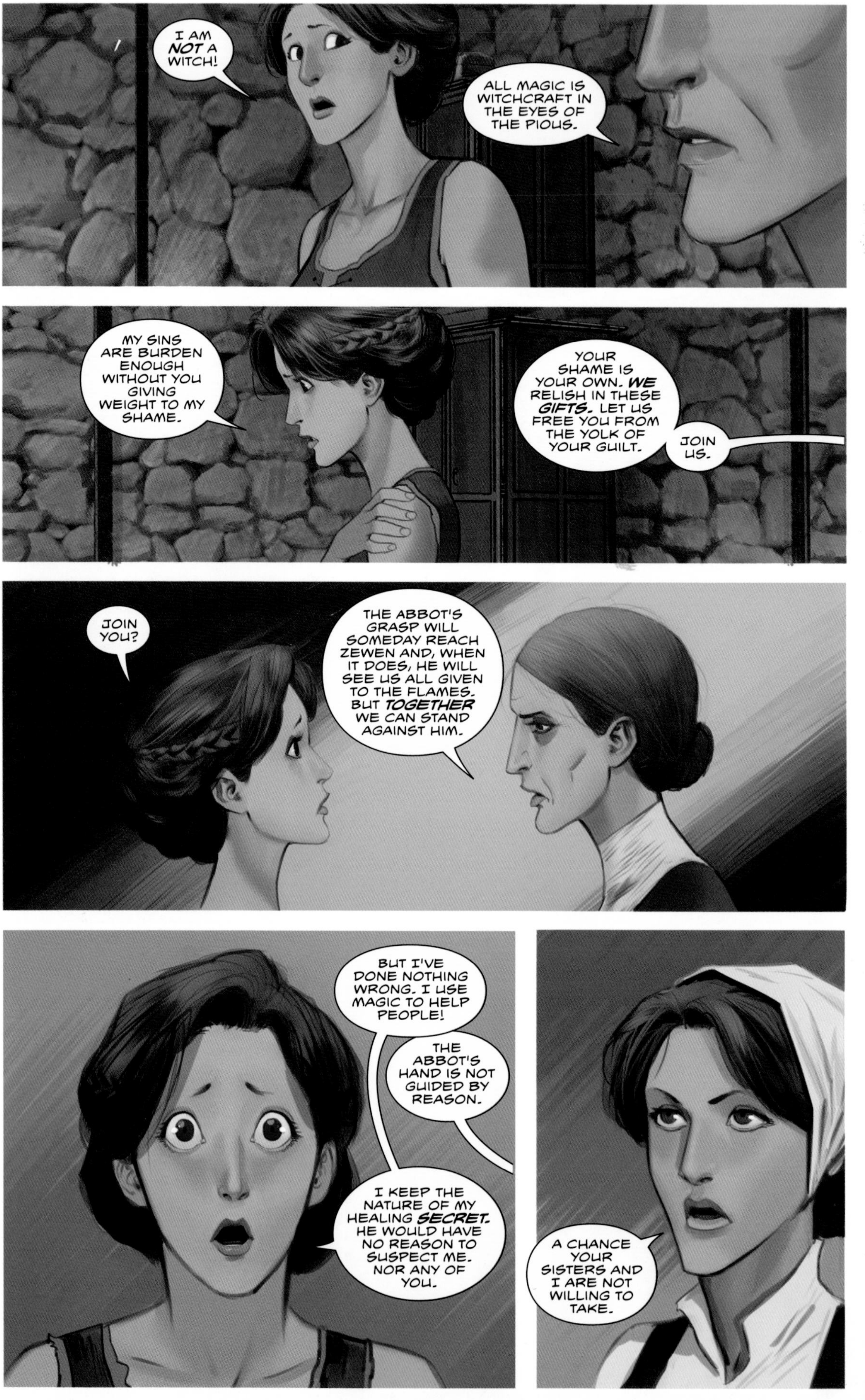

I AM NOT A WITCH!
ALL MAGIC IS WITCHCRAFT IN THE EYES OF THE PIOUS.
MY SINS ARE BURDEN ENOUGH WITHOUT YOU GIVING WEIGHT TO MY SHAME.
YOUR SHAME IS YOUR OWN. WE RELISH IN THESE GIFTS. LET US FREE YOU FROM THE YOLK OF YOUR GUILT.
JOIN US.
JOIN YOU?
THE ABBOT'S GRASP WILL SOMEDAY REACH ZEWEN AND, WHEN IT DOES, HE WILL SEE US ALL GIVEN TO THE FLAMES. BUT TOGETHER WE CAN STAND AGAINST HIM.
BUT I'VE DONE NOTHING WRONG. I USE MAGIC TO HELP PEOPLE!
THE ABBOT'S HAND IS NOT GUIDED BY REASON.
I KEEP THE NATURE OF MY HEALING SECRET. HE WOULD HAVE NO REASON TO SUSPECT ME. NOR ANY OF YOU.
A CHANCE YOUR SISTERS AND I ARE NOT WILLING TO TAKE.

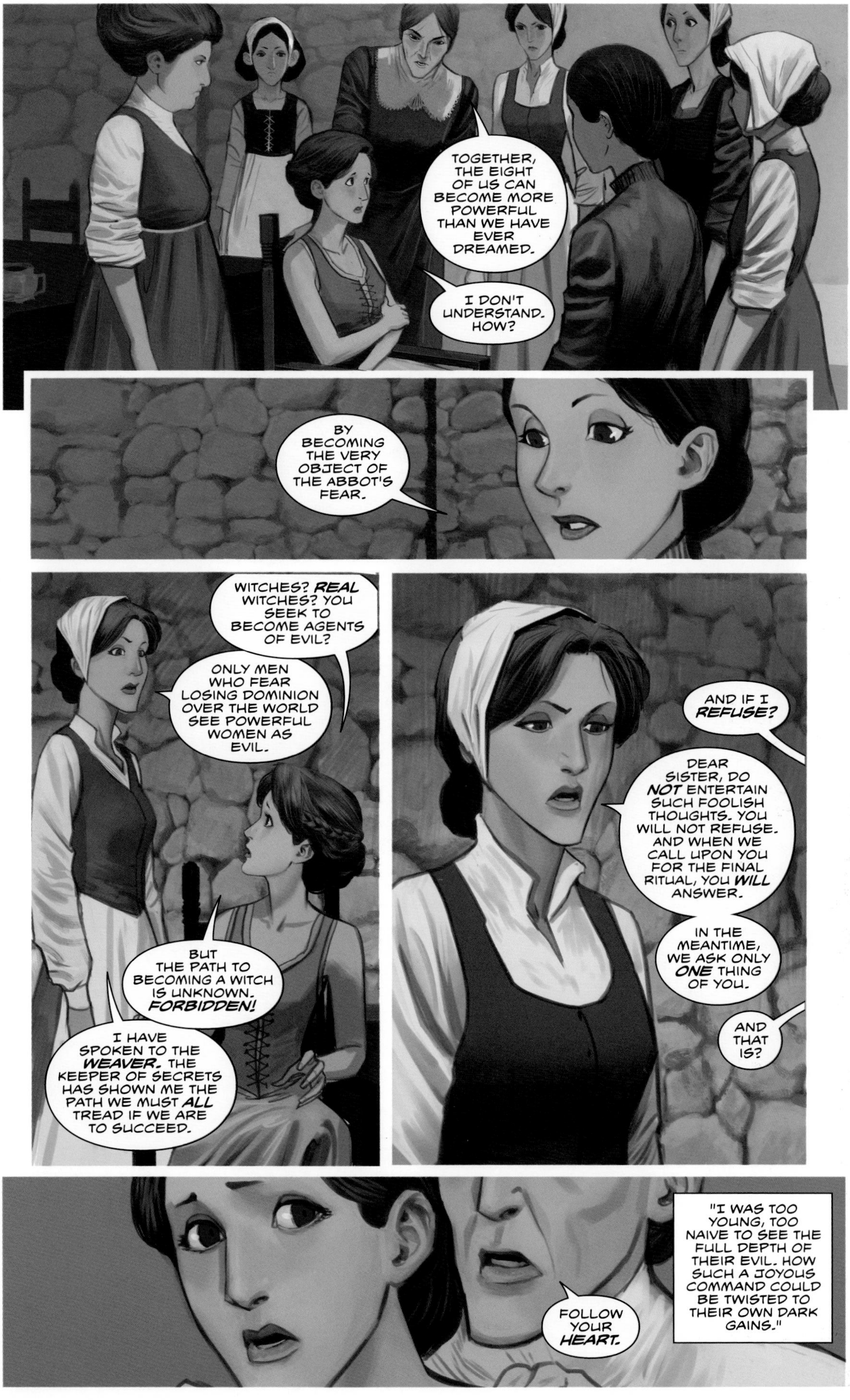
TOGETHER, THE EIGHT OF US CAN BECOME MORE POWERFUL THAN WE HAVE EVER DREAMED.
I DON'T UNDERSTAND. HOW?
BY BECOMING THE VERY OBJECT OF THE ABBOT'S FEAR.
WITCHES? REAL WITCHES? YOU SEEK TO BECOME AGENTS OF EVIL?
ONLY MEN WHO FEAR LOSING DOMINION OVER THE WORLD SEE POWERFUL WOMEN AS EVIL.
BUT THE PATH TO BECOMING A WITCH IS UNKNOWN. FORBIDDEN!
I HAVE SPOKEN TO THE WEAVER. THE KEEPER OF SECRETS HAS SHOWN ME THE PATH WE MUST ALL TREAD IF WE ARE TO SUCCEED.
AND IF I REFUSE?
DEAR SISTER, DO NOT ENTERTAIN SUCH FOOLISH THOUGHTS. YOU WILL NOT REFUSE. AND WHEN WE CALL UPON YOU FOR THE FINAL RITUAL, YOU WILL ANSWER.
IN THE MEANTIME, WE ASK ONLY ONE THING OF YOU.
AND THAT IS?
FOLLOW YOUR HEART.
"I WAS TOO YOUNG, TOO NAIVE TO SEE THE FULL DEPTH OF THEIR EVIL. HOW SUCH A JOYOUS COMMAND COULD BE TWISTED TO THEIR OWN DARK GAINS."

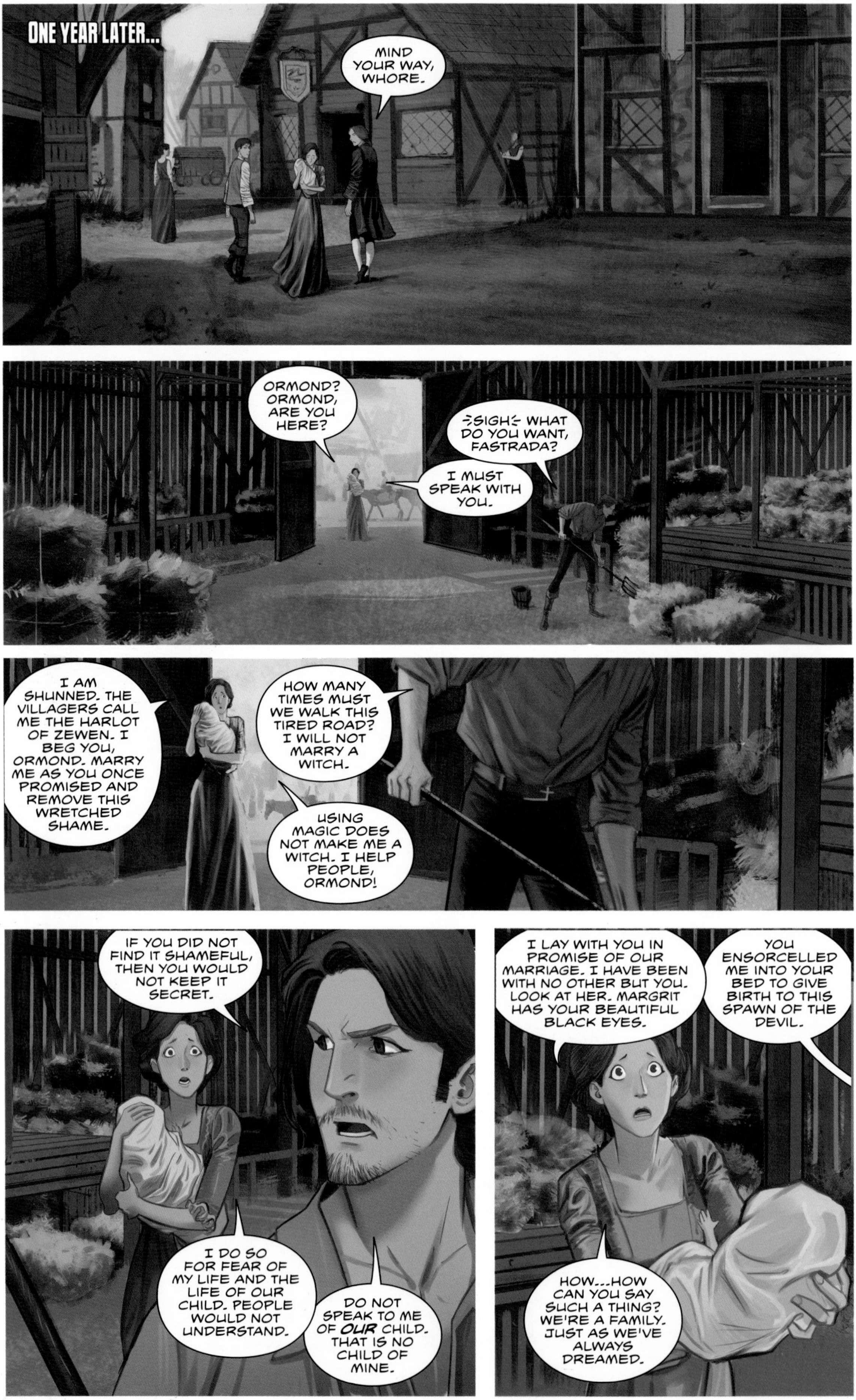
ONE YEAR LATER...
MIND YOUR WAY, WHORE.
ORMOND? ORMOND, ARE YOU HERE?
-SIGH- WHAT DO YOU WANT, FASTRADA?
I MUST SPEAK WITH YOU.
I AM SHUNNED. THE VILLAGERS CALL ME THE HARLOT OF ZEWEN. I BEG YOU, ORMOND. MARRY ME AS YOU ONCE PROMISED AND REMOVE THIS WRETCHED SHAME.
HOW MANY TIMES MUST WE WALK THIS TIRED ROAD? I WILL NOT MARRY A WITCH.
USING MAGIC DOES NOT MAKE ME A WITCH. I HELP PEOPLE, ORMOND!
IF YOU DID NOT FIND IT SHAMEFUL, THEN YOU WOULD NOT KEEP IT SECRET.
I DO SO FOR FEAR OF MY LIFE AND THE LIFE OF OUR CHILD. PEOPLE WOULD NOT UNDERSTAND.
DO NOT SPEAK TO ME OF OUR CHILD. THAT IS NO CHILD OF MINE.
I LAY WITH YOU IN PROMISE OF OUR MARRIAGE. I HAVE BEEN WITH NO OTHER BUT YOU. LOOK AT HER. MARGRIT HAS YOUR BEAUTIFUL BLACK EYES.
YOU ENSORCELLED ME INTO YOUR BED TO GIVE BIRTH TO THIS SPAWN OF THE DEVIL.
HOW...HOW CAN YOU SAY SUCH A THING? WE'RE A FAMILY. JUST AS WE'VE ALWAYS DREAMED.

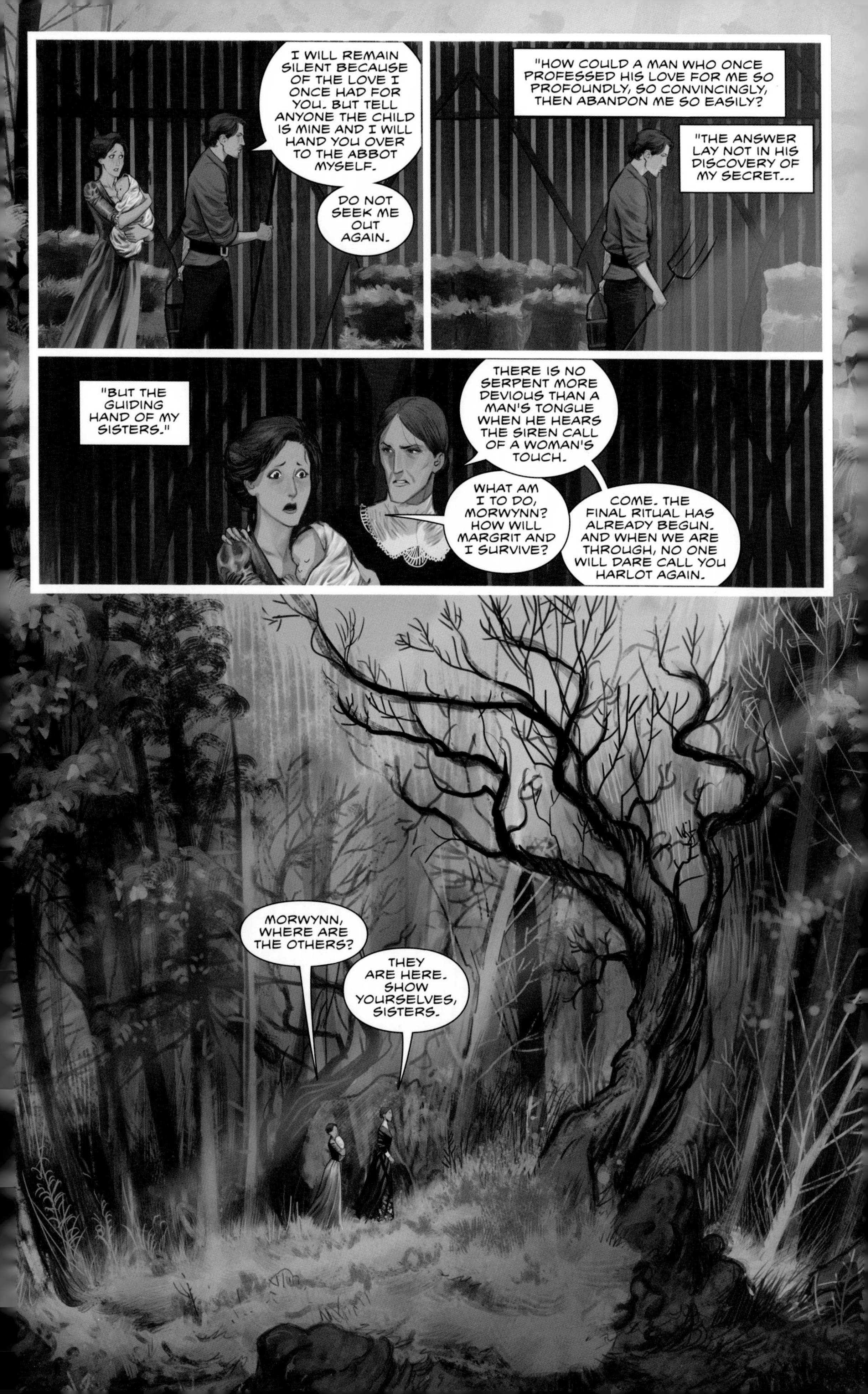
I WILL REMAIN SILENT BECAUSE OF THE LOVE I ONCE HAD FOR YOU. BUT TELL ANYONE THE CHILD IS MINE AND I WILL HAND YOU OVER TO THE ABBOT MYSELF.
DO NOT SEEK ME OUT AGAIN.
"HOW COULD A MAN WHO ONCE PROFESSED HIS LOVE FOR ME SO PROFOUNDLY, SO CONVINCINGLY, THEN ABANDON ME SO EASILY?
"THE ANSWER LAY NOT IN HIS DISCOVERY OF MY SECRET...
"BUT THE GUIDING HAND OF MY SISTERS."
THERE IS NO SERPENT MORE DEVIOUS THAN A MAN'S TONGUE WHEN HE HEARS THE SIREN CALL OF A WOMAN'S TOUCH.
WHAT AM I TO DO, MORWYNN? HOW WILL MARGRIT AND I SURVIVE?
COME. THE FINAL RITUAL HAS ALREADY BEGUN. AND WHEN WE ARE THROUGH, NO ONE WILL DARE CALL YOU HARLOT AGAIN.
MORWYNN, WHERE ARE THE OTHERS?
THEY ARE HERE. SHOW YOURSELVES, SISTERS.

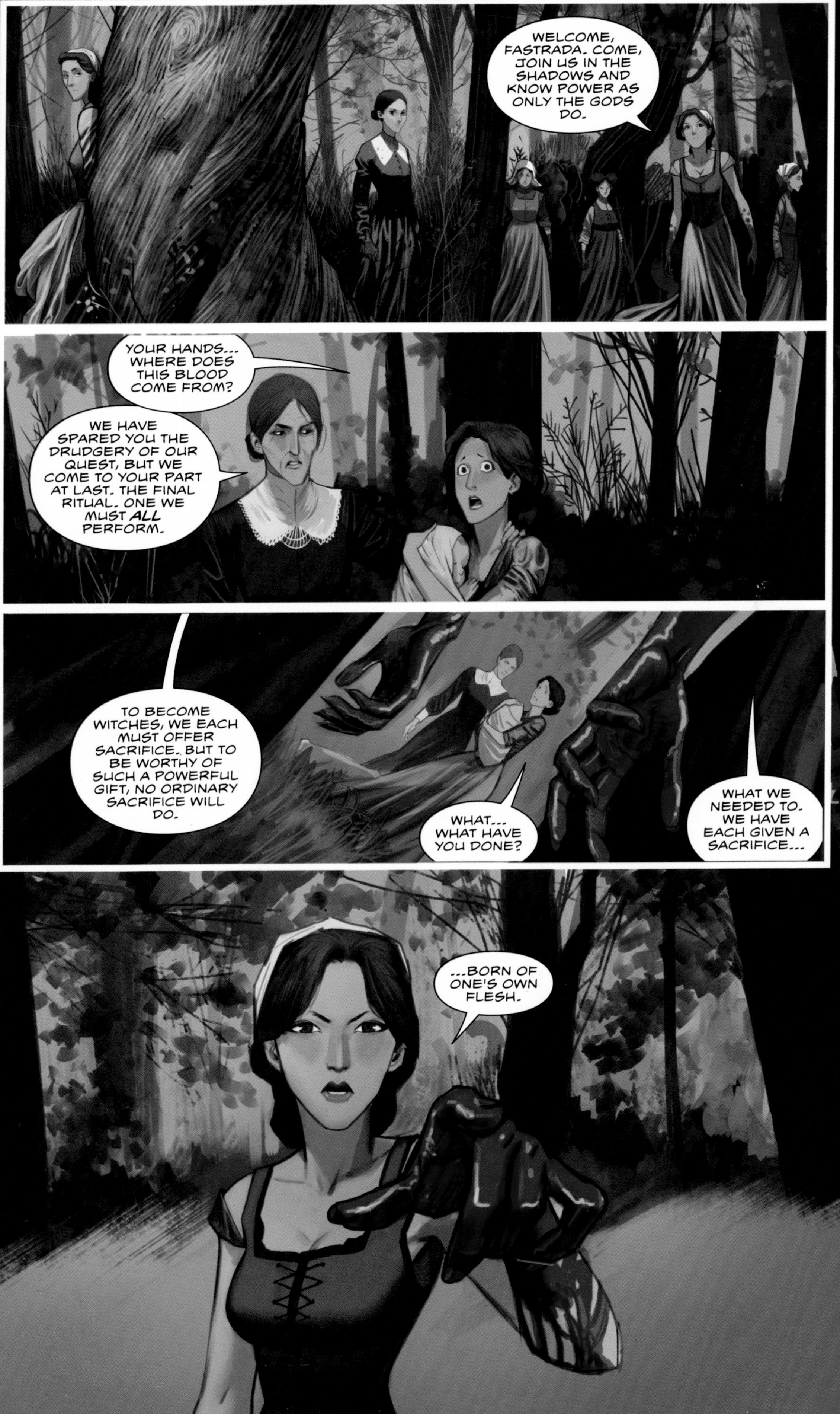
WELCOME, FASTRADA. COME, JOIN US IN THE SHADOWS AND KNOW POWER AS ONLY THE GODS DO.
YOUR HANDS... WHERE DOES THIS BLOOD COME FROM?
WE HAVE SPARED YOU THE DRUDGERY OF OUR QUEST, BUT WE COME TO YOUR PART AT LAST. THE FINAL RITUAL. ONE WE MUST ALL PERFORM.
TO BECOME WITCHES, WE EACH MUST OFFER SACRIFICE. BUT TO BE WORTHY OF SUCH A POWERFUL GIFT, NO ORDINARY SACRIFICE WILL DO.
WHAT... WHAT HAVE YOU DONE?
WHAT WE NEEDED TO. WE HAVE EACH GIVEN A SACRIFICE...
...BORN OF ONE'S OWN FLESH.

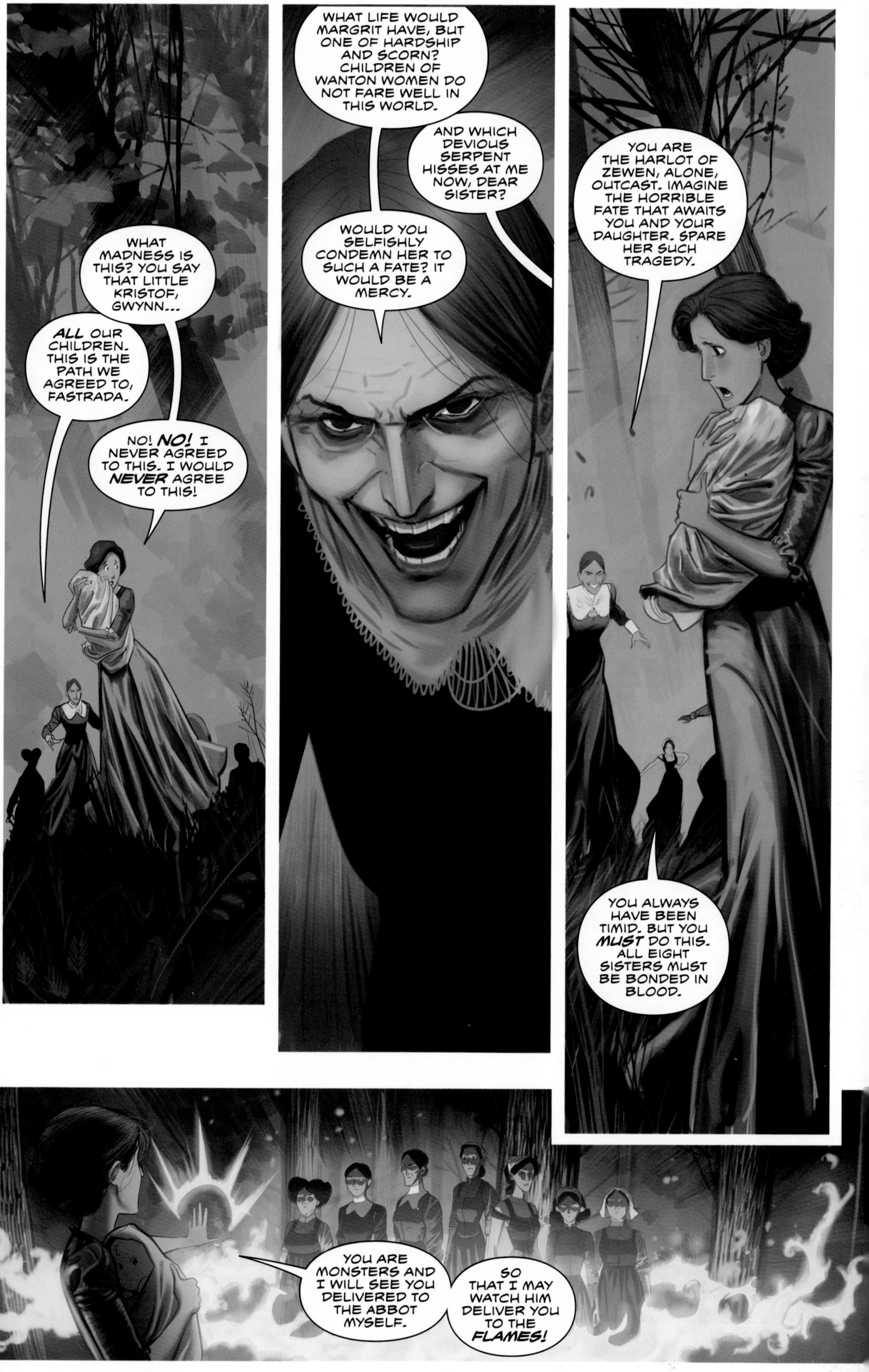
WHAT MADNESS IS THIS? YOU SAY THAT LITTLE KRISTOF, GWYNN...
ALL OUR CHILDREN. THIS IS THE PATH WE AGREED TO, FASTRADA.
NO! NO! I NEVER AGREED TO THIS. I WOULD NEVER AGREE TO THIS!
WHAT LIFE WOULD MARGRIT HAVE, BUT ONE OF HARDSHIP AND SCORN? CHILDREN OF WANTON WOMEN DO NOT FARE WELL IN THIS WORLD.
WOULD YOU SELFISHLY CONDEMN HER TO SUCH A FATE? IT WOULD BE A MERCY.
AND WHICH DEVIOUS SERPENT HISSES AT ME NOW, DEAR SISTER?
YOU ARE THE HARLOT OF ZEWEN, ALONE, OUTCAST. IMAGINE THE HORRIBLE FATE THAT AWAITS YOU AND YOUR DAUGHTER. SPARE HER SUCH TRAGEDY.
YOU ALWAYS HAVE BEEN TIMID. BUT YOU MUST DO THIS. ALL EIGHT SISTERS MUST BE BONDED IN BLOOD.
YOU ARE MONSTERS AND I WILL SEE YOU DELIVERED TO THE ABBOT MYSELF.
SO THAT I MAY WATCH HIM DELIVER YOU TO THE FLAMES!

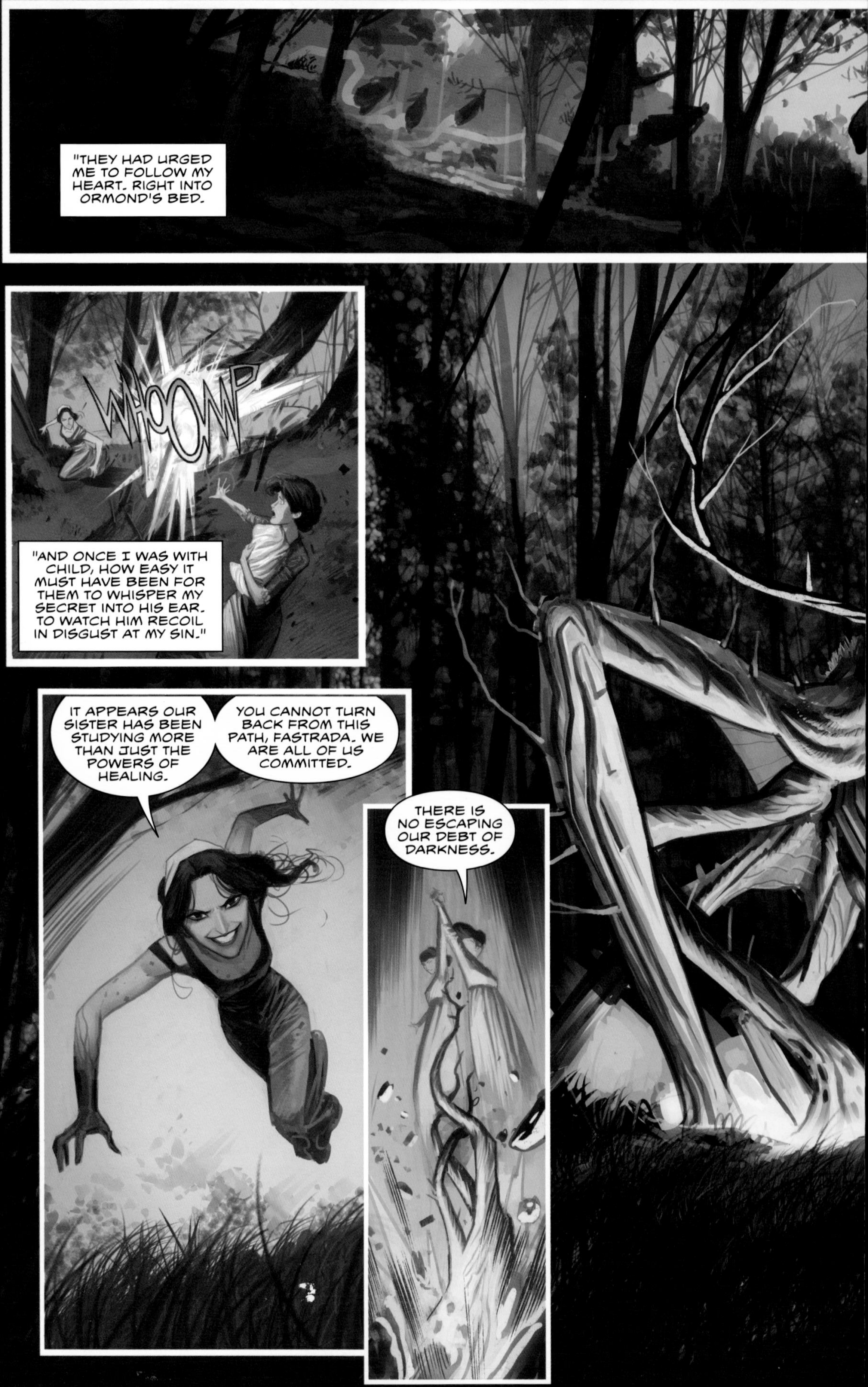
"THEY HAD URGED ME TO FOLLOW MY HEART. RIGHT INTO ORMOND'S BED.
WHOOMP
"AND ONCE I WAS WITH CHILD, HOW EASY IT MUST HAVE BEEN FOR THEM TO WHISPER MY SECRET INTO HIS EAR. TO WATCH HIM RECOIL IN DISGUST AT MY SIN."
IT APPEARS OUR SISTER HAS BEEN STUDYING MORE THAN JUST THE POWERS OF HEALING.
YOU CANNOT TURN BACK FROM THIS PATH, FASTRADA. WE ARE ALL OF US COMMITTED.
THERE IS NO ESCAPING OUR DEBT OF DARKNESS.

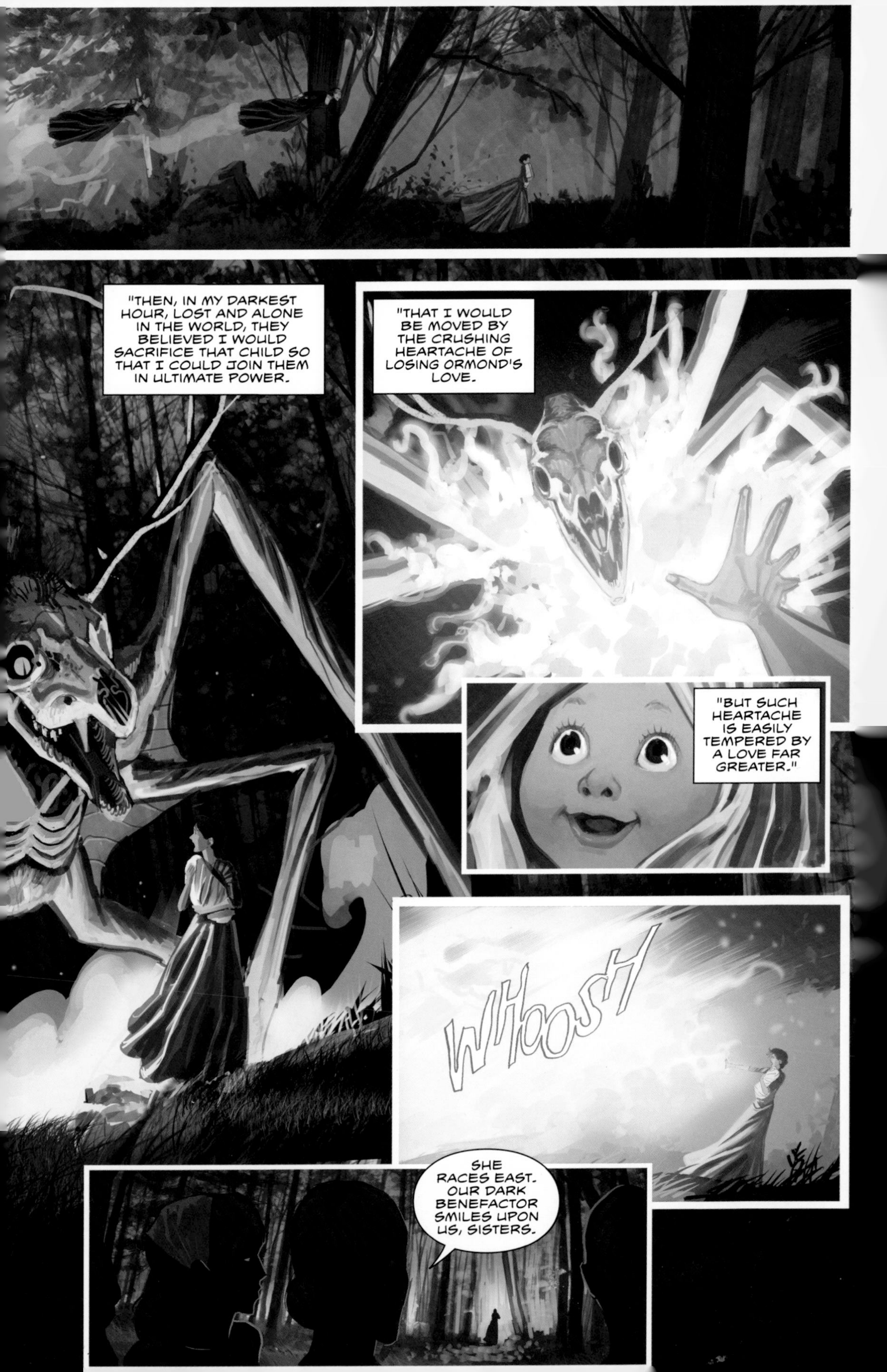
"THEN, IN MY DARKEST HOUR, LOST AND ALONE IN THE WORLD, THEY BELIEVED I WOULD SACRIFICE THAT CHILD SO THAT I COULD JOIN THEM IN ULTIMATE POWER.
"THAT I WOULD BE MOVED BY THE CRUSHING HEARTACHE OF LOSING ORMOND'S LOVE.
"BUT SUCH HEARTACHE IS EASILY TEMPERED BY A LOVE FAR GREATER."
WHOOSH
SHE RACES EAST. OUR DARK BENEFACTOR SMILES UPON US, SISTERS.

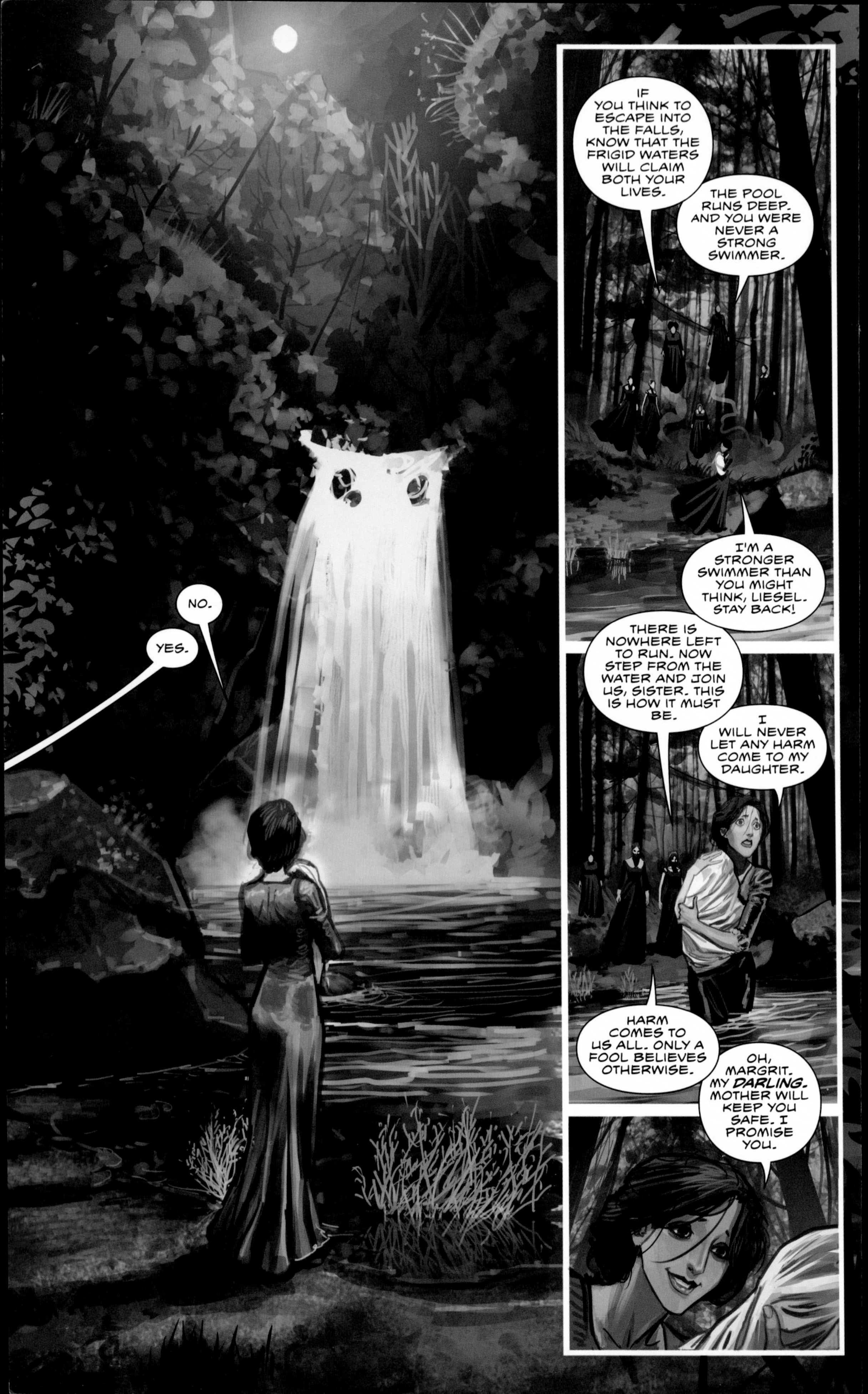
NO.
YES.
IF YOU THINK TO ESCAPE INTO THE FALLS, KNOW THAT THE FRIGID WATERS WILL CLAIM BOTH YOUR LIVES.
THE POOL RUNS DEEP. AND YOU WERE NEVER A STRONG SWIMMER.
I'M A STRONGER SWIMMER THAN YOU MIGHT THINK, LIESEL. STAY BACK!
THERE IS NOWHERE LEFT TO RUN. NOW STEP FROM THE WATER AND JOIN US, SISTER. THIS IS HOW IT MUST BE.
I WILL NEVER LET ANY HARM COME TO MY DAUGHTER.
HARM COMES TO US ALL. ONLY A FOOL BELIEVES OTHERWISE.
OH, MARGRIT. MY ***DARLING.*** MOTHER WILL KEEP YOU SAFE. I PROMISE YOU.

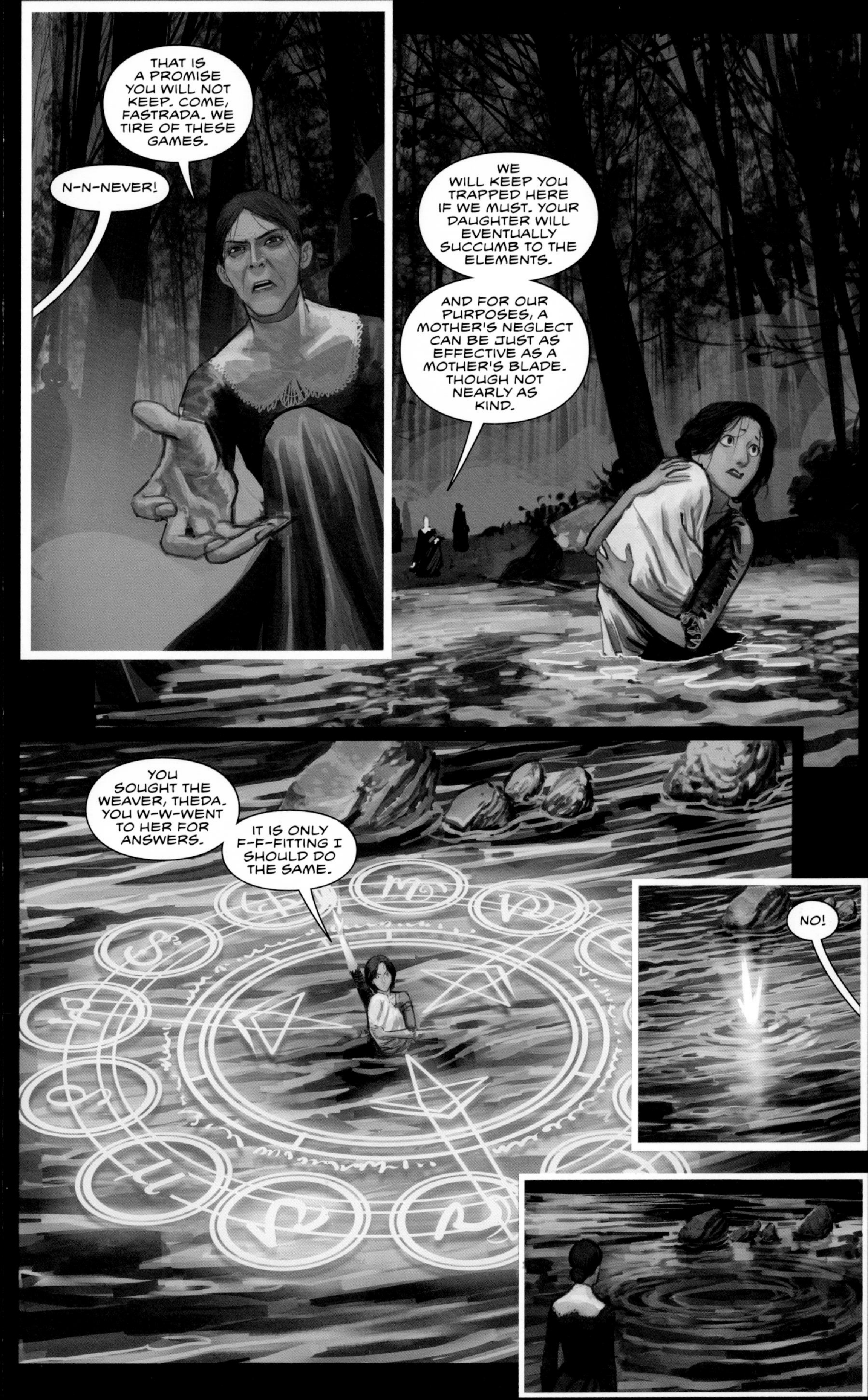
THAT IS A PROMISE YOU WILL NOT KEEP. COME, FASTRADA. WE TIRE OF THESE GAMES.
N-N-NEVER!
WE WILL KEEP YOU TRAPPED HERE IF WE MUST. YOUR DAUGHTER WILL EVENTUALLY SUCCUMB TO THE ELEMENTS.
AND FOR OUR PURPOSES, A MOTHER'S NEGLECT CAN BE JUST AS EFFECTIVE AS A MOTHER'S BLADE. THOUGH NOT NEARLY AS KIND.
YOU SOUGHT THE WEAVER, THEDA. YOU W-W-WENT TO HER FOR ANSWERS.
IT IS ONLY F-F-FITTING I SHOULD DO THE SAME.
NO!

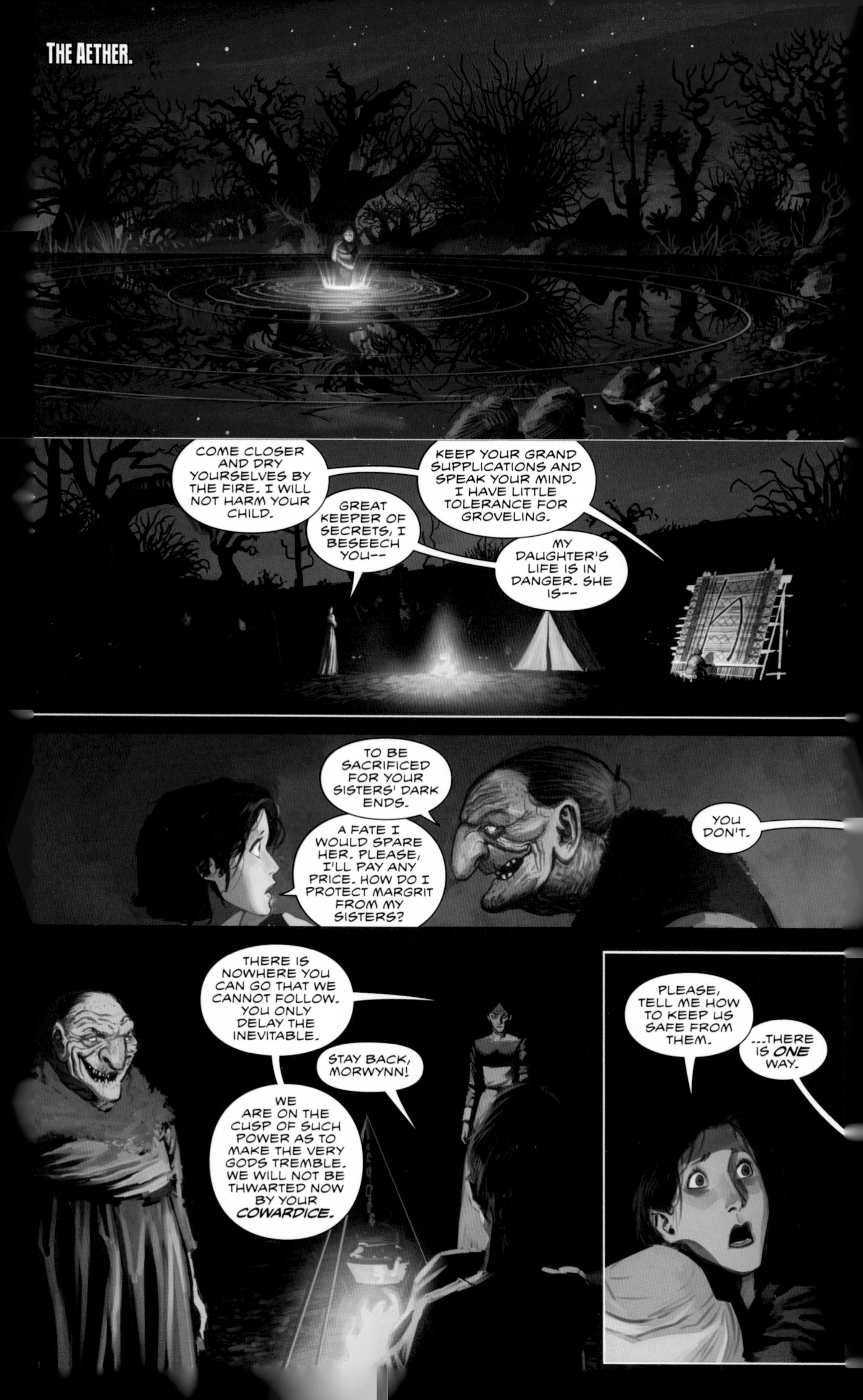
THE AETHER.
COME CLOSER AND DRY YOURSELVES BY THE FIRE. I WILL NOT HARM YOUR CHILD.
KEEP YOUR GRAND SUPPLICATIONS AND SPEAK YOUR MIND. I HAVE LITTLE TOLERANCE FOR GROVELING.
GREAT KEEPER OF SECRETS, I BESEECH YOU--
MY DAUGHTER'S LIFE IS IN DANGER. SHE IS--
TO BE SACRIFICED FOR YOUR SISTERS' DARK ENDS.
A FATE I WOULD SPARE HER. PLEASE, I'LL PAY ANY PRICE. HOW DO I PROTECT MARGRIT FROM MY SISTERS?
YOU DON'T.
THERE IS NOWHERE YOU CAN GO THAT WE CANNOT FOLLOW. YOU ONLY DELAY THE INEVITABLE.
STAY BACK, MORWYNN!
WE ARE ON THE CUSP OF SUCH POWER AS TO MAKE THE VERY GODS TREMBLE. WE WILL NOT BE THWARTED NOW BY YOUR COWARDICE.
PLEASE, TELL ME HOW TO KEEP US SAFE FROM THEM.
...THERE IS ONE WAY.

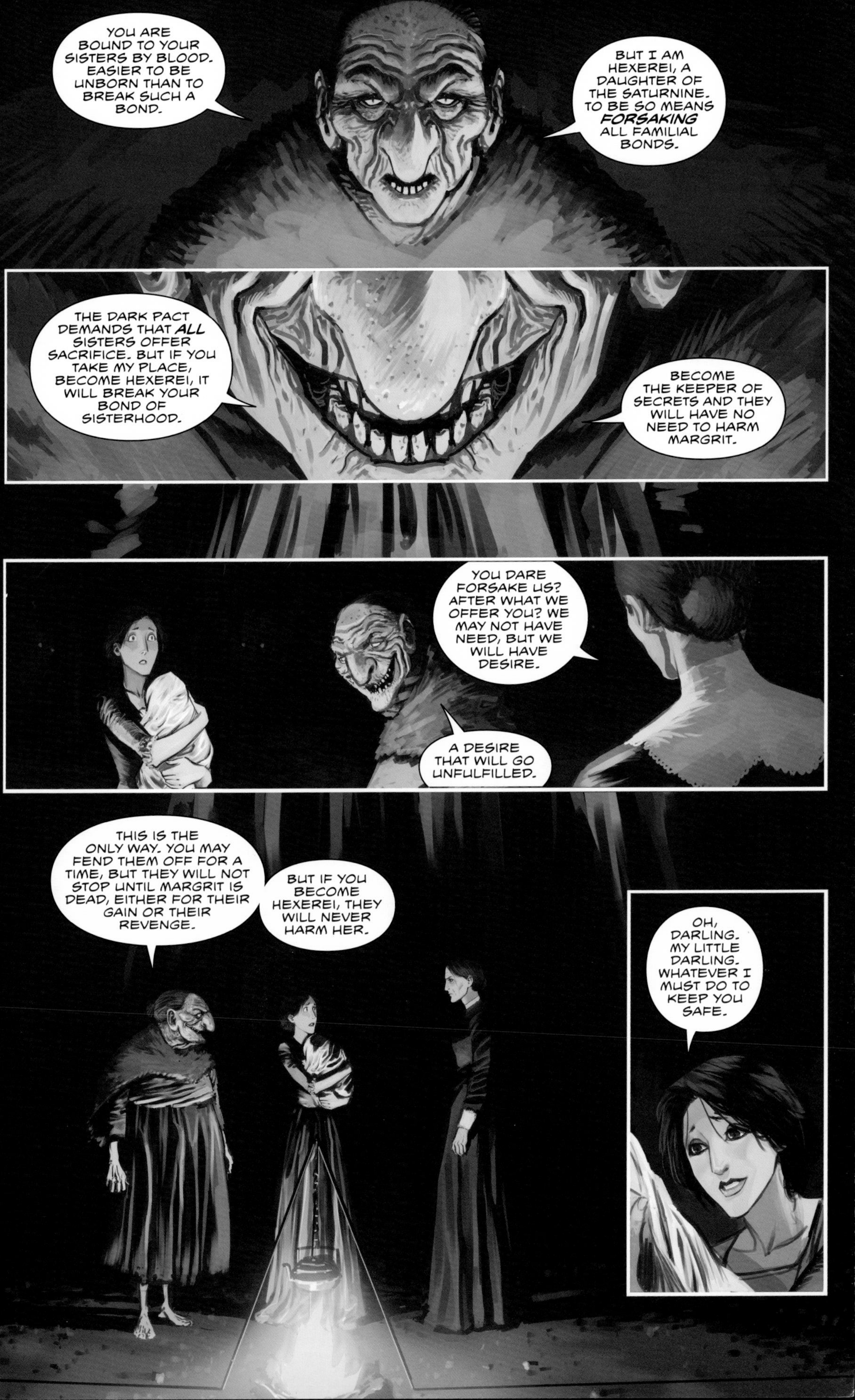
YOU ARE BOUND TO YOUR SISTERS BY BLOOD. EASIER TO BE UNBORN THAN TO BREAK SUCH A BOND.
BUT I AM HEXEREI, A DAUGHTER OF THE SATURNINE. TO BE SO MEANS FORSAKING ALL FAMILIAL BONDS.
THE DARK PACT DEMANDS THAT ALL SISTERS OFFER SACRIFICE. BUT IF YOU TAKE MY PLACE, BECOME HEXEREI, IT WILL BREAK YOUR BOND OF SISTERHOOD.
BECOME THE KEEPER OF SECRETS AND THEY WILL HAVE NO NEED TO HARM MARGRIT.
YOU DARE FORSAKE US? AFTER WHAT WE OFFER YOU? WE MAY NOT HAVE NEED, BUT WE WILL HAVE DESIRE.
A DESIRE THAT WILL GO UNFULFILLED.
THIS IS THE ONLY WAY. YOU MAY FEND THEM OFF FOR A TIME, BUT THEY WILL NOT STOP UNTIL MARGRIT IS DEAD, EITHER FOR THEIR GAIN OR THEIR REVENGE.
BUT IF YOU BECOME HEXEREI, THEY WILL NEVER HARM HER.
OH, DARLING. MY LITTLE DARLING. WHATEVER I MUST DO TO KEEP YOU SAFE.

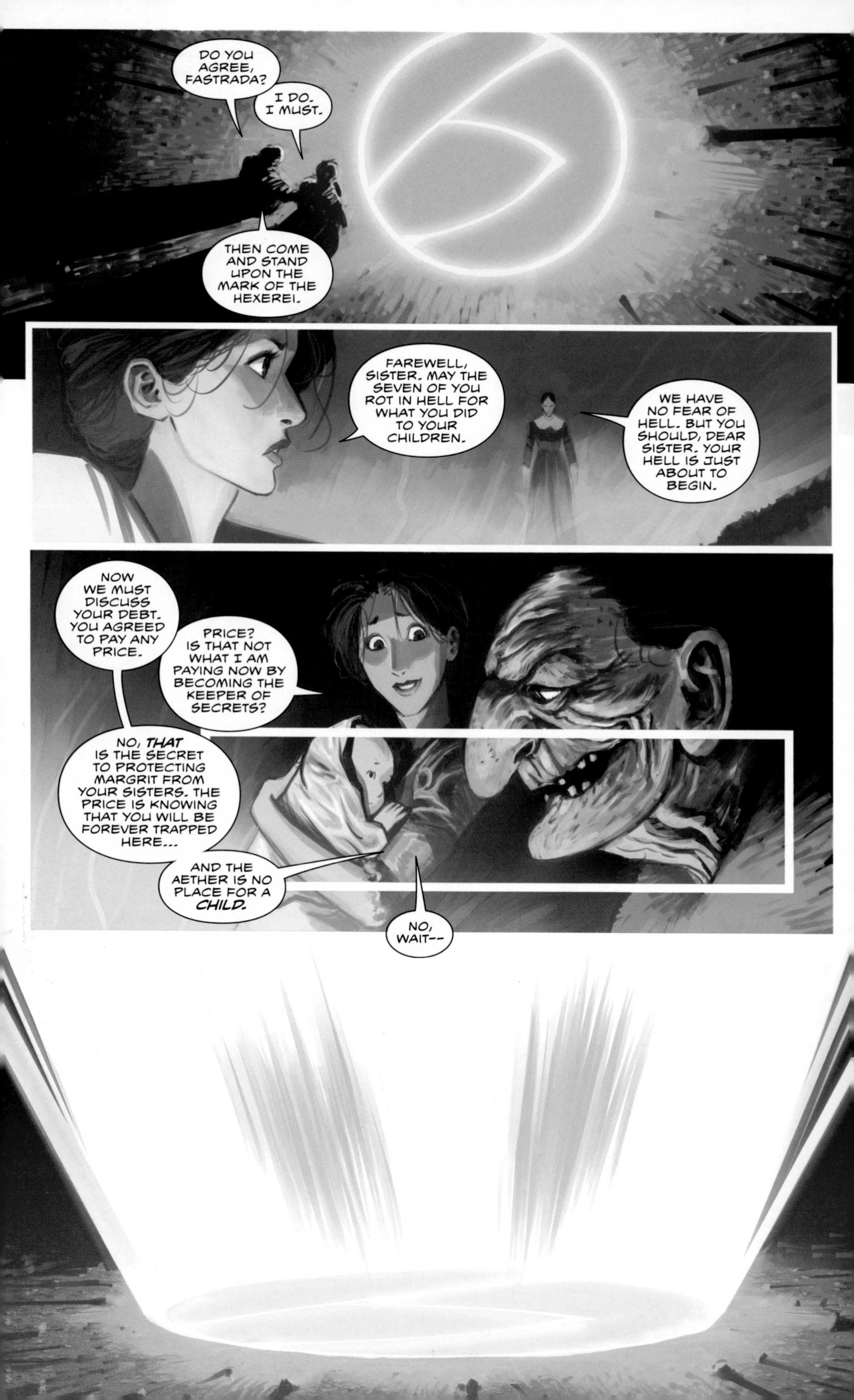
DO YOU AGREE, FASTRADA?
I DO. I MUST.
THEN COME AND STAND UPON THE MARK OF THE HEXEREI.
FAREWELL, SISTER. MAY THE SEVEN OF YOU ROT IN HELL FOR WHAT YOU DID TO YOUR CHILDREN.
WE HAVE NO FEAR OF HELL. BUT YOU SHOULD, DEAR SISTER. YOUR HELL IS JUST ABOUT TO BEGIN.
NOW WE MUST DISCUSS YOUR DEBT. YOU AGREED TO PAY ANY PRICE.
PRICE? IS THAT NOT WHAT I AM PAYING NOW BY BECOMING THE KEEPER OF SECRETS?
NO, ***THAT*** IS THE SECRET TO PROTECTING MARGRIT FROM YOUR SISTERS. THE PRICE IS KNOWING THAT YOU WILL BE FOREVER TRAPPED HERE...
AND THE AETHER IS NO PLACE FOR A ***CHILD.***
NO, WAIT--

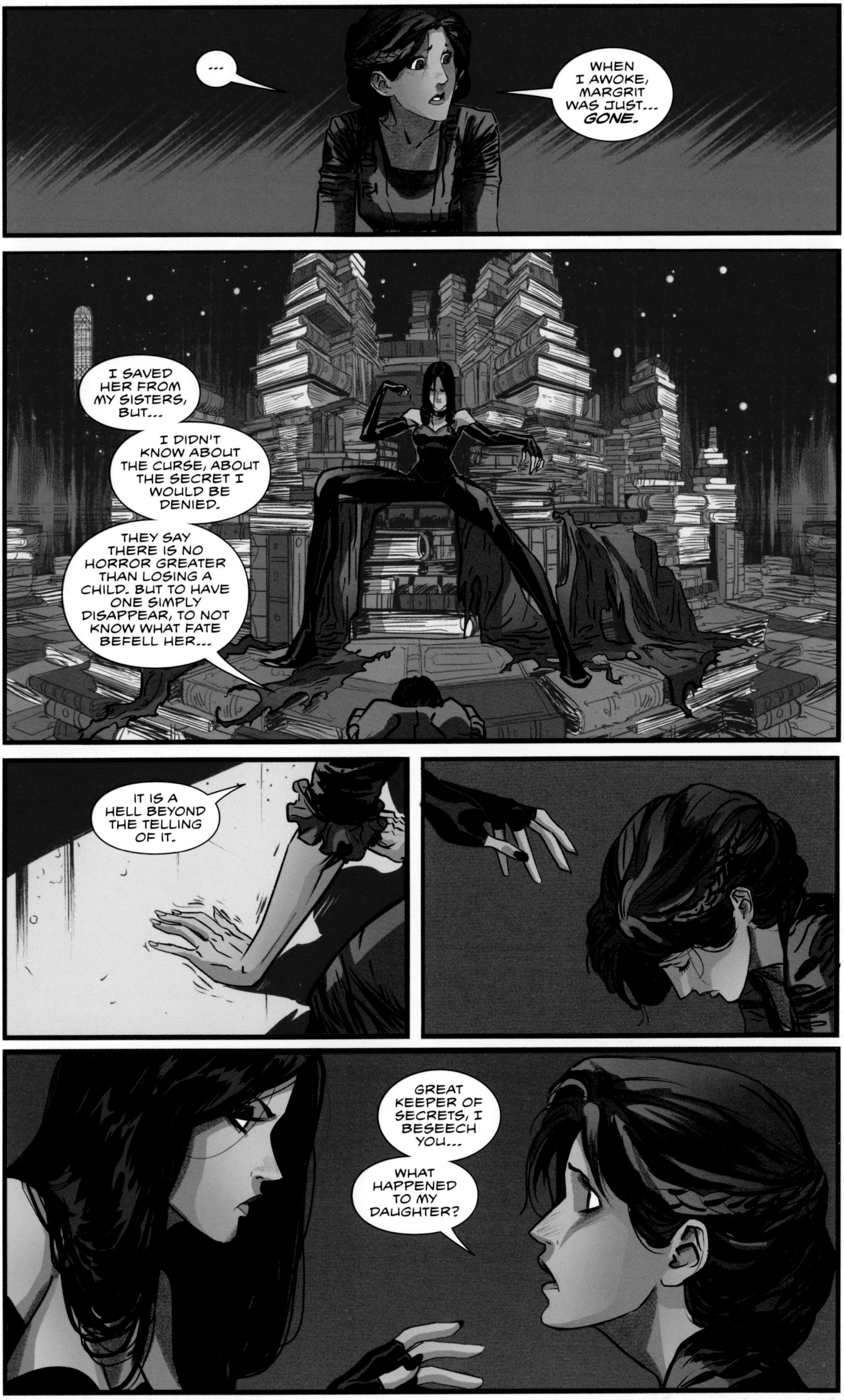
...
WHEN I AWOKE, MARGRIT WAS JUST... GONE.
I SAVED HER FROM MY SISTERS, BUT...
I DIDN'T KNOW ABOUT THE CURSE, ABOUT THE SECRET I WOULD BE DENIED.
THEY SAY THERE IS NO HORROR GREATER THAN LOSING A CHILD. BUT TO HAVE ONE SIMPLY DISAPPEAR, TO NOT KNOW WHAT FATE BEFELL HER...
IT IS A HELL BEYOND THE TELLING OF IT.
GREAT KEEPER OF SECRETS, I BESEECH YOU...
WHAT HAPPENED TO MY DAUGHTER?

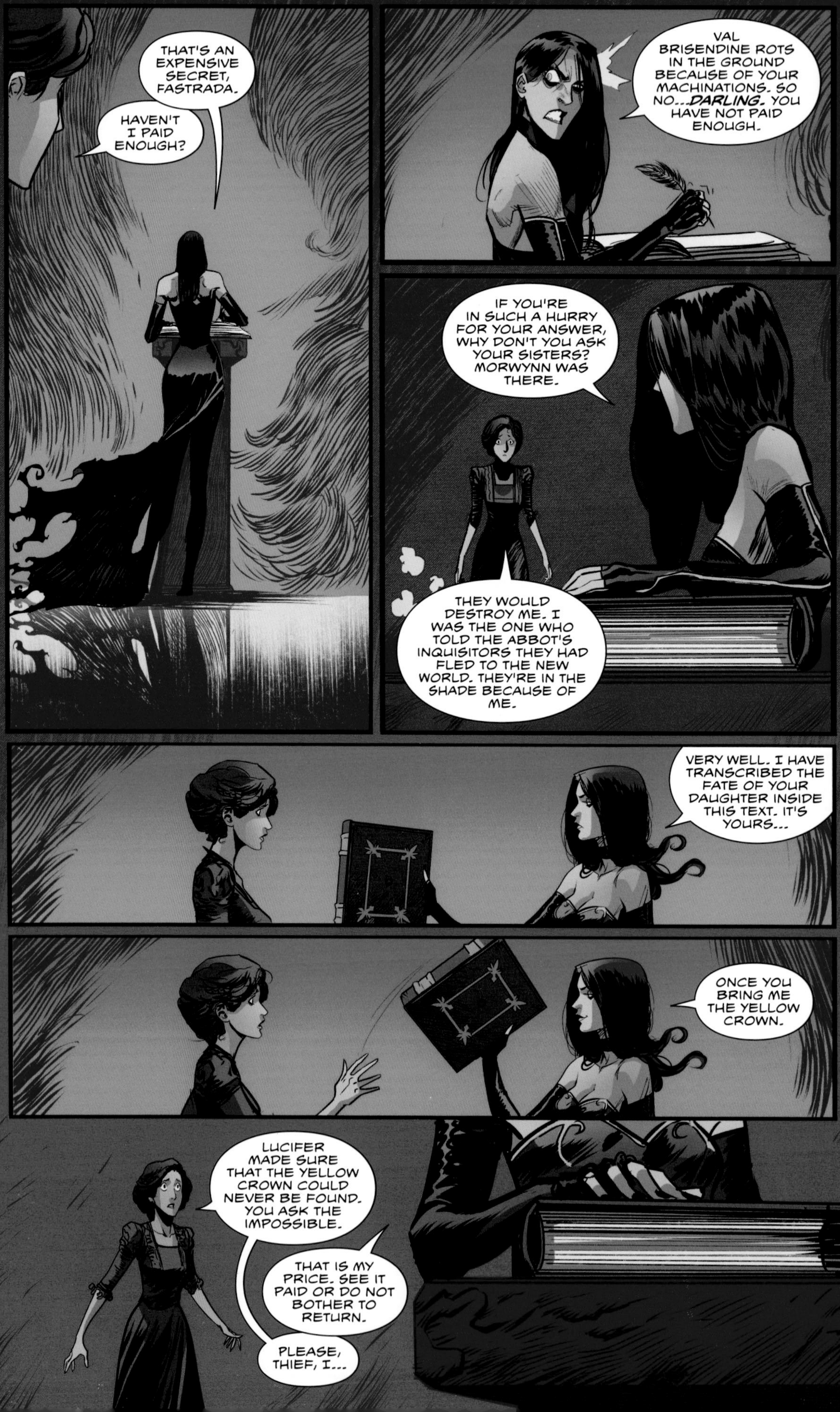

THAT'S AN EXPENSIVE SECRET, FASTRADA.
HAVEN'T I PAID ENOUGH?
VAL BRISENDINE ROTS IN THE GROUND BECAUSE OF YOUR MACHINATIONS. SO NO...DARLING. YOU HAVE NOT PAID ENOUGH.
IF YOU'RE IN SUCH A HURRY FOR YOUR ANSWER, WHY DON'T YOU ASK YOUR SISTERS? MORWYNN WAS THERE.
THEY WOULD DESTROY ME. I WAS THE ONE WHO TOLD THE ABBOT'S INQUISITORS THEY HAD FLED TO THE NEW WORLD. THEY'RE IN THE SHADE BECAUSE OF ME.
VERY WELL. I HAVE TRANSCRIBED THE FATE OF YOUR DAUGHTER INSIDE THIS TEXT. IT'S YOURS...
ONCE YOU BRING ME THE YELLOW CROWN.
LUCIFER MADE SURE THAT THE YELLOW CROWN COULD NEVER BE FOUND. YOU ASK THE IMPOSSIBLE.
THAT IS MY PRICE. SEE IT PAID OR DO NOT BOTHER TO RETURN.
PLEASE, THIEF, I...

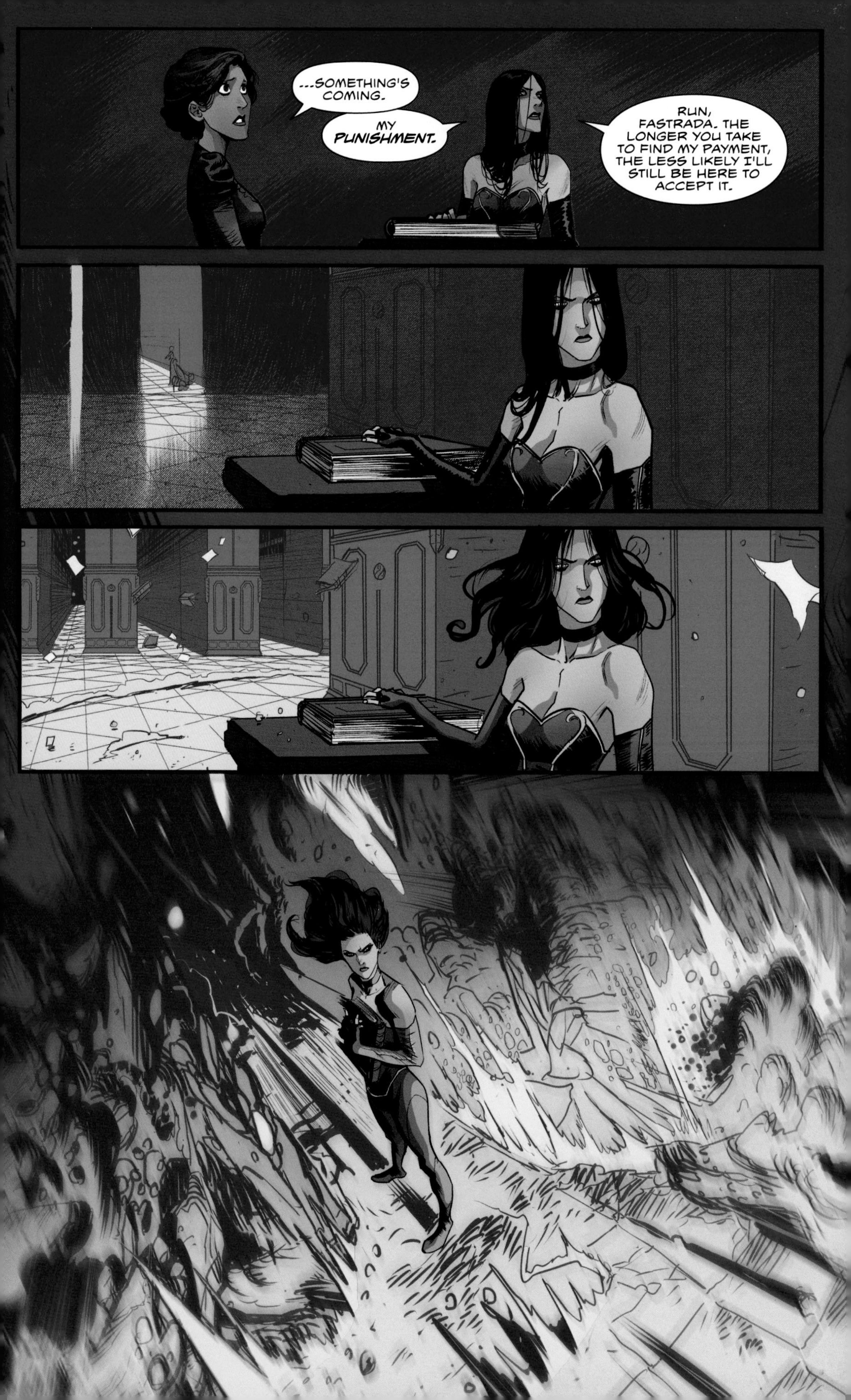
...SOMETHING'S COMING.
MY PUNISHMENT.
RUN, FASTRADA. THE LONGER YOU TAKE TO FIND MY PAYMENT, THE LESS LIKELY I'LL STILL BE HERE TO ACCEPT IT.

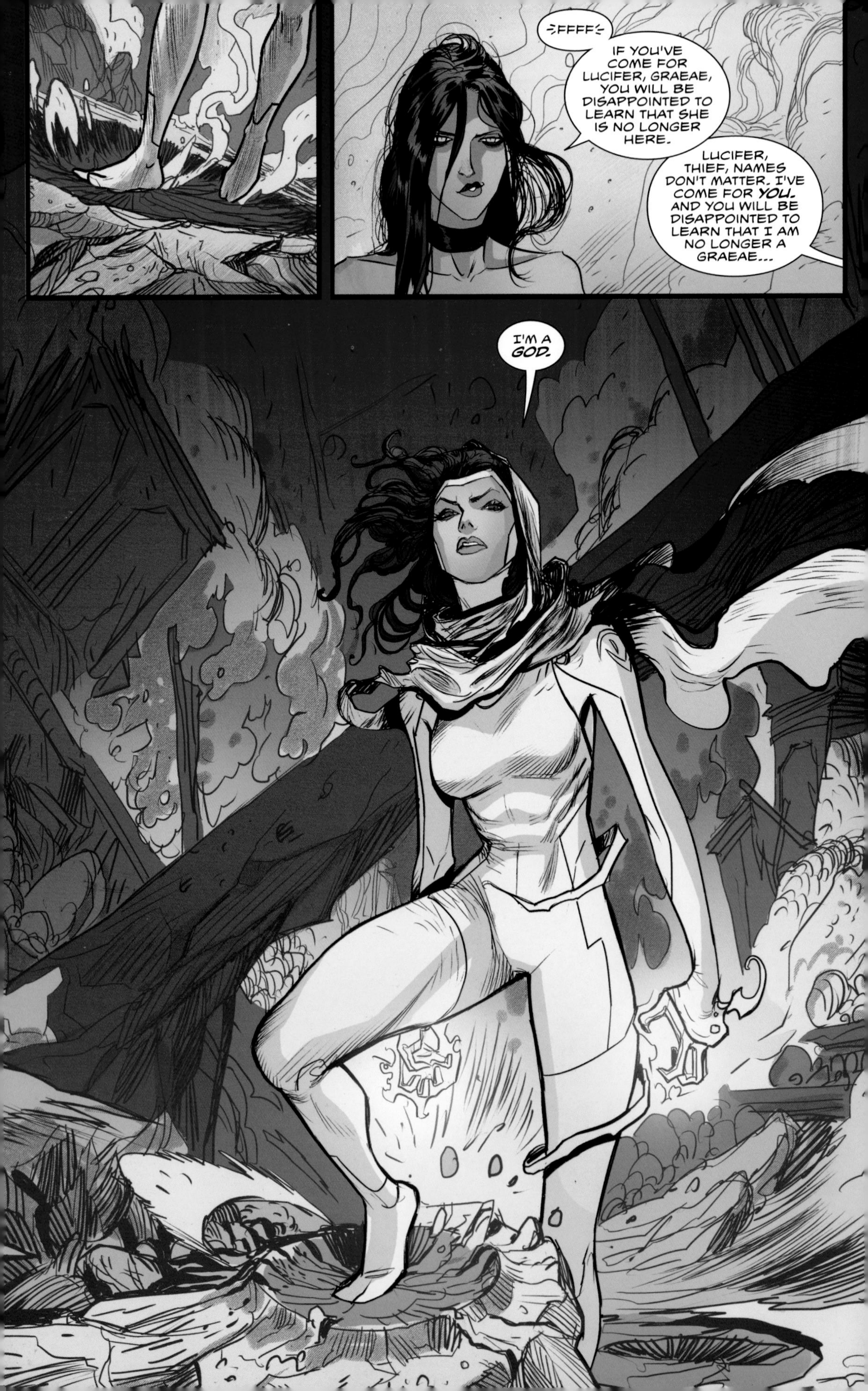

FFFF
IF YOU'VE COME FOR LUCIFER, GRAEAE, YOU WILL BE DISAPPOINTED TO LEARN THAT SHE IS NO LONGER HERE.
LUCIFER, THIEF, NAMES DON'T MATTER. I'VE COME FOR YOU. AND YOU WILL BE DISAPPOINTED TO LEARN THAT I AM NO LONGER A GRAEAE...
I'M A GOD.

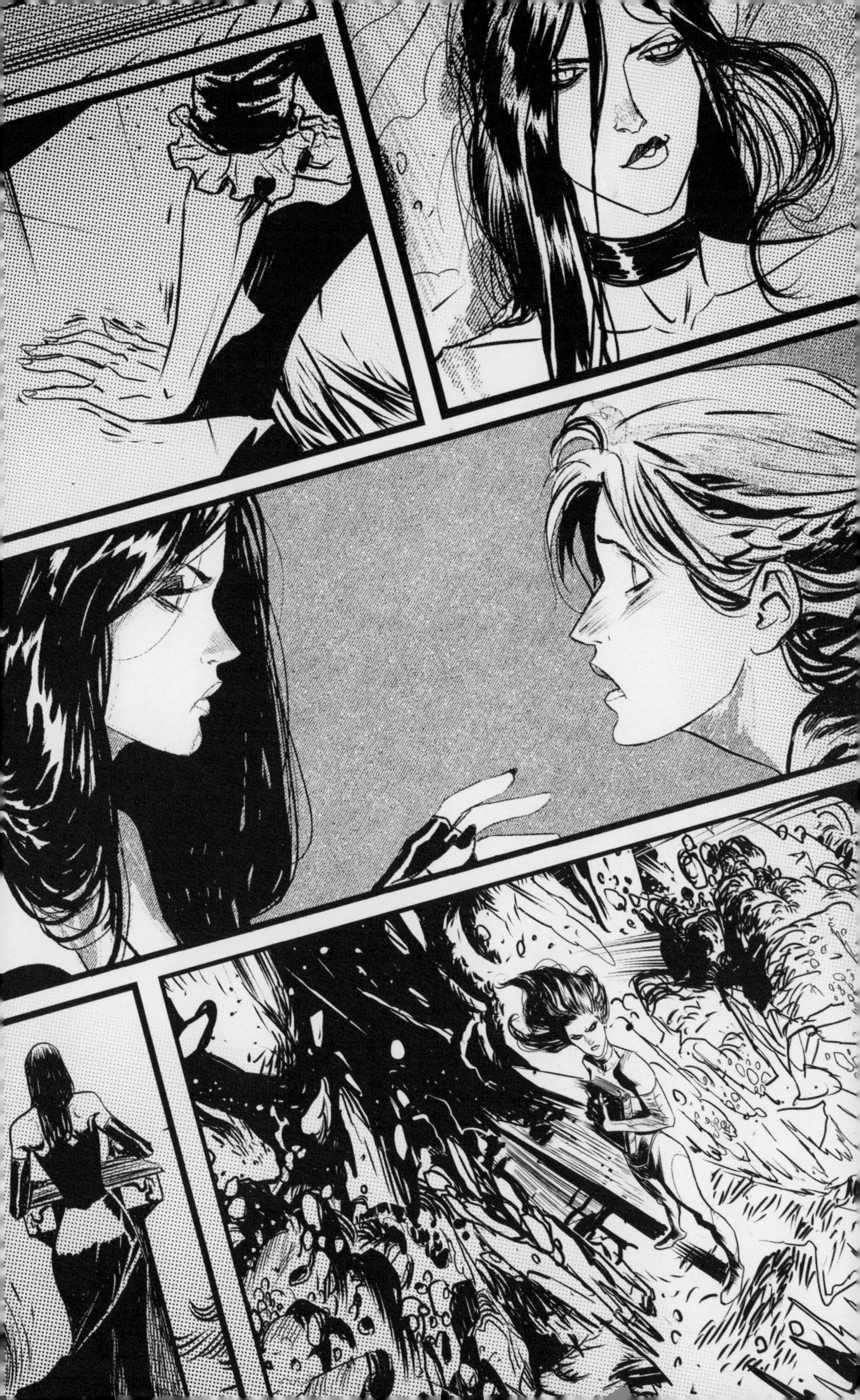

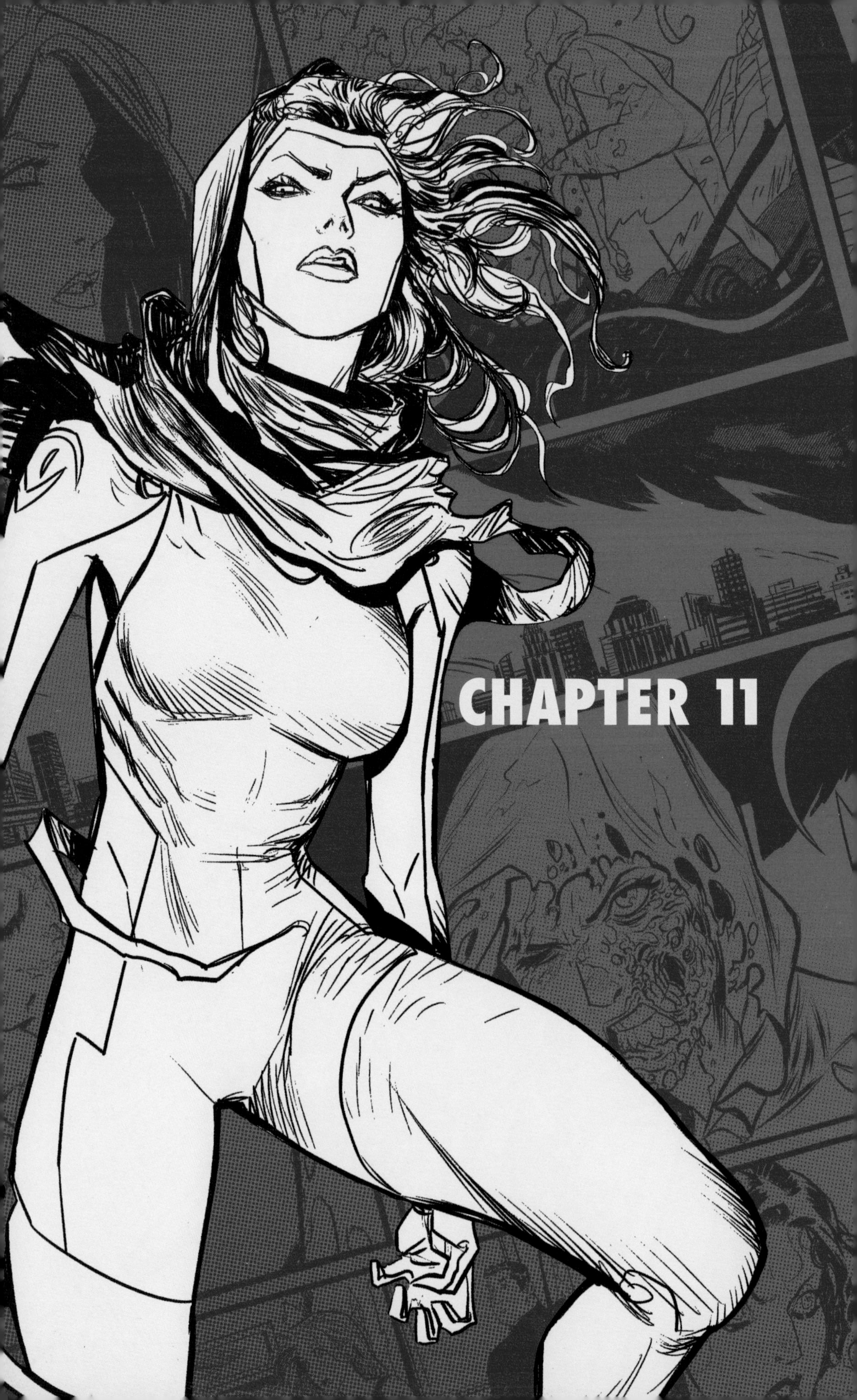

CHAPTER 11

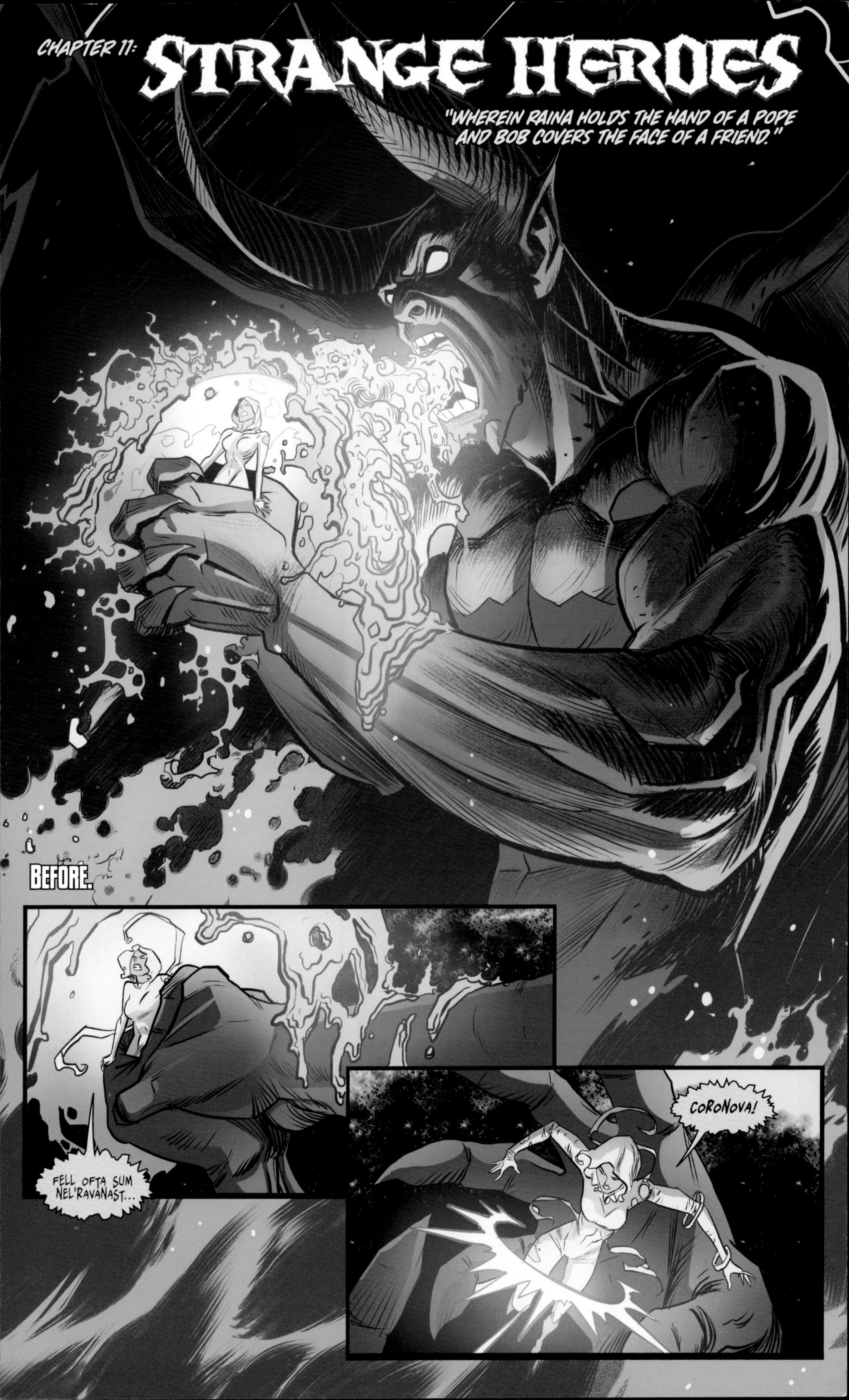
CHAPTER 11: STRANGE HEROES
"WHEREIN RAINA HOLDS THE HAND OF A POPE AND BOB COVERS THE FACE OF A FRIEND."
BEFORE.
FELL OFTA SUM NEL'RAVANAST...
CORONOVA!

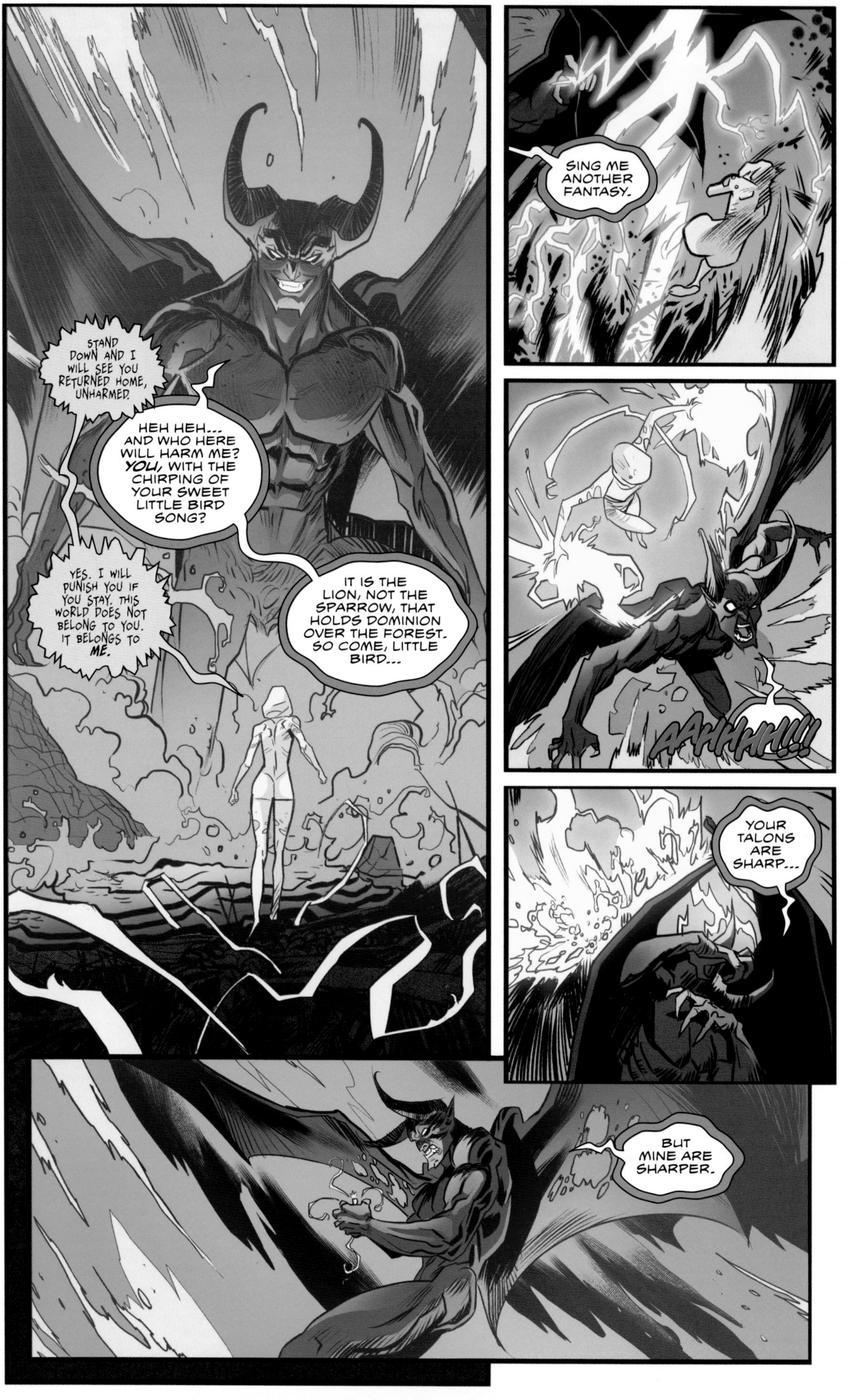
STAND DOWN AND I WILL SEE YOU RETURNED HOME, UNHARMED.
HEH HEH... AND WHO HERE WILL HARM ME? YOU, WITH THE CHIRPING OF YOUR SWEET LITTLE BIRD SONG?
YES. I WILL PUNISH YOU IF YOU STAY. THIS WORLD DOES NOT BELONG TO YOU. IT BELONGS TO ME.
IT IS THE LION, NOT THE SPARROW, THAT HOLDS DOMINION OVER THE FOREST. SO COME, LITTLE BIRD...
SING ME ANOTHER FANTASY.
AAHHHH!!!
YOUR TALONS ARE SHARP...
BUT MINE ARE SHARPER.

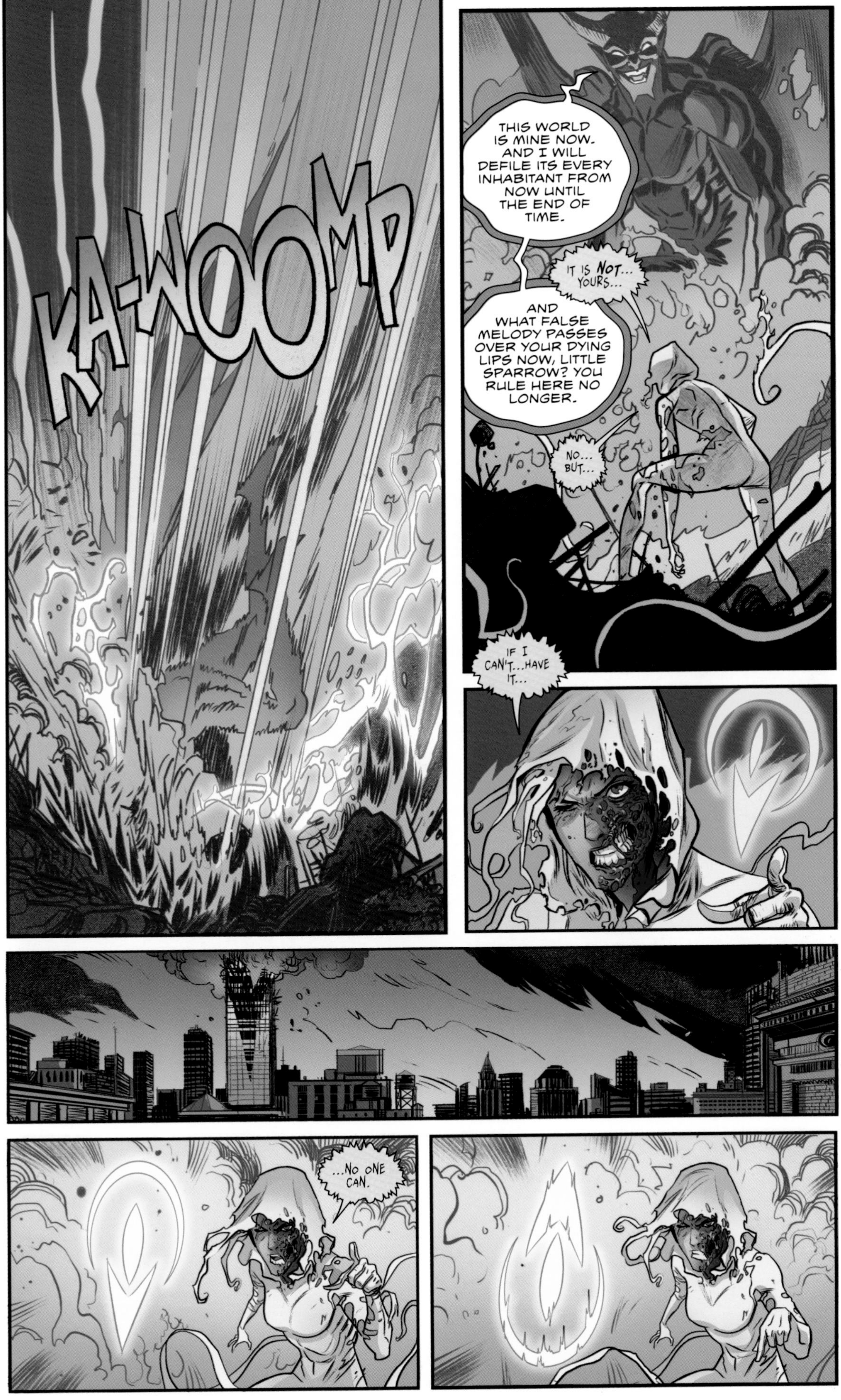
KA-WOOMP
THIS WORLD IS MINE NOW. AND I WILL DEFILE ITS EVERY INHABITANT FROM NOW UNTIL THE END OF TIME.
IT IS NOT... YOURS...
AND WHAT FALSE MELODY PASSES OVER YOUR DYING LIPS NOW, LITTLE SPARROW? YOU RULE HERE NO LONGER.
NO... BUT...
IF I CAN'T...HAVE IT...
...NO ONE CAN.

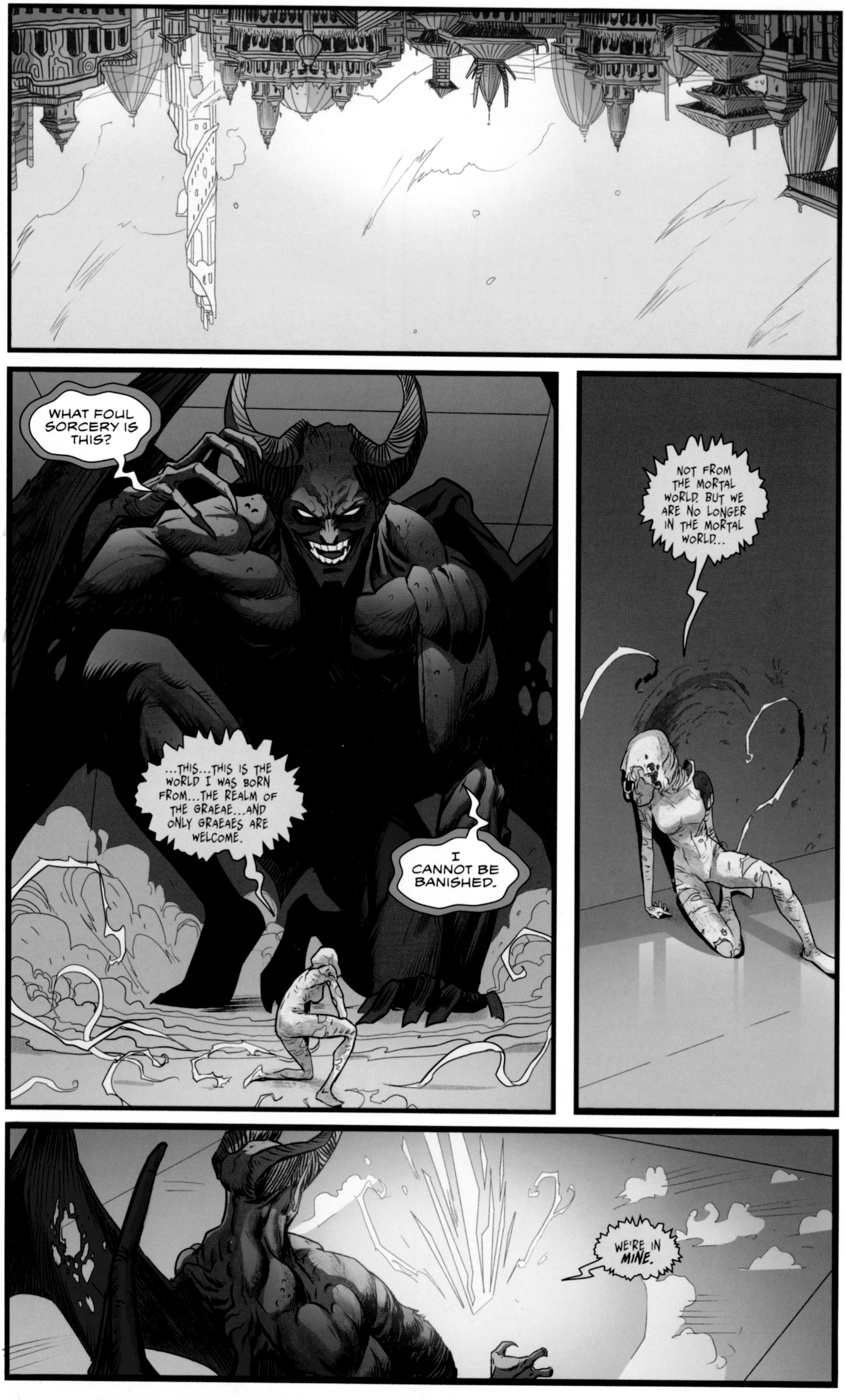
WHAT FOUL SORCERY IS THIS?
NOT FROM THE MORTAL WORLD. BUT WE ARE NO LONGER IN THE MORTAL WORLD...
...THIS...THIS IS THE WORLD I WAS BORN FROM...THE REALM OF THE GRAEAE...AND ONLY GRAEAES ARE WELCOME.
I CANNOT BE BANISHED.
WE'RE IN MINE.

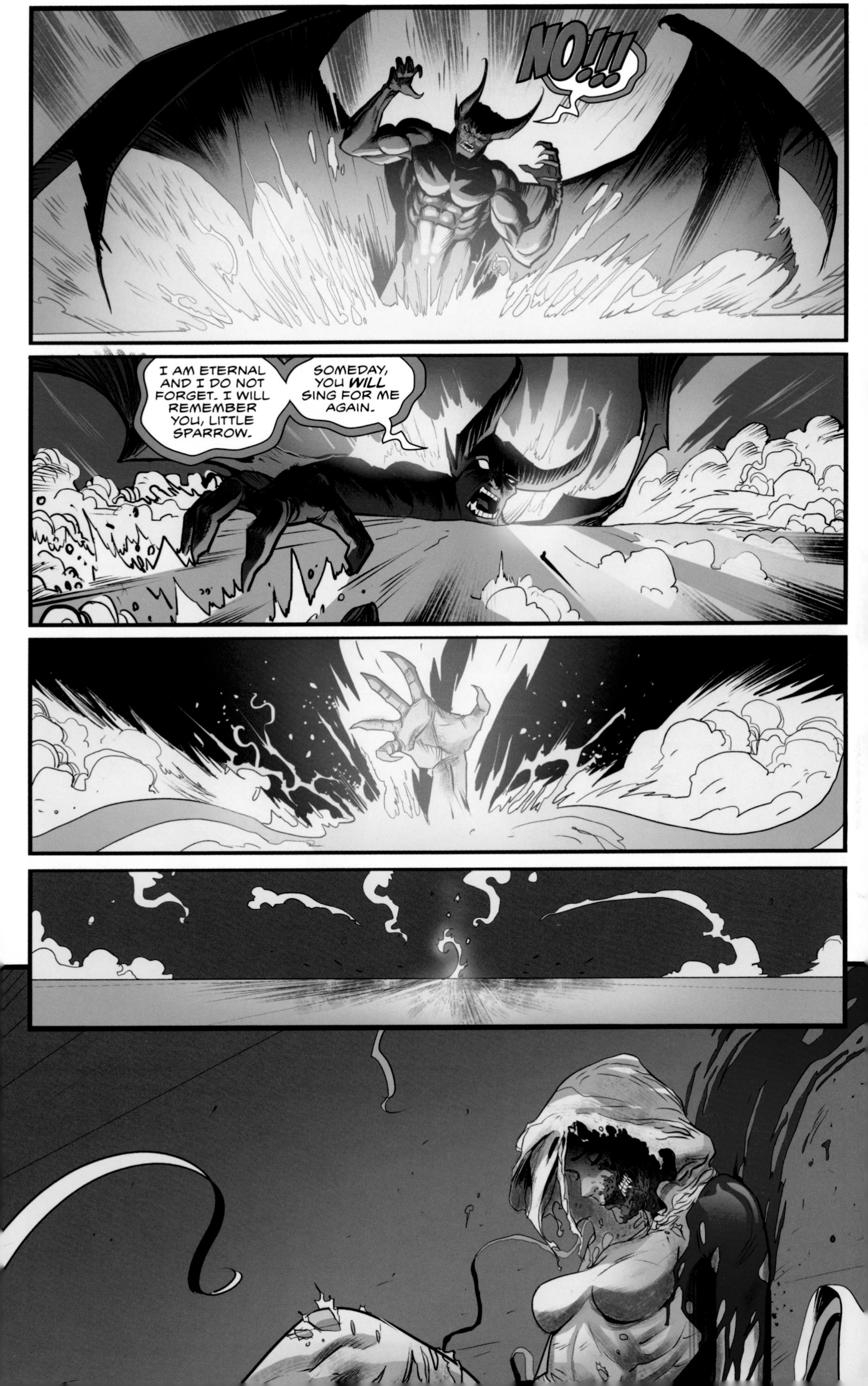
NO!!!...
I AM ETERNAL AND I DO NOT FORGET. I WILL REMEMBER YOU, LITTLE SPARROW.
SOMEDAY, YOU WILL SING FOR ME AGAIN.

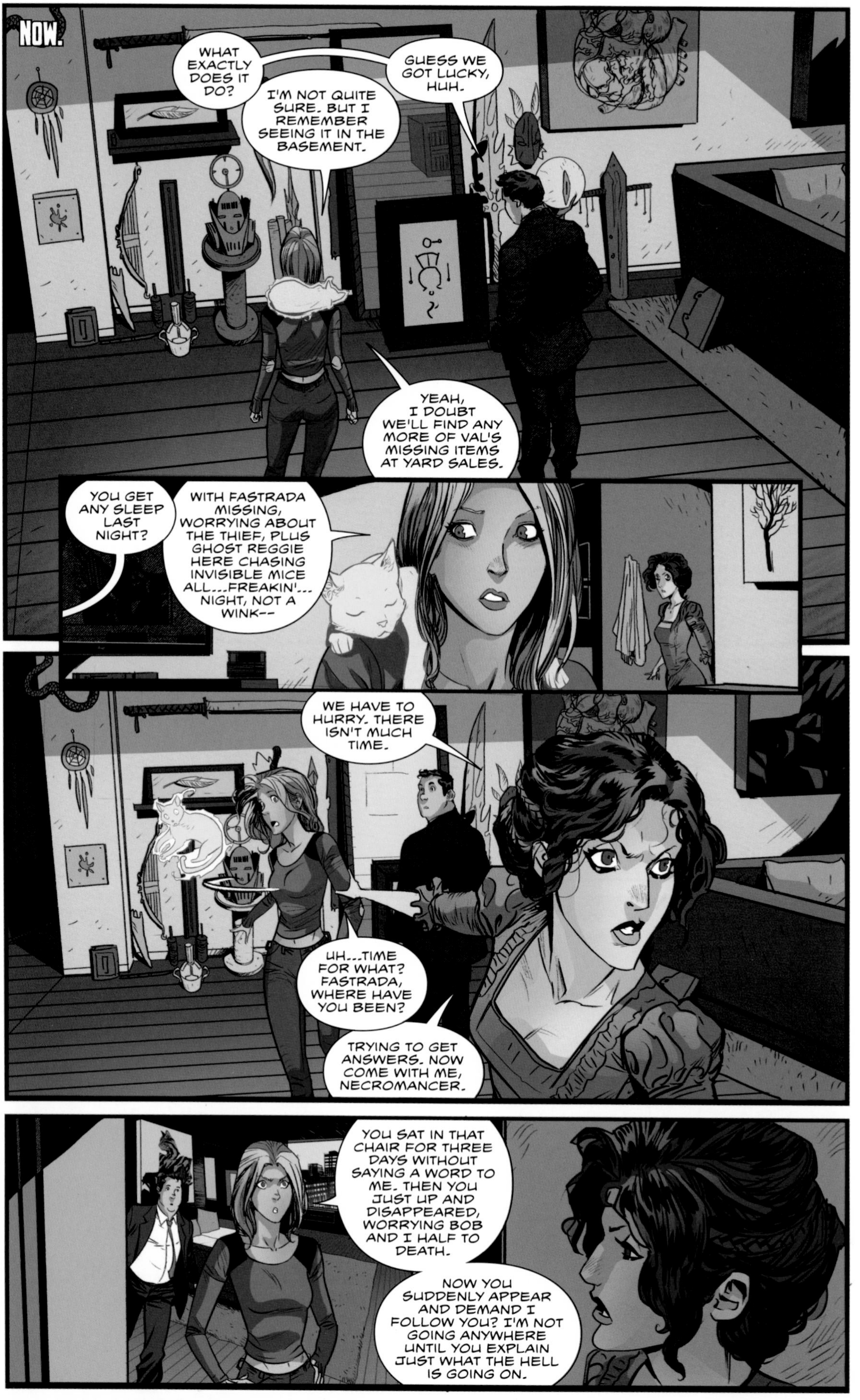
NOW.
WHAT EXACTLY DOES IT DO?
I'M NOT QUITE SURE. BUT I REMEMBER SEEING IT IN THE BASEMENT.
GUESS WE GOT LUCKY, HUH.
YEAH, I DOUBT WE'LL FIND ANY MORE OF VAL'S MISSING ITEMS AT YARD SALES.
YOU GET ANY SLEEP LAST NIGHT?
WITH FASTRADA MISSING, WORRYING ABOUT THE THIEF, PLUS GHOST REGGIE HERE CHASING INVISIBLE MICE ALL...FREAKIN'... NIGHT, NOT A WINK--
WE HAVE TO HURRY. THERE ISN'T MUCH TIME.
UH...TIME FOR WHAT? FASTRADA, WHERE HAVE YOU BEEN?
TRYING TO GET ANSWERS. NOW COME WITH ME, NECROMANCER.
YOU SAT IN THAT CHAIR FOR THREE DAYS WITHOUT SAYING A WORD TO ME. THEN YOU JUST UP AND DISAPPEARED, WORRYING BOB AND I HALF TO DEATH.
NOW YOU SUDDENLY APPEAR AND DEMAND I FOLLOW YOU? I'M NOT GOING ANYWHERE UNTIL YOU EXPLAIN JUST WHAT THE HELL IS GOING ON.

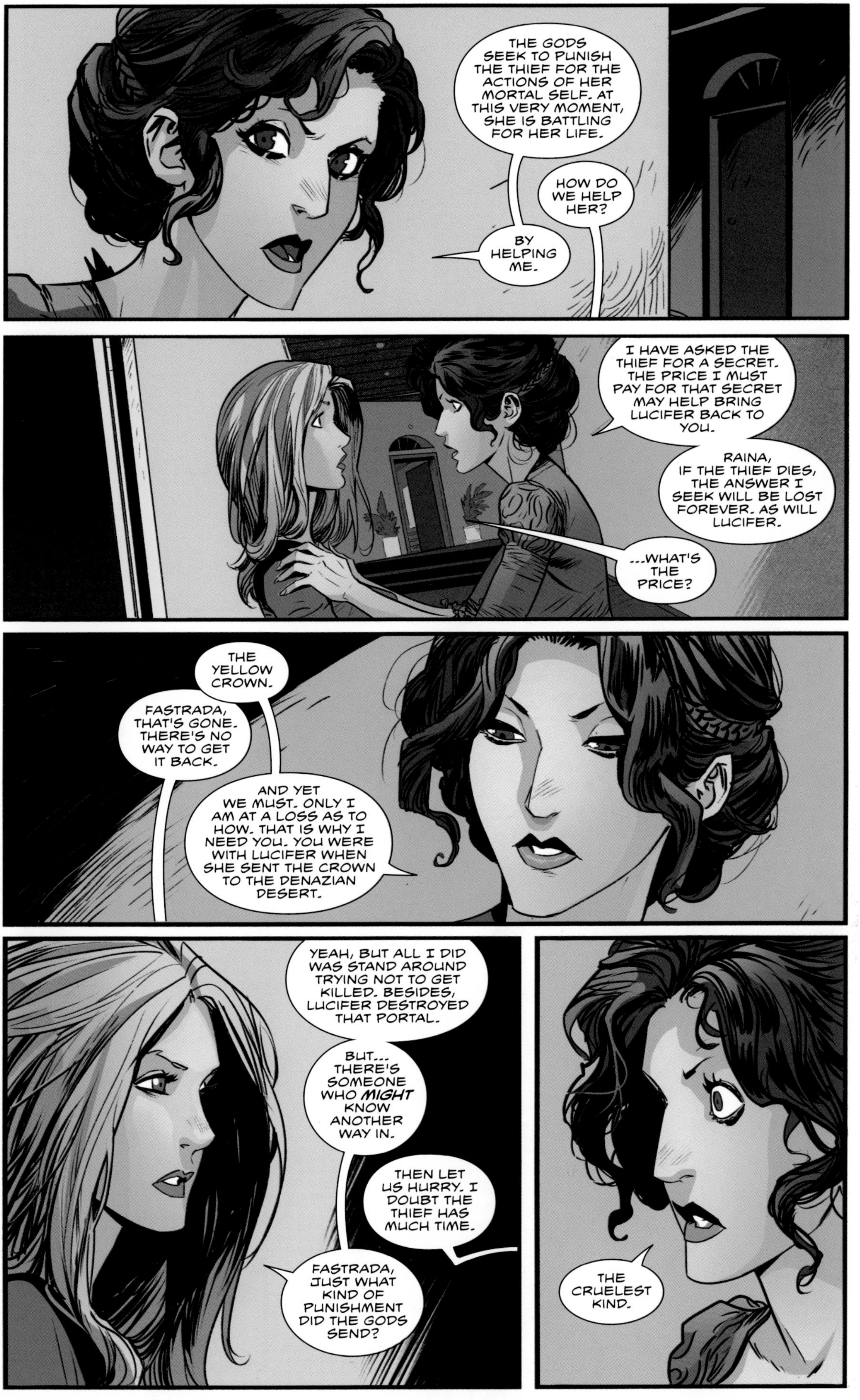
THE GODS SEEK TO PUNISH THE THIEF FOR THE ACTIONS OF HER MORTAL SELF. AT THIS VERY MOMENT, SHE IS BATTLING FOR HER LIFE.
HOW DO WE HELP HER?
BY HELPING ME.
I HAVE ASKED THE THIEF FOR A SECRET. THE PRICE I MUST PAY FOR THAT SECRET MAY HELP BRING LUCIFER BACK TO YOU.
RAINA, IF THE THIEF DIES, THE ANSWER I SEEK WILL BE LOST FOREVER. AS WILL LUCIFER.
...WHAT'S THE PRICE?
THE YELLOW CROWN.
FASTRADA, THAT'S GONE. THERE'S NO WAY TO GET IT BACK.
AND YET WE MUST. ONLY I AM AT A LOSS AS TO HOW. THAT IS WHY I NEED YOU. YOU WERE WITH LUCIFER WHEN SHE SENT THE CROWN TO THE DENAZIAN DESERT.
YEAH, BUT ALL I DID WAS STAND AROUND TRYING NOT TO GET KILLED. BESIDES, LUCIFER DESTROYED THAT PORTAL.
BUT... THERE'S SOMEONE WHO *MIGHT* KNOW ANOTHER WAY IN.
THEN LET US HURRY. I DOUBT THE THIEF HAS MUCH TIME.
FASTRADA, JUST WHAT KIND OF PUNISHMENT DID THE GODS SEND?
THE CRUELEST KIND.

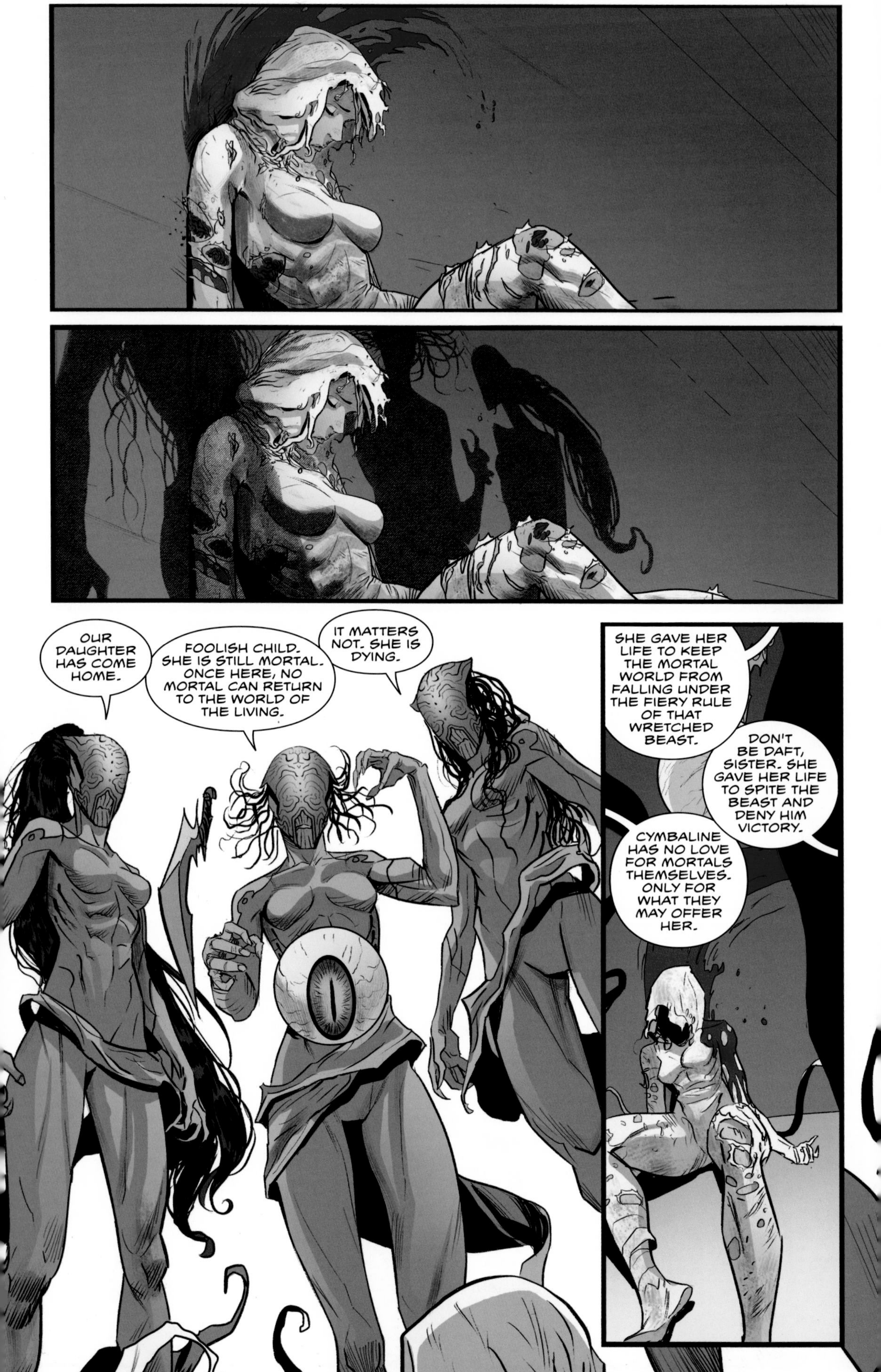
OUR DAUGHTER HAS COME HOME.
FOOLISH CHILD. SHE IS STILL MORTAL. ONCE HERE, NO MORTAL CAN RETURN TO THE WORLD OF THE LIVING.
IT MATTERS NOT. SHE IS DYING.
SHE GAVE HER LIFE TO KEEP THE MORTAL WORLD FROM FALLING UNDER THE FIERY RULE OF THAT WRETCHED BEAST.
DON'T BE DAFT, SISTER. SHE GAVE HER LIFE TO SPITE THE BEAST AND DENY HIM VICTORY.
CYMBALINE HAS NO LOVE FOR MORTALS THEMSELVES. ONLY FOR WHAT THEY MAY OFFER HER.

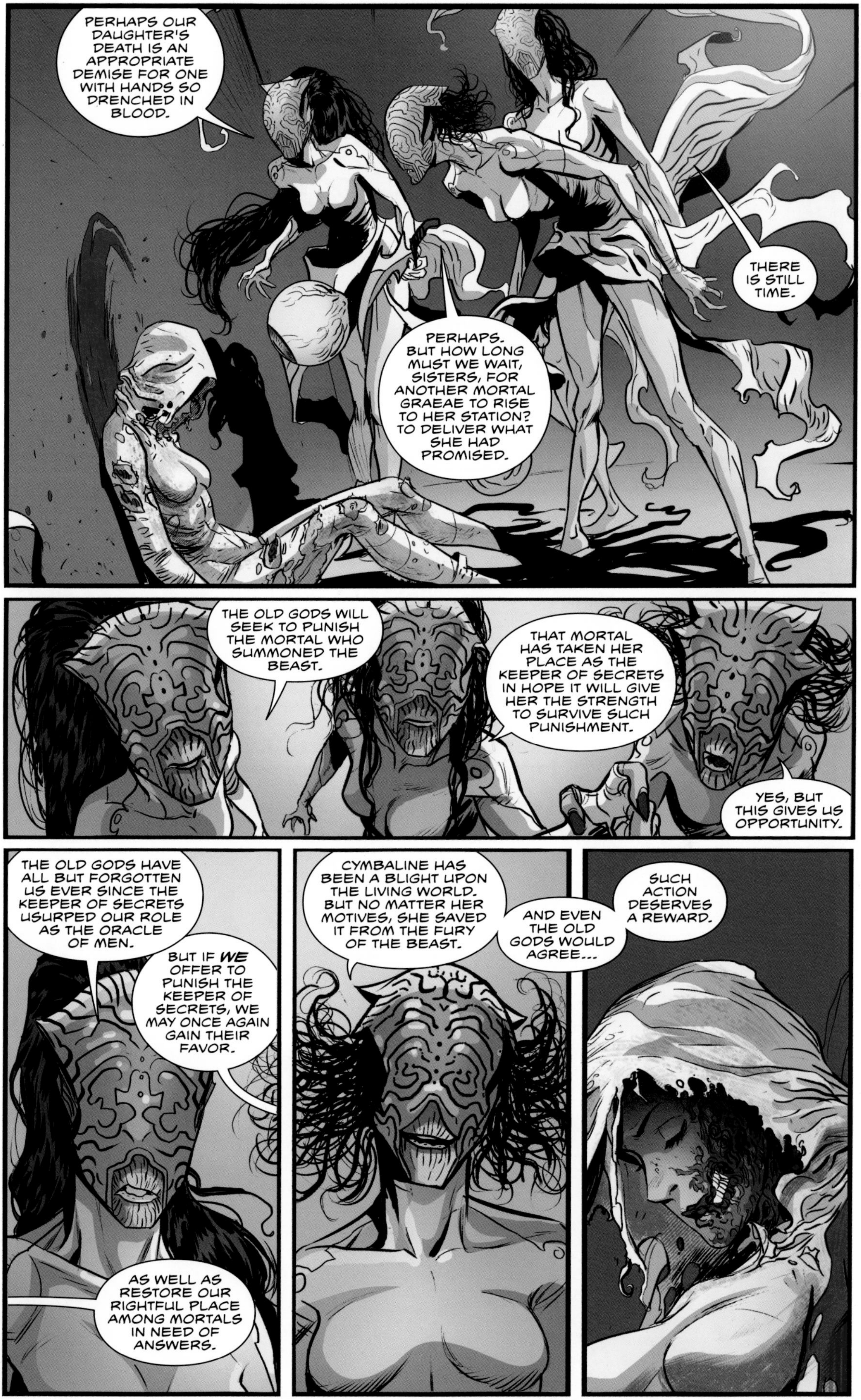
PERHAPS OUR DAUGHTER'S DEATH IS AN APPROPRIATE DEMISE FOR ONE WITH HANDS SO DRENCHED IN BLOOD.
PERHAPS. BUT HOW LONG MUST WE WAIT, SISTERS, FOR ANOTHER MORTAL GRAEAE TO RISE TO HER STATION? TO DELIVER WHAT SHE HAD PROMISED.
THERE IS STILL TIME.
THE OLD GODS WILL SEEK TO PUNISH THE MORTAL WHO SUMMONED THE BEAST.
THAT MORTAL HAS TAKEN HER PLACE AS THE KEEPER OF SECRETS IN HOPE IT WILL GIVE HER THE STRENGTH TO SURVIVE SUCH PUNISHMENT.
YES, BUT THIS GIVES US OPPORTUNITY.
THE OLD GODS HAVE ALL BUT FORGOTTEN US EVER SINCE THE KEEPER OF SECRETS USURPED OUR ROLE AS THE ORACLE OF MEN.
BUT IF WE OFFER TO PUNISH THE KEEPER OF SECRETS, WE MAY ONCE AGAIN GAIN THEIR FAVOR.
AS WELL AS RESTORE OUR RIGHTFUL PLACE AMONG MORTALS IN NEED OF ANSWERS.
CYMBALINE HAS BEEN A BLIGHT UPON THE LIVING WORLD. BUT NO MATTER HER MOTIVES, SHE SAVED IT FROM THE FURY OF THE BEAST.
AND EVEN THE OLD GODS WOULD AGREE...
SUCH ACTION DESERVES A REWARD.

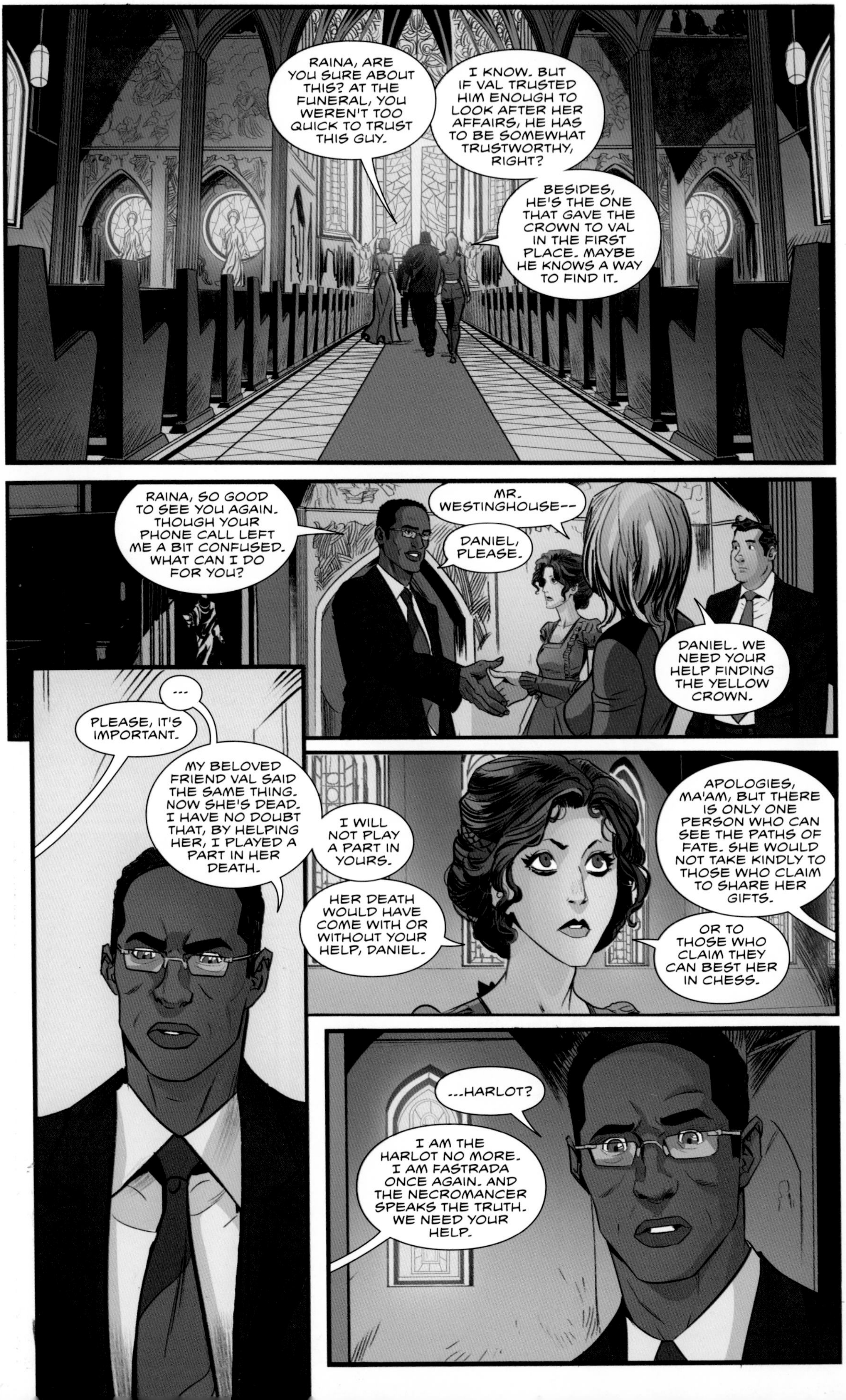
RAINA, ARE YOU SURE ABOUT THIS? AT THE FUNERAL, YOU WEREN'T TOO QUICK TO TRUST THIS GUY.
I KNOW. BUT IF VAL TRUSTED HIM ENOUGH TO LOOK AFTER HER AFFAIRS, HE HAS TO BE SOMEWHAT TRUSTWORTHY, RIGHT?
BESIDES, HE'S THE ONE THAT GAVE THE CROWN TO VAL IN THE FIRST PLACE. MAYBE HE KNOWS A WAY TO FIND IT.
RAINA, SO GOOD TO SEE YOU AGAIN. THOUGH YOUR PHONE CALL LEFT ME A BIT CONFUSED. WHAT CAN I DO FOR YOU?
MR. WESTINGHOUSE--
DANIEL, PLEASE.
DANIEL. WE NEED YOUR HELP FINDING THE YELLOW CROWN.
...
PLEASE, IT'S IMPORTANT.
MY BELOVED FRIEND VAL SAID THE SAME THING. NOW SHE'S DEAD. I HAVE NO DOUBT THAT, BY HELPING HER, I PLAYED A PART IN HER DEATH.
I WILL NOT PLAY A PART IN YOURS.
HER DEATH WOULD HAVE COME WITH OR WITHOUT YOUR HELP, DANIEL.
APOLOGIES, MA'AM, BUT THERE IS ONLY ONE PERSON WHO CAN SEE THE PATHS OF FATE. SHE WOULD NOT TAKE KINDLY TO THOSE WHO CLAIM TO SHARE HER GIFTS.
OR TO THOSE WHO CLAIM THEY CAN BEST HER IN CHESS.
...HARLOT?
I AM THE HARLOT NO MORE. I AM FASTRADA ONCE AGAIN. AND THE NECROMANCER SPEAKS THE TRUTH. WE NEED YOUR HELP.

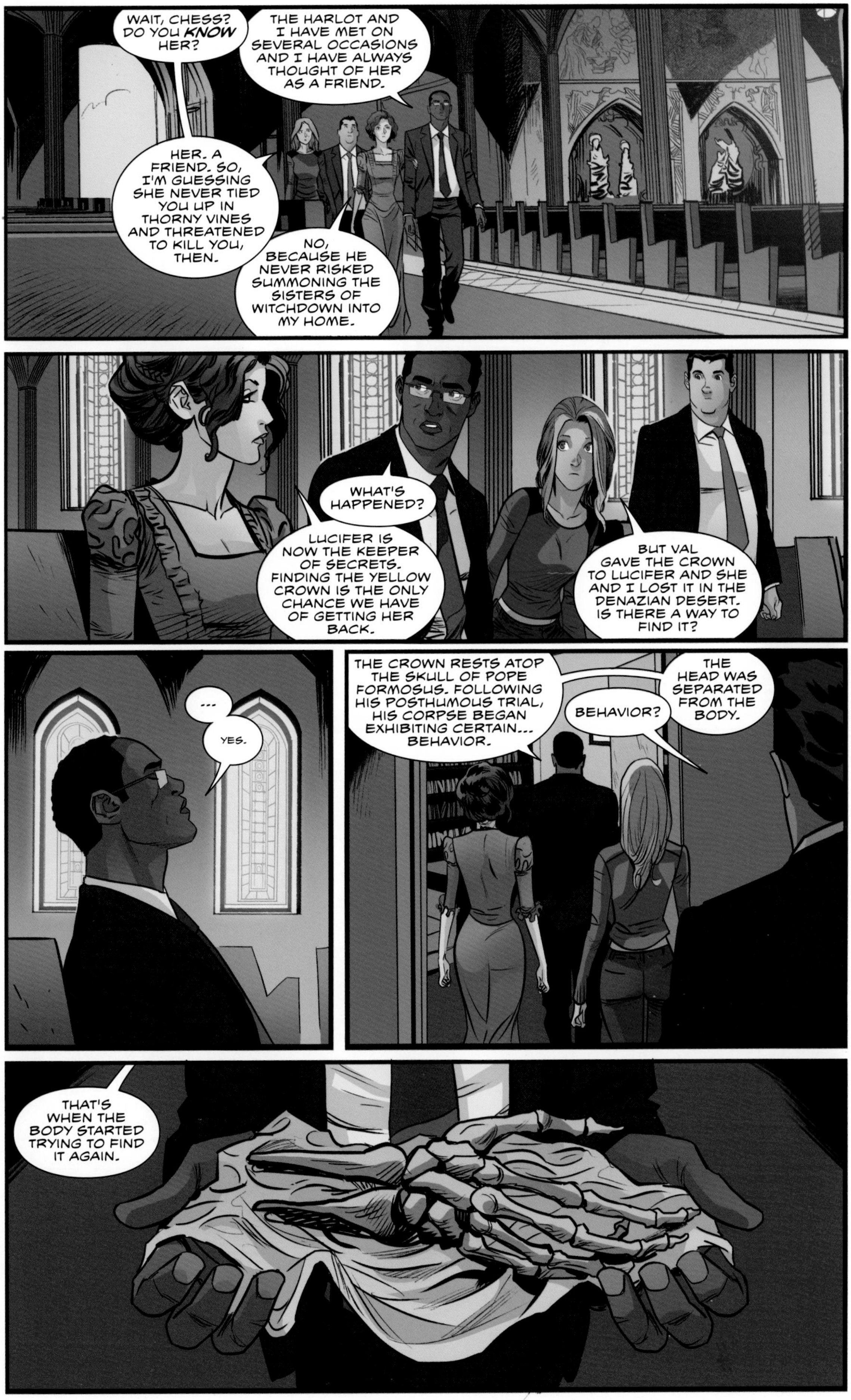
WAIT, CHESS? DO YOU KNOW HER?
THE HARLOT AND I HAVE MET ON SEVERAL OCCASIONS AND I HAVE ALWAYS THOUGHT OF HER AS A FRIEND.
HER. A FRIEND. SO, I'M GUESSING SHE NEVER TIED YOU UP IN THORNY VINES AND THREATENED TO KILL YOU, THEN.
NO, BECAUSE HE NEVER RISKED SUMMONING THE SISTERS OF WITCHDOWN INTO MY HOME.
WHAT'S HAPPENED?
LUCIFER IS NOW THE KEEPER OF SECRETS. FINDING THE YELLOW CROWN IS THE ONLY CHANCE WE HAVE OF GETTING HER BACK.
BUT VAL GAVE THE CROWN TO LUCIFER AND SHE AND I LOST IT IN THE DENAZIAN DESERT. IS THERE A WAY TO FIND IT?
...
YES.
THE CROWN RESTS ATOP THE SKULL OF POPE FORMOSUS. FOLLOWING HIS POSTHUMOUS TRIAL, HIS CORPSE BEGAN EXHIBITING CERTAIN... BEHAVIOR.
BEHAVIOR?
THE HEAD WAS SEPARATED FROM THE BODY.
THAT'S WHEN THE BODY STARTED TRYING TO FIND IT AGAIN.

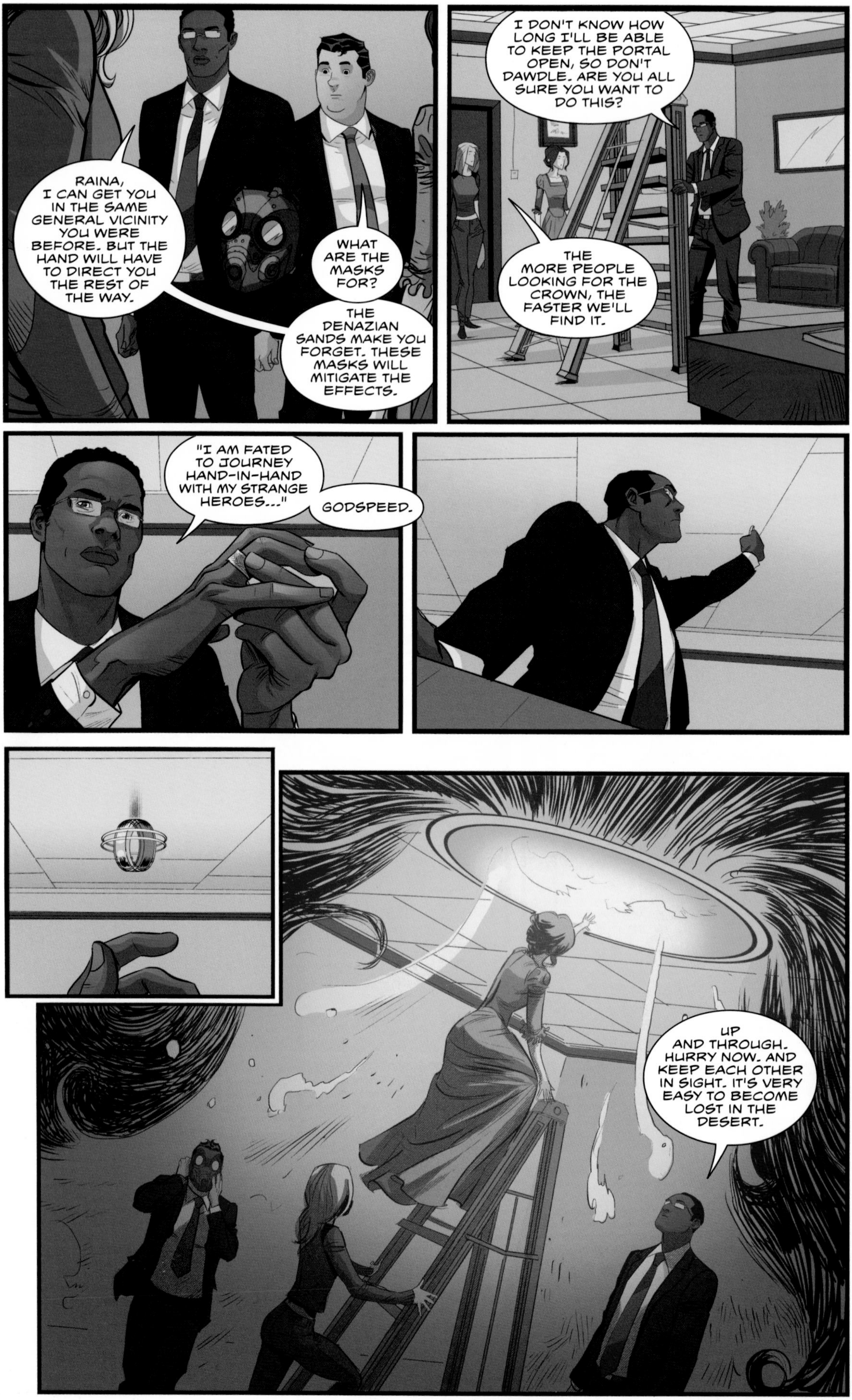
RAINA, I CAN GET YOU IN THE SAME GENERAL VICINITY YOU WERE BEFORE. BUT THE HAND WILL HAVE TO DIRECT YOU THE REST OF THE WAY.
WHAT ARE THE MASKS FOR?
THE DENAZIAN SANDS MAKE YOU FORGET. THESE MASKS WILL MITIGATE THE EFFECTS.
I DON'T KNOW HOW LONG I'LL BE ABLE TO KEEP THE PORTAL OPEN, SO DON'T DAWDLE. ARE YOU ALL SURE YOU WANT TO DO THIS?
THE MORE PEOPLE LOOKING FOR THE CROWN, THE FASTER WE'LL FIND IT.
"I AM FATED TO JOURNEY HAND-IN-HAND WITH MY STRANGE HEROES..."
GODSPEED.
UP AND THROUGH. HURRY NOW. AND KEEP EACH OTHER IN SIGHT. IT'S VERY EASY TO BECOME LOST IN THE DESERT.

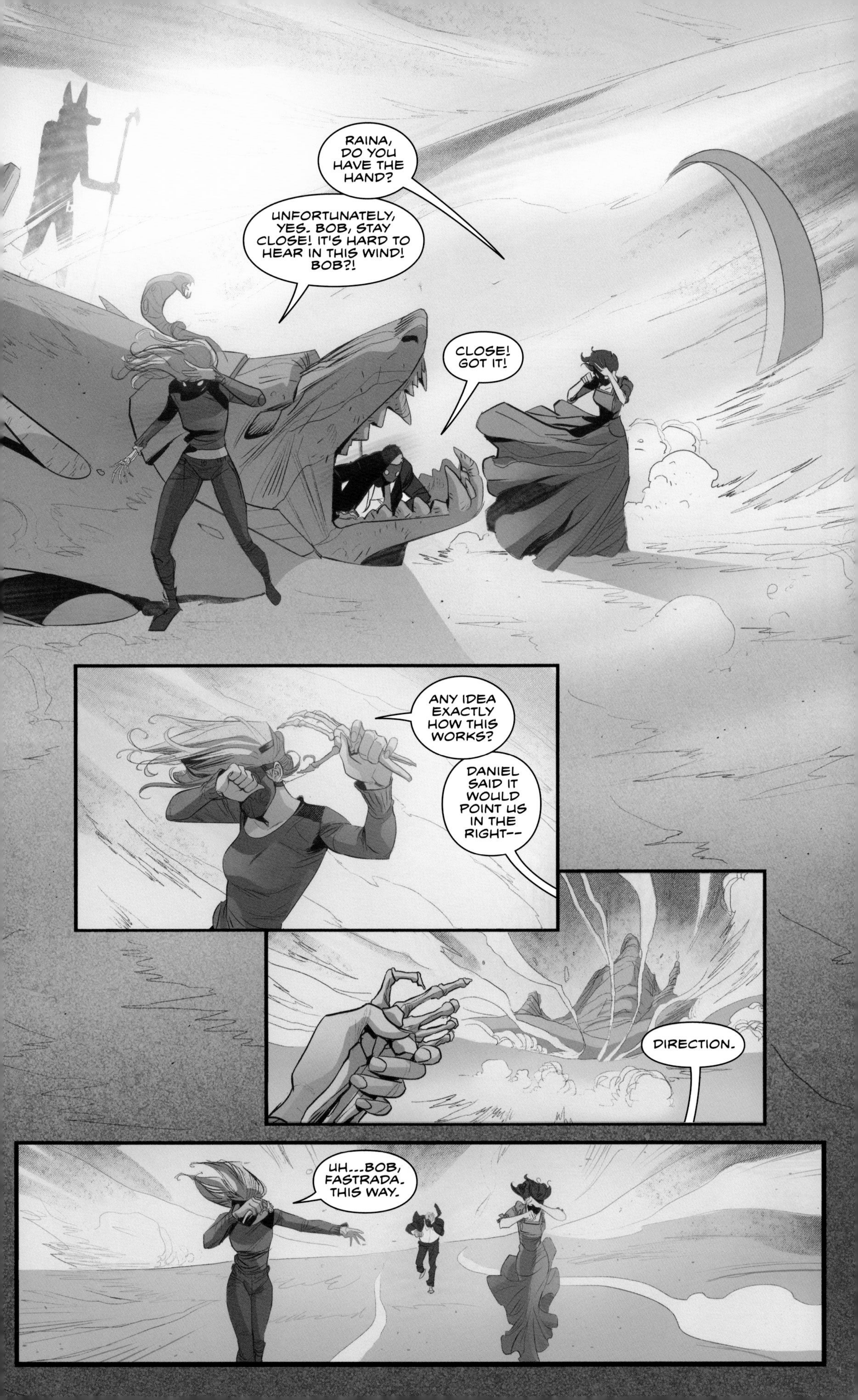
RAINA, DO YOU HAVE THE HAND?
UNFORTUNATELY, YES. BOB, STAY CLOSE! IT'S HARD TO HEAR IN THIS WIND! BOB?!
CLOSE! GOT IT!
ANY IDEA EXACTLY HOW THIS WORKS?
DANIEL SAID IT WOULD POINT US IN THE RIGHT--
DIRECTION.
UH...BOB, FASTRADA. THIS WAY.

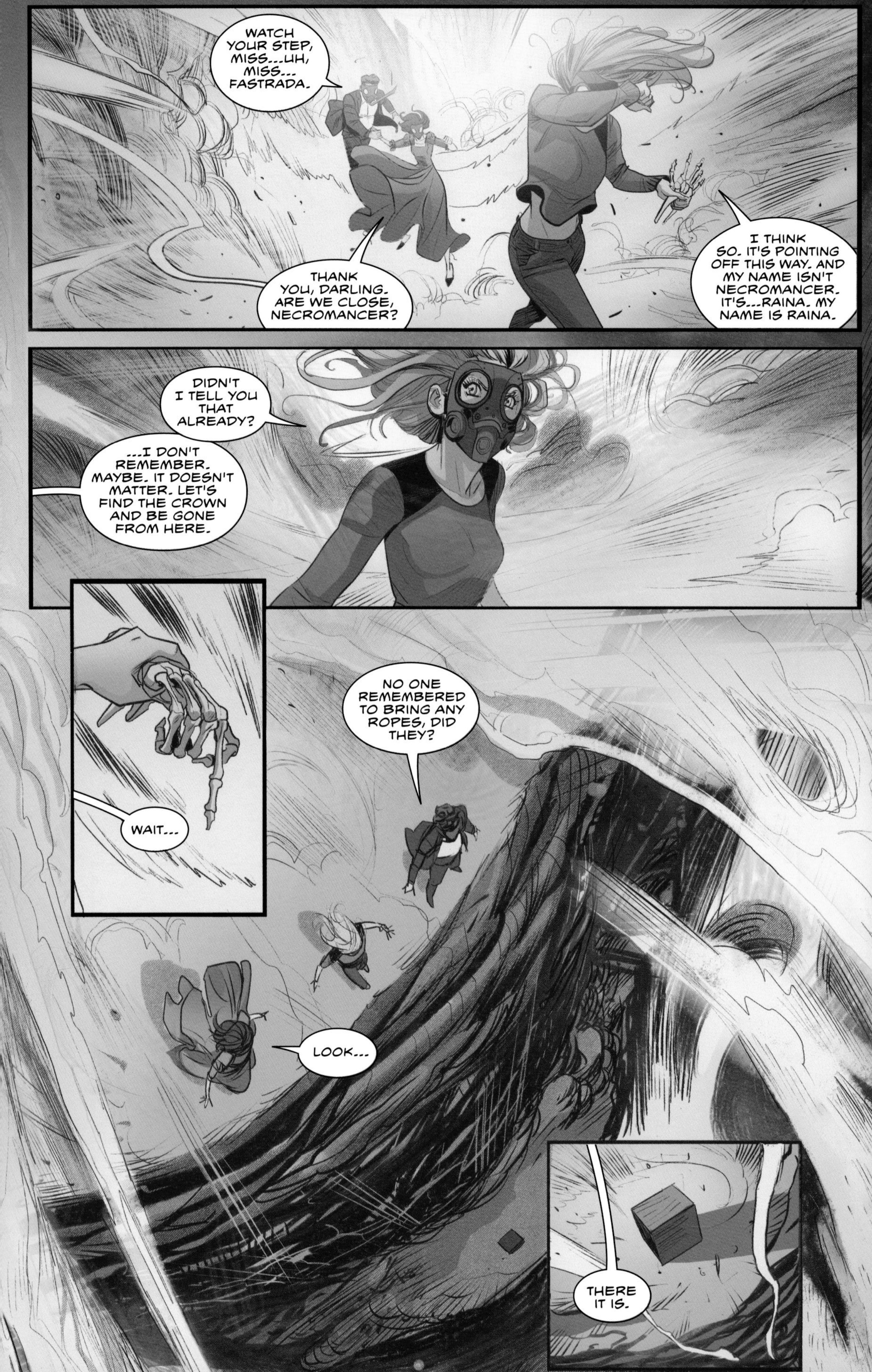

WATCH YOUR STEP, MISS...UH, MISS... FASTRADA.
THANK YOU, DARLING. ARE WE CLOSE, NECROMANCER?
I THINK SO. IT'S POINTING OFF THIS WAY. AND MY NAME ISN'T NECROMANCER. IT'S...RAINA. MY NAME IS RAINA.
DIDN'T I TELL YOU THAT ALREADY?
...I DON'T REMEMBER. MAYBE. IT DOESN'T MATTER. LET'S FIND THE CROWN AND BE GONE FROM HERE.
WAIT...
NO ONE REMEMBERED TO BRING ANY ROPES, DID THEY?
LOOK...
THERE IT IS.

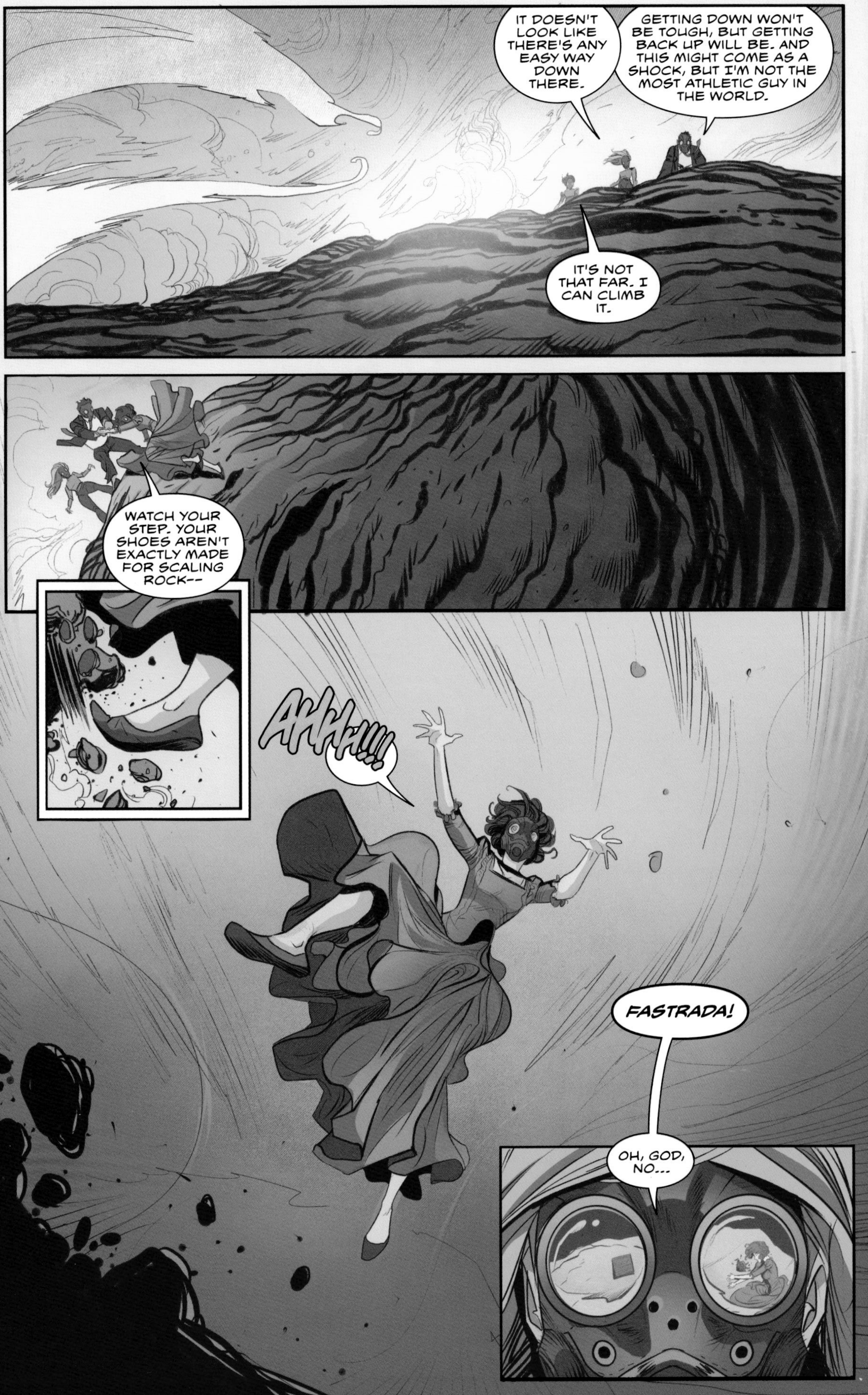
IT DOESN'T LOOK LIKE THERE'S ANY EASY WAY DOWN THERE.
GETTING DOWN WON'T BE TOUGH, BUT GETTING BACK UP WILL BE. AND THIS MIGHT COME AS A SHOCK, BUT I'M NOT THE MOST ATHLETIC GUY IN THE WORLD.
IT'S NOT THAT FAR. I CAN CLIMB IT.
WATCH YOUR STEP. YOUR SHOES AREN'T EXACTLY MADE FOR SCALING ROCK--
AHHH!!!!
FASTRADA!
OH, GOD, NO...

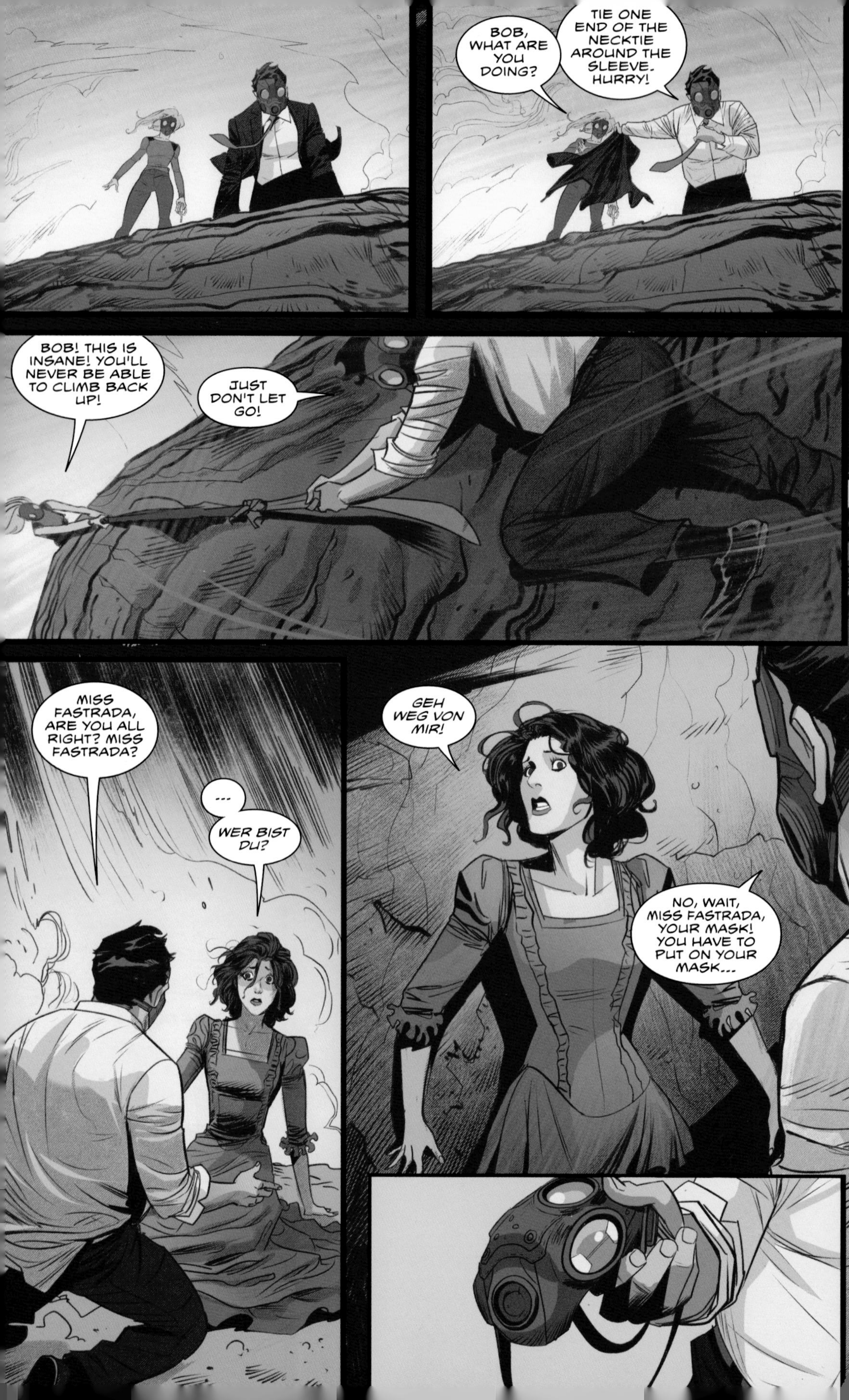
BOB, WHAT ARE YOU DOING?
TIE ONE END OF THE NECKTIE AROUND THE SLEEVE. HURRY!
BOB! THIS IS INSANE! YOU'LL NEVER BE ABLE TO CLIMB BACK UP!
JUST DON'T LET GO!
MISS FASTRADA, ARE YOU ALL RIGHT? MISS FASTRADA?
...
WER BIST DU?
GEH WEG VON MIR!
NO, WAIT, MISS FASTRADA, YOUR MASK! YOU HAVE TO PUT ON YOUR MASK...

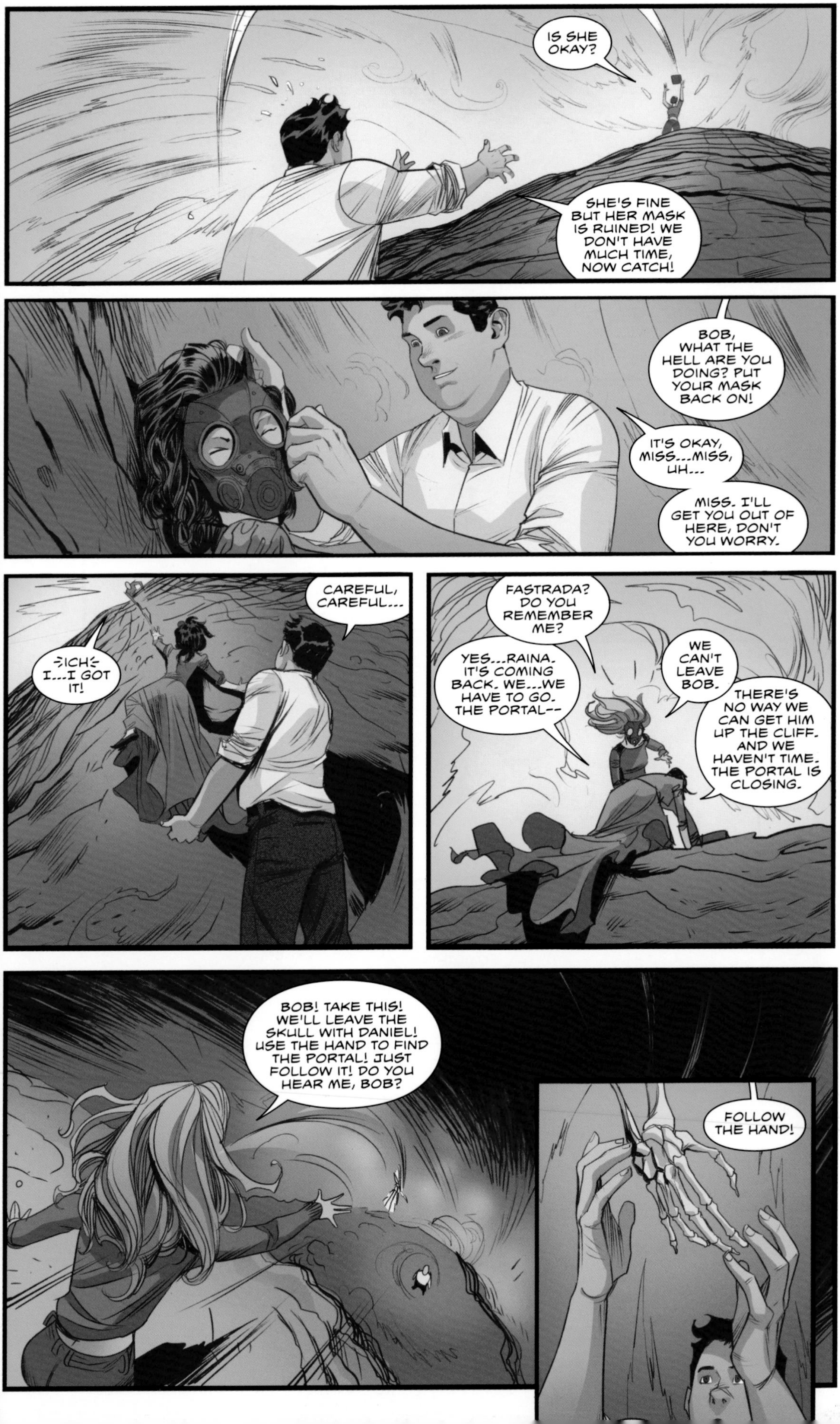

IS SHE OKAY?
SHE'S FINE BUT HER MASK IS RUINED! WE DON'T HAVE MUCH TIME, NOW CATCH!
BOB, WHAT THE HELL ARE YOU DOING? PUT YOUR MASK BACK ON!
IT'S OKAY, MISS...MISS, UH...
MISS. I'LL GET YOU OUT OF HERE, DON'T YOU WORRY.
CAREFUL, CAREFUL...
ICH I...I GOT IT!
FASTRADA? DO YOU REMEMBER ME?
YES...RAINA. IT'S COMING BACK. WE...WE HAVE TO GO. THE PORTAL--
WE CAN'T LEAVE BOB.
THERE'S NO WAY WE CAN GET HIM UP THE CLIFF. AND WE HAVEN'T TIME. THE PORTAL IS CLOSING.
BOB! TAKE THIS! WE'LL LEAVE THE SKULL WITH DANIEL! USE THE HAND TO FIND THE PORTAL! JUST FOLLOW IT! DO YOU HEAR ME, BOB?
FOLLOW THE HAND!

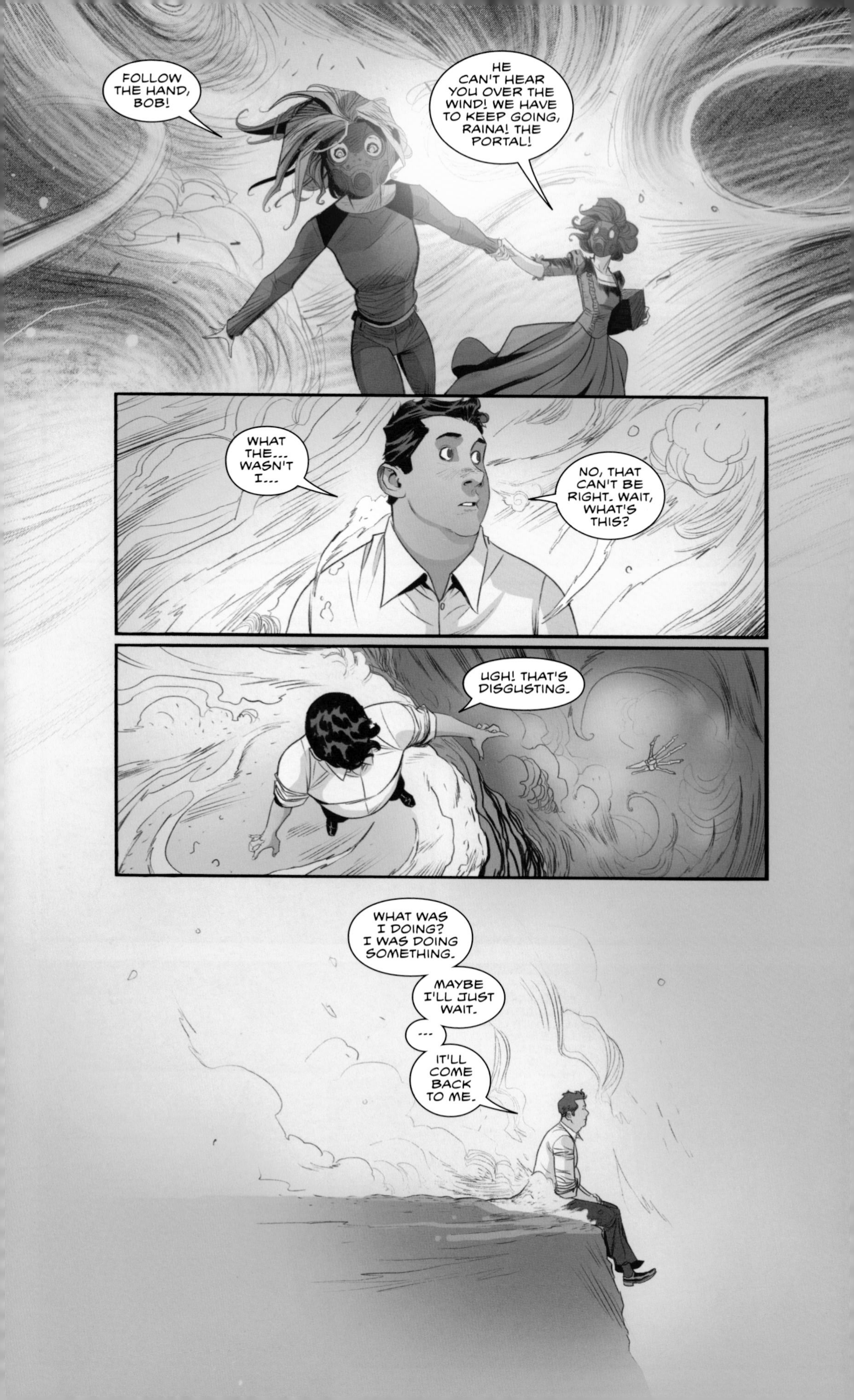
FOLLOW THE HAND, BOB!
HE CAN'T HEAR YOU OVER THE WIND! WE HAVE TO KEEP GOING, RAINA! THE PORTAL!
WHAT THE... WASN'T I...
NO, THAT CAN'T BE RIGHT. WAIT, WHAT'S THIS?
UGH! THAT'S DISGUSTING.
WHAT WAS I DOING? I WAS DOING SOMETHING.
MAYBE I'LL JUST WAIT.
...
IT'LL COME BACK TO ME.

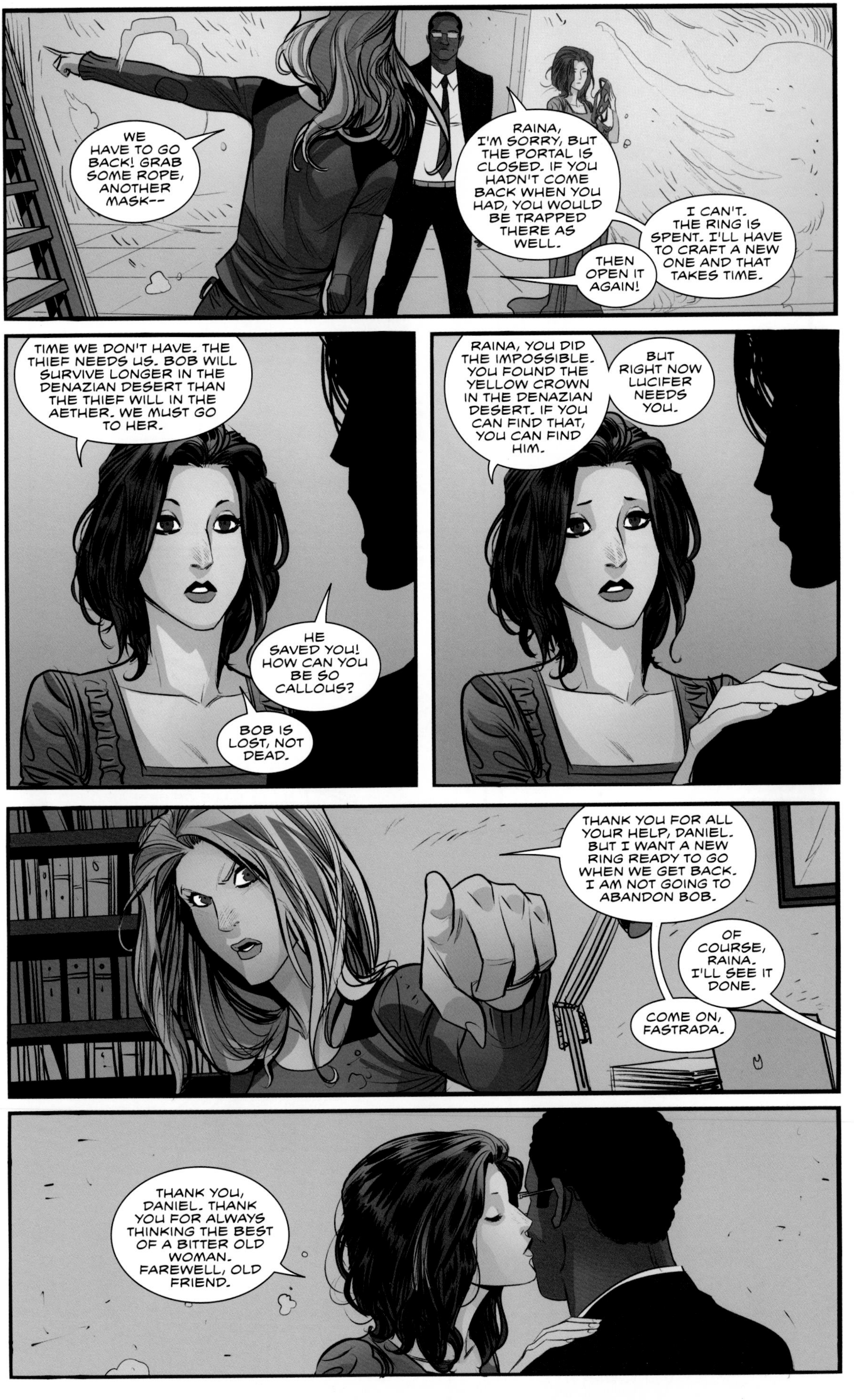
WE HAVE TO GO BACK! GRAB SOME ROPE, ANOTHER MASK--
RAINA, I'M SORRY, BUT THE PORTAL IS CLOSED. IF YOU HADN'T COME BACK WHEN YOU HAD, YOU WOULD BE TRAPPED THERE AS WELL.
THEN OPEN IT AGAIN!
I CAN'T. THE RING IS SPENT. I'LL HAVE TO CRAFT A NEW ONE AND THAT TAKES TIME.
TIME WE DON'T HAVE. THE THIEF NEEDS US. BOB WILL SURVIVE LONGER IN THE DENAZIAN DESERT THAN THE THIEF WILL IN THE AETHER. WE MUST GO TO HER.
HE SAVED YOU! HOW CAN YOU BE SO CALLOUS?
BOB IS LOST, NOT DEAD.
RAINA, YOU DID THE IMPOSSIBLE. YOU FOUND THE YELLOW CROWN IN THE DENAZIAN DESERT. IF YOU CAN FIND THAT, YOU CAN FIND HIM.
BUT RIGHT NOW LUCIFER NEEDS YOU.
THANK YOU FOR ALL YOUR HELP, DANIEL. BUT I WANT A NEW RING READY TO GO WHEN WE GET BACK. I AM NOT GOING TO ABANDON BOB.
OF COURSE, RAINA. I'LL SEE IT DONE.
COME ON, FASTRADA.
THANK YOU, DANIEL. THANK YOU FOR ALWAYS THINKING THE BEST OF A BITTER OLD WOMAN. FAREWELL, OLD FRIEND.

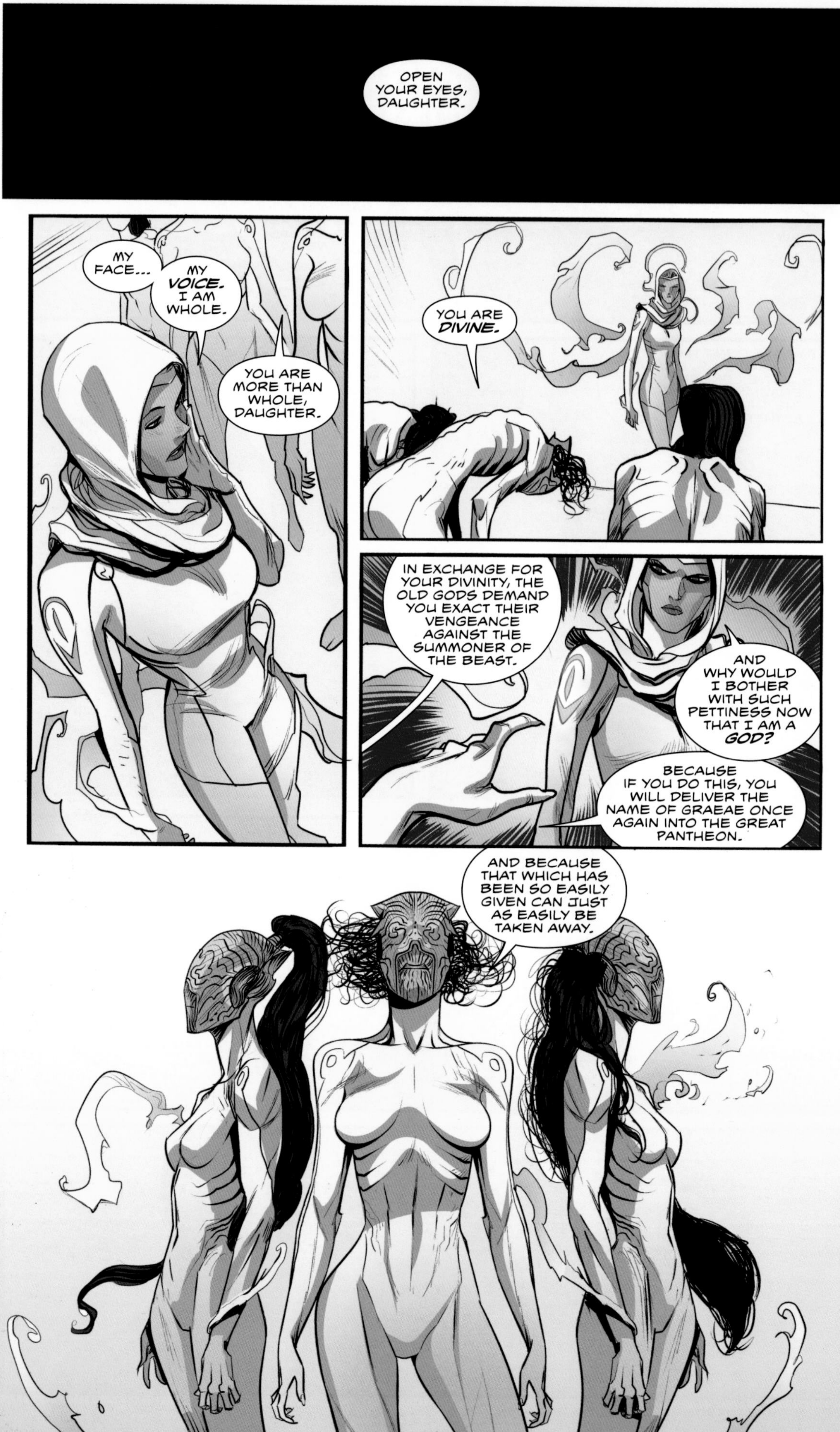
OPEN YOUR EYES, DAUGHTER.
MY FACE...
MY *VOICE.* I AM WHOLE.
YOU ARE MORE THAN WHOLE, DAUGHTER.
YOU ARE *DIVINE.*
IN EXCHANGE FOR YOUR DIVINITY, THE OLD GODS DEMAND YOU EXACT THEIR VENGEANCE AGAINST THE SUMMONER OF THE BEAST.
AND WHY WOULD I BOTHER WITH SUCH PETTINESS NOW THAT I AM A *GOD?*
BECAUSE IF YOU DO THIS, YOU WILL DELIVER THE NAME OF GRAEAE ONCE AGAIN INTO THE GREAT PANTHEON.
AND BECAUSE THAT WHICH HAS BEEN SO EASILY GIVEN CAN JUST AS EASILY BE TAKEN AWAY.

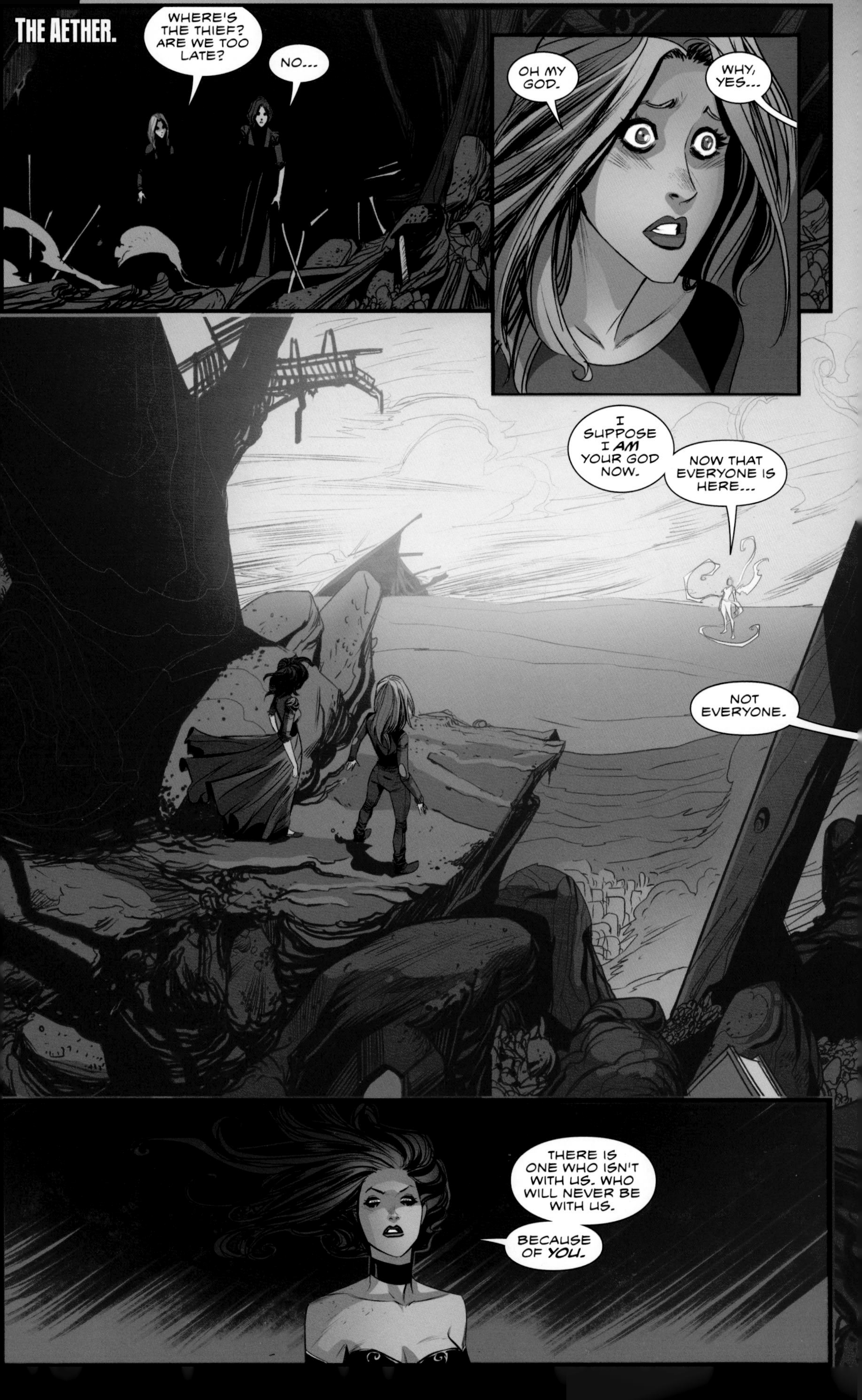
THE AETHER.
WHERE'S THE THIEF? ARE WE TOO LATE?
NO...
OH MY GOD.
WHY, YES...
I SUPPOSE I AM YOUR GOD NOW.
NOW THAT EVERYONE IS HERE...
NOT EVERYONE.
THERE IS ONE WHO ISN'T WITH US. WHO WILL NEVER BE WITH US.
BECAUSE OF YOU.

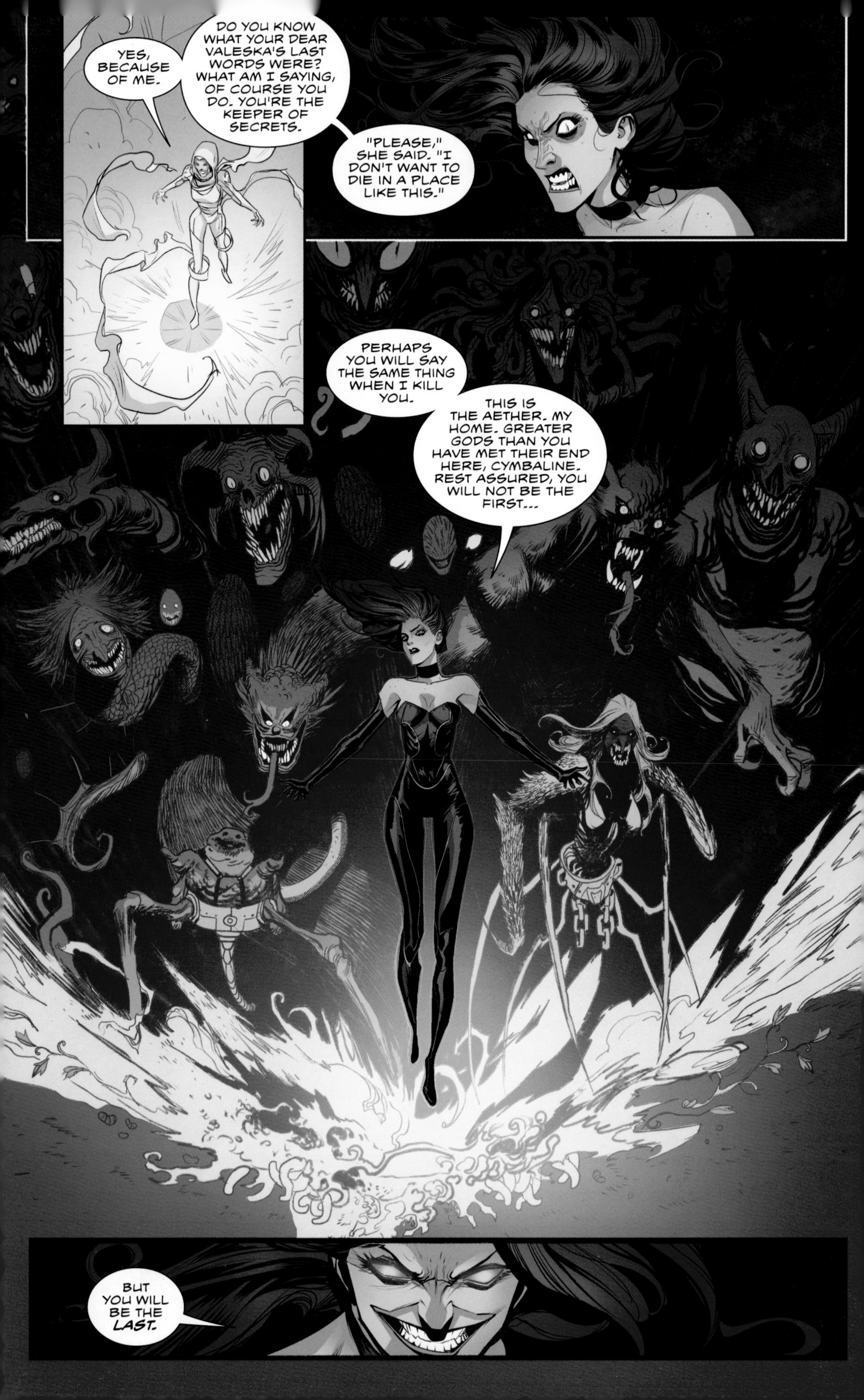
YES, BECAUSE OF ME.
DO YOU KNOW WHAT YOUR DEAR VALESKA'S LAST WORDS WERE? WHAT AM I SAYING, OF COURSE YOU DO. YOU'RE THE KEEPER OF SECRETS.
"PLEASE," SHE SAID. "I DON'T WANT TO DIE IN A PLACE LIKE THIS."
PERHAPS YOU WILL SAY THE SAME THING WHEN I KILL YOU.
THIS IS THE AETHER. MY HOME. GREATER GODS THAN YOU HAVE MET THEIR END HERE, CYMBALINE. REST ASSURED, YOU WILL NOT BE THE FIRST...
BUT YOU WILL BE THE *LAST.*

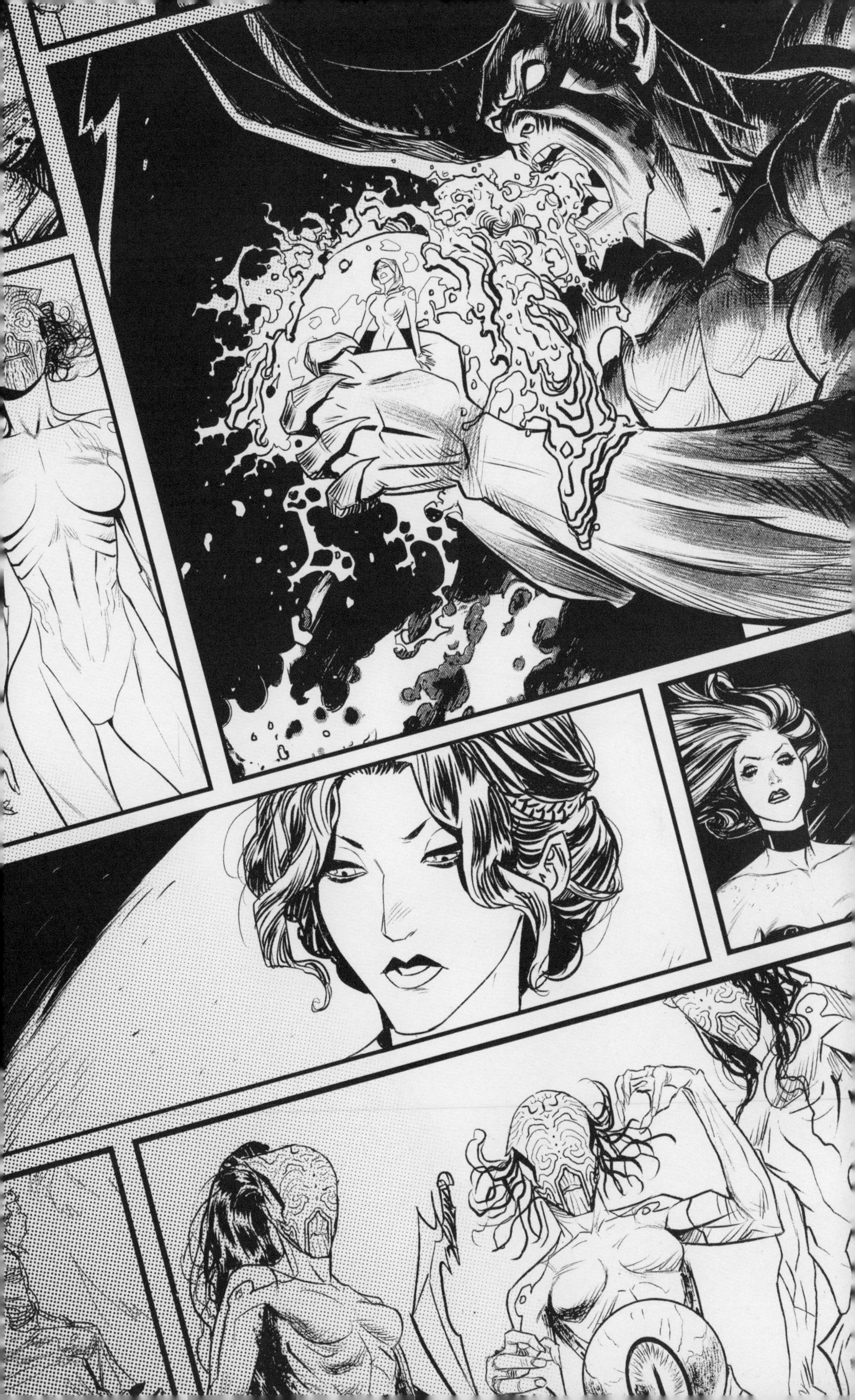

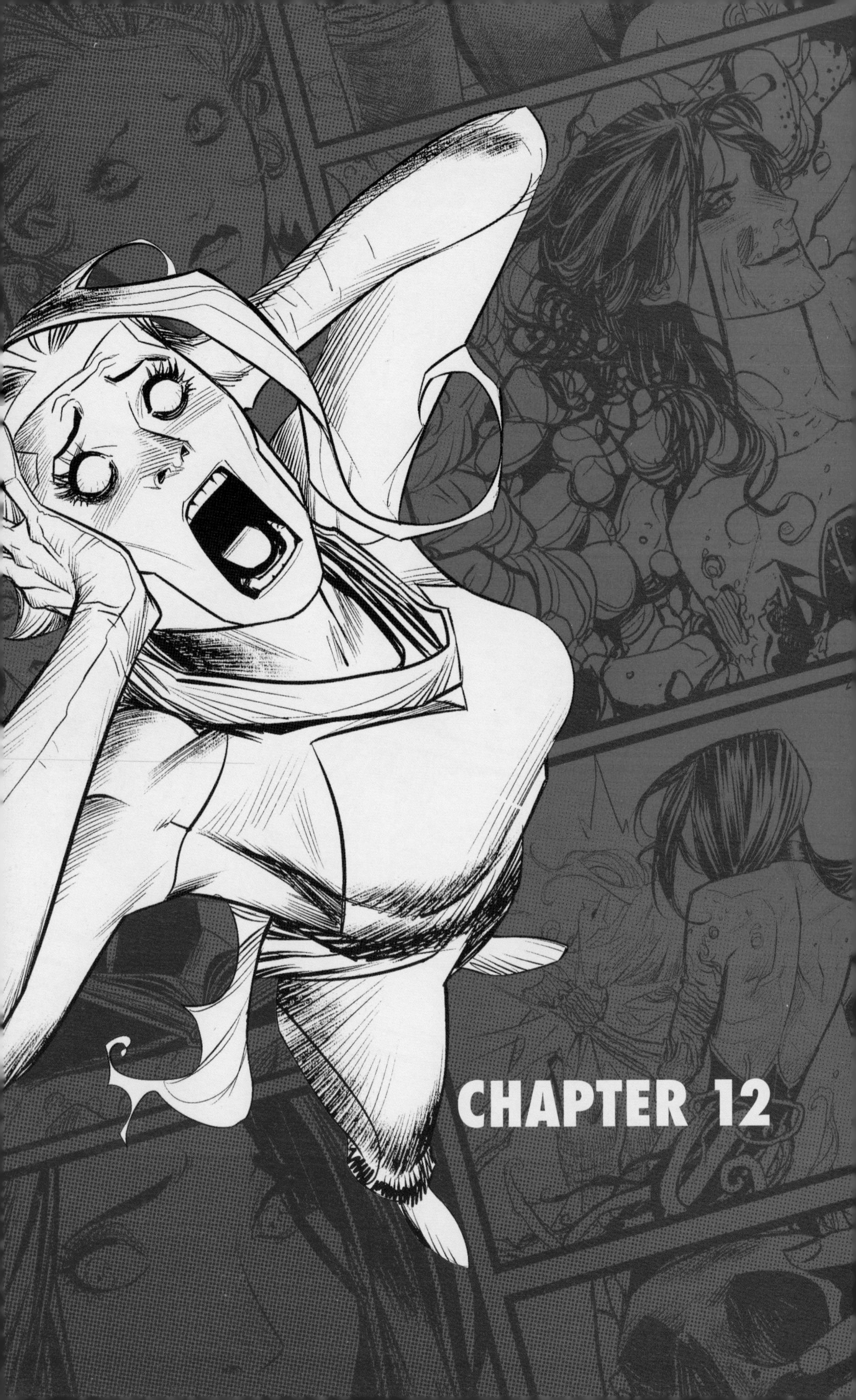

CHAPTER 12

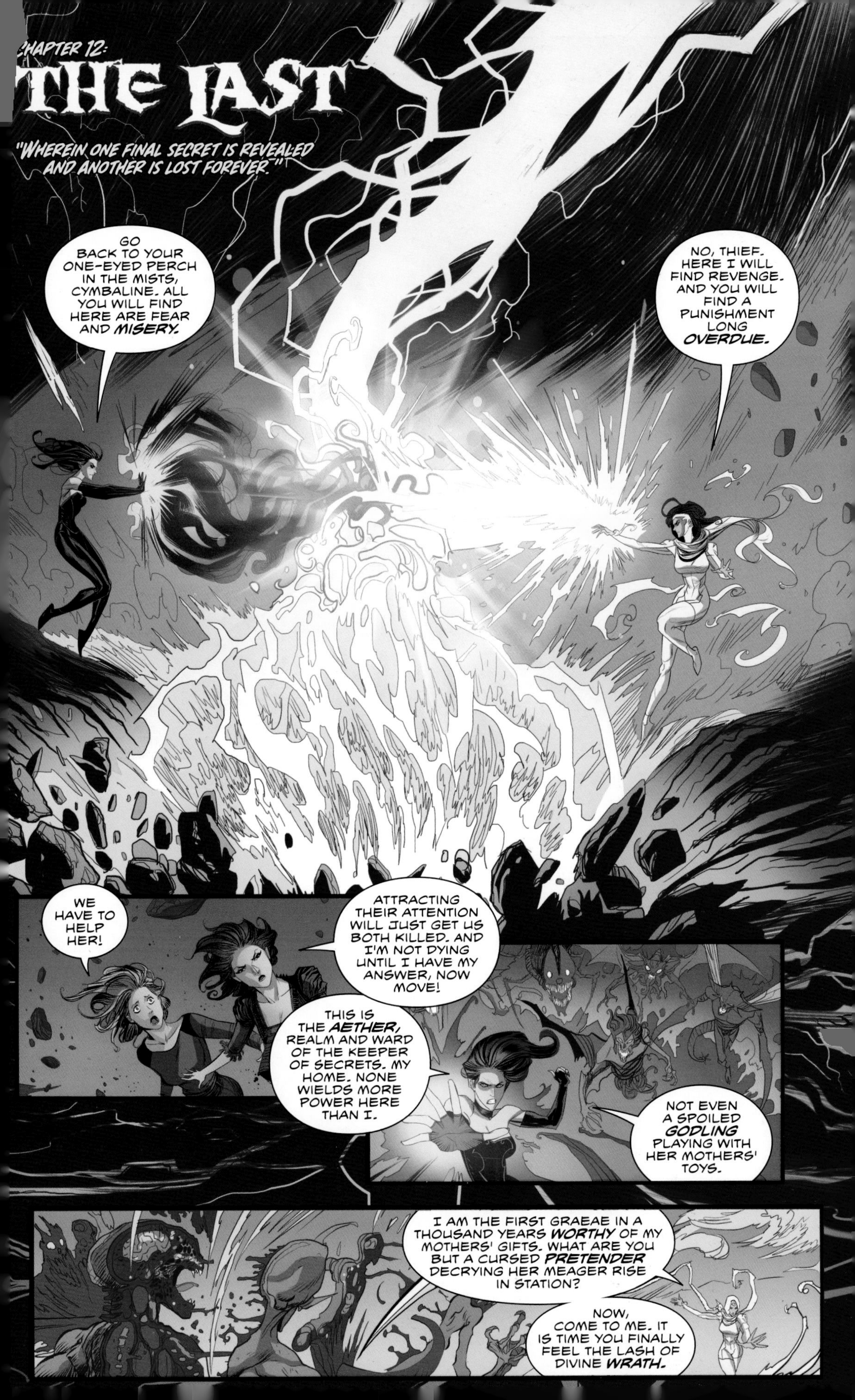
CHAPTER 12:
THE LAST
"WHEREIN ONE FINAL SECRET IS REVEALED AND ANOTHER IS LOST FOREVER."
GO BACK TO YOUR ONE-EYED PERCH IN THE MISTS, CYMBALINE. ALL YOU WILL FIND HERE ARE FEAR AND MISERY.
NO, THIEF. HERE I WILL FIND REVENGE. AND YOU WILL FIND A PUNISHMENT LONG OVERDUE.
WE HAVE TO HELP HER!
ATTRACTING THEIR ATTENTION WILL JUST GET US BOTH KILLED. AND I'M NOT DYING UNTIL I HAVE MY ANSWER, NOW MOVE!
THIS IS THE AETHER, REALM AND WARD OF THE KEEPER OF SECRETS. MY HOME. NONE WIELDS MORE POWER HERE THAN I.
NOT EVEN A SPOILED GODLING PLAYING WITH HER MOTHERS' TOYS.
I AM THE FIRST GRAEAE IN A THOUSAND YEARS WORTHY OF MY MOTHERS' GIFTS. WHAT ARE YOU BUT A CURSED PRETENDER DECRYING HER MEAGER RISE IN STATION?
NOW, COME TO ME. IT IS TIME YOU FINALLY FEEL THE LASH OF DIVINE WRATH.

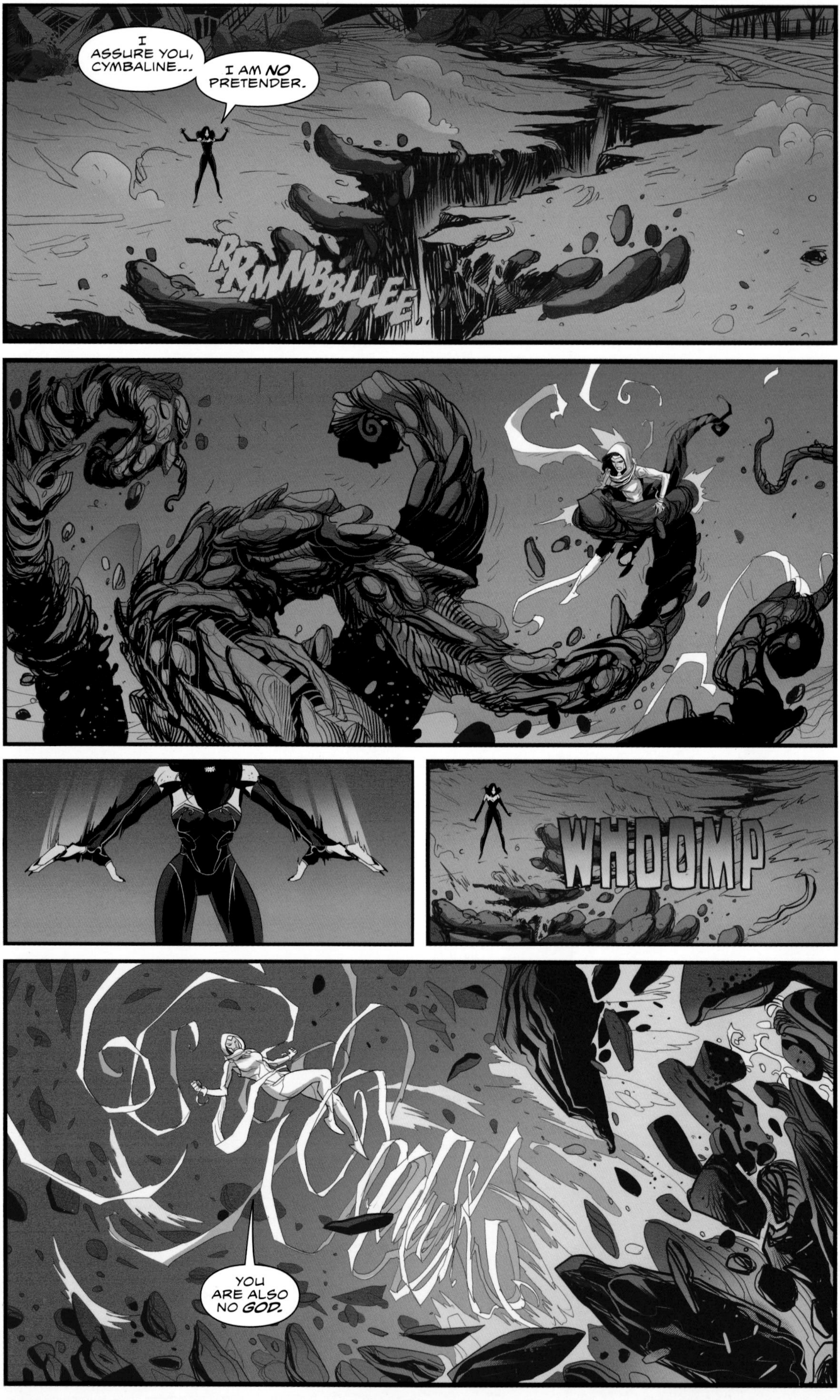
I ASSURE YOU, CYMBALINE...
I AM NO PRETENDER.
RRMMBBLLEE
WHOOMP
YOU ARE ALSO NO GOD.

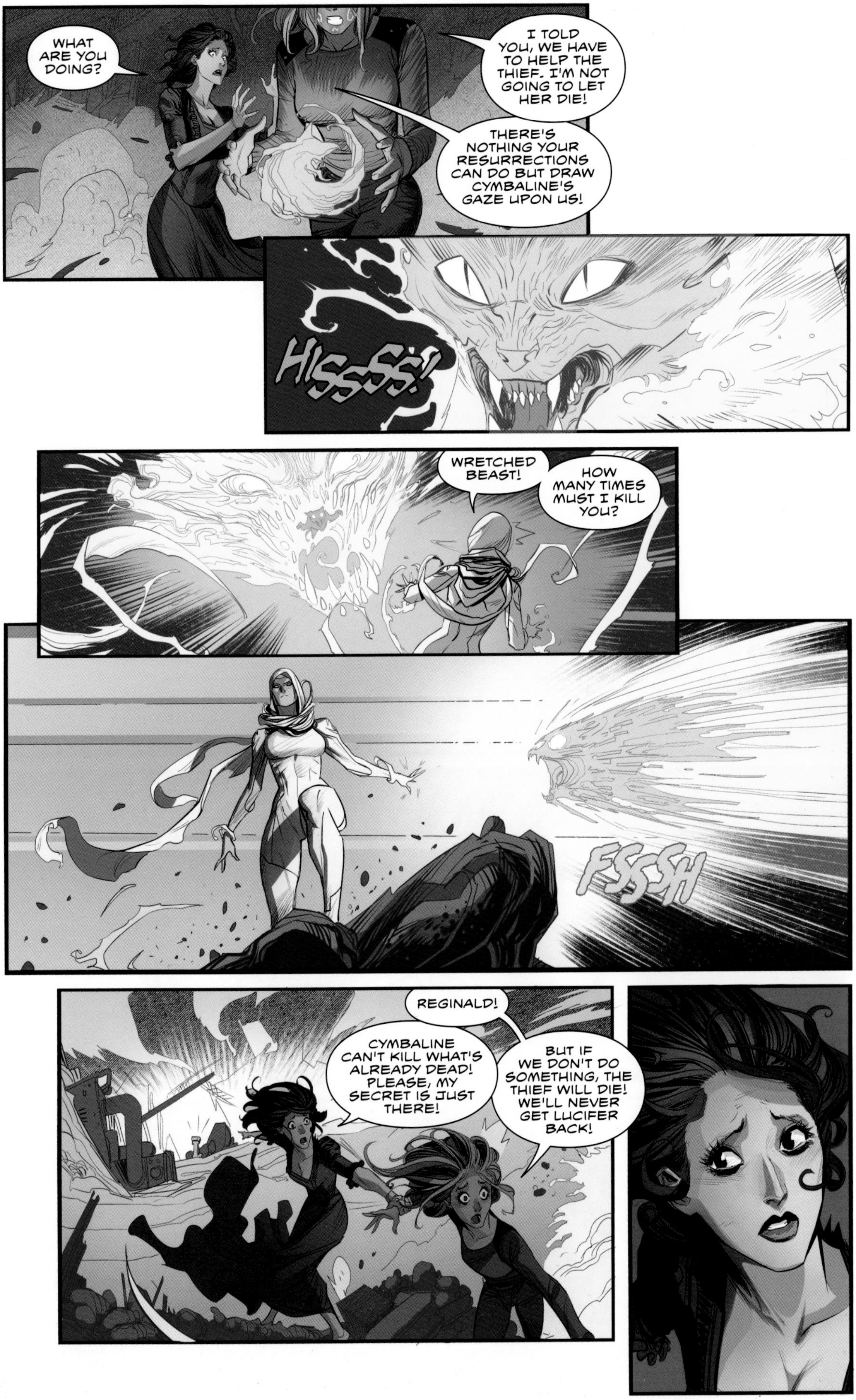
WHAT ARE YOU DOING?
I TOLD YOU, WE HAVE TO HELP THE THIEF. I'M NOT GOING TO LET HER DIE!
THERE'S NOTHING YOUR RESURRECTIONS CAN DO BUT DRAW CYMBALINE'S GAZE UPON US!
HISSSSS!
WRETCHED BEAST!
HOW MANY TIMES MUST I KILL YOU?
FSSSH
REGINALD!
CYMBALINE CAN'T KILL WHAT'S ALREADY DEAD! PLEASE, MY SECRET IS JUST THERE!
BUT IF WE DON'T DO SOMETHING, THE THIEF WILL DIE! WE'LL NEVER GET LUCIFER BACK!

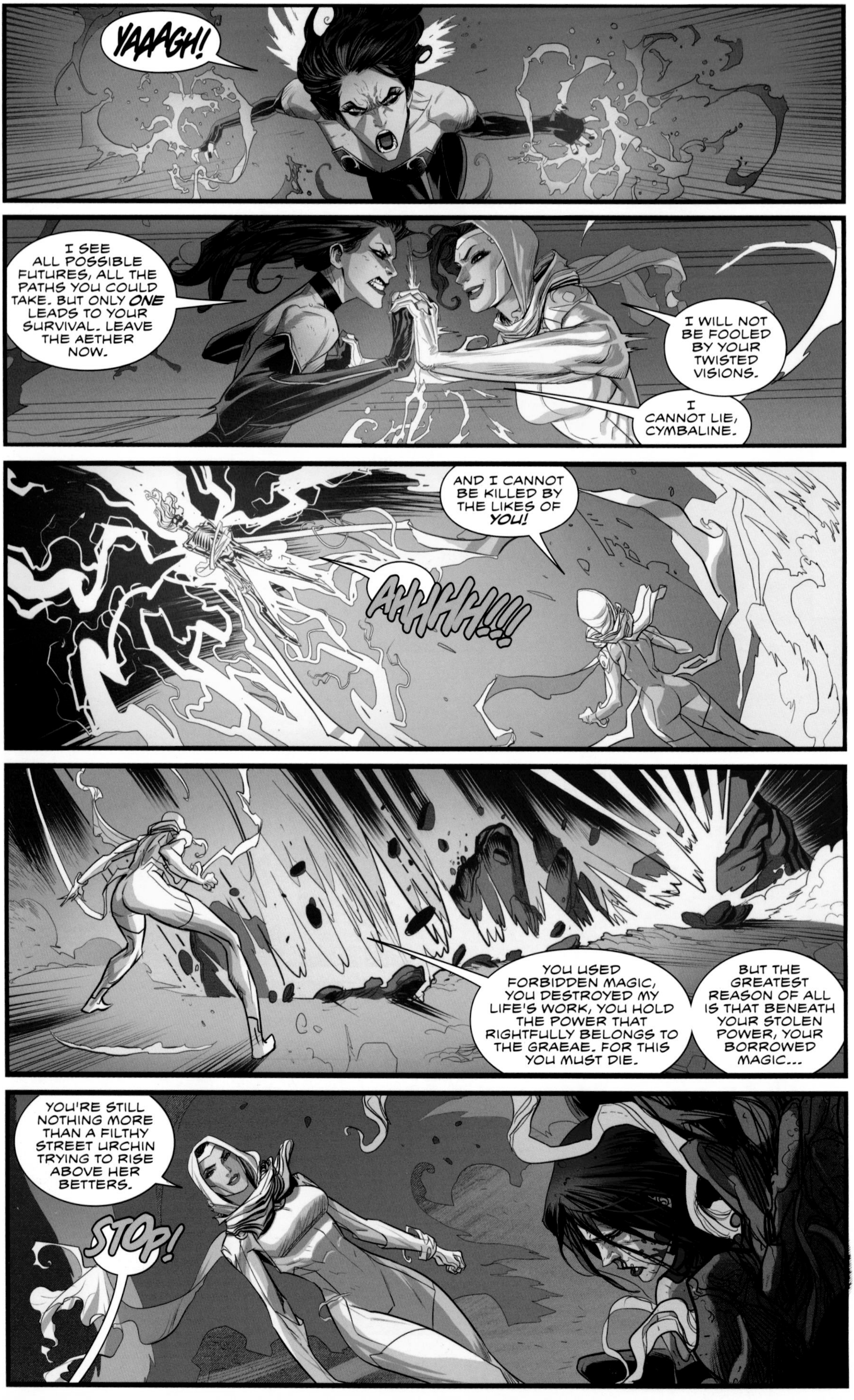
YAAAGH!
I SEE ALL POSSIBLE FUTURES, ALL THE PATHS YOU COULD TAKE. BUT ONLY ONE LEADS TO YOUR SURVIVAL. LEAVE THE AETHER NOW.
I WILL NOT BE FOOLED BY YOUR TWISTED VISIONS.
I CANNOT LIE, CYMBALINE.
AND I CANNOT BE KILLED BY THE LIKES OF YOU!
AHHHH!!!
YOU USED FORBIDDEN MAGIC, YOU DESTROYED MY LIFE'S WORK, YOU HOLD THE POWER THAT RIGHTFULLY BELONGS TO THE GRAEAE. FOR THIS YOU MUST DIE.
BUT THE GREATEST REASON OF ALL IS THAT BENEATH YOUR STOLEN POWER, YOUR BORROWED MAGIC...
YOU'RE STILL NOTHING MORE THAN A FILTHY STREET URCHIN TRYING TO RISE ABOVE HER BETTERS.
STOP!

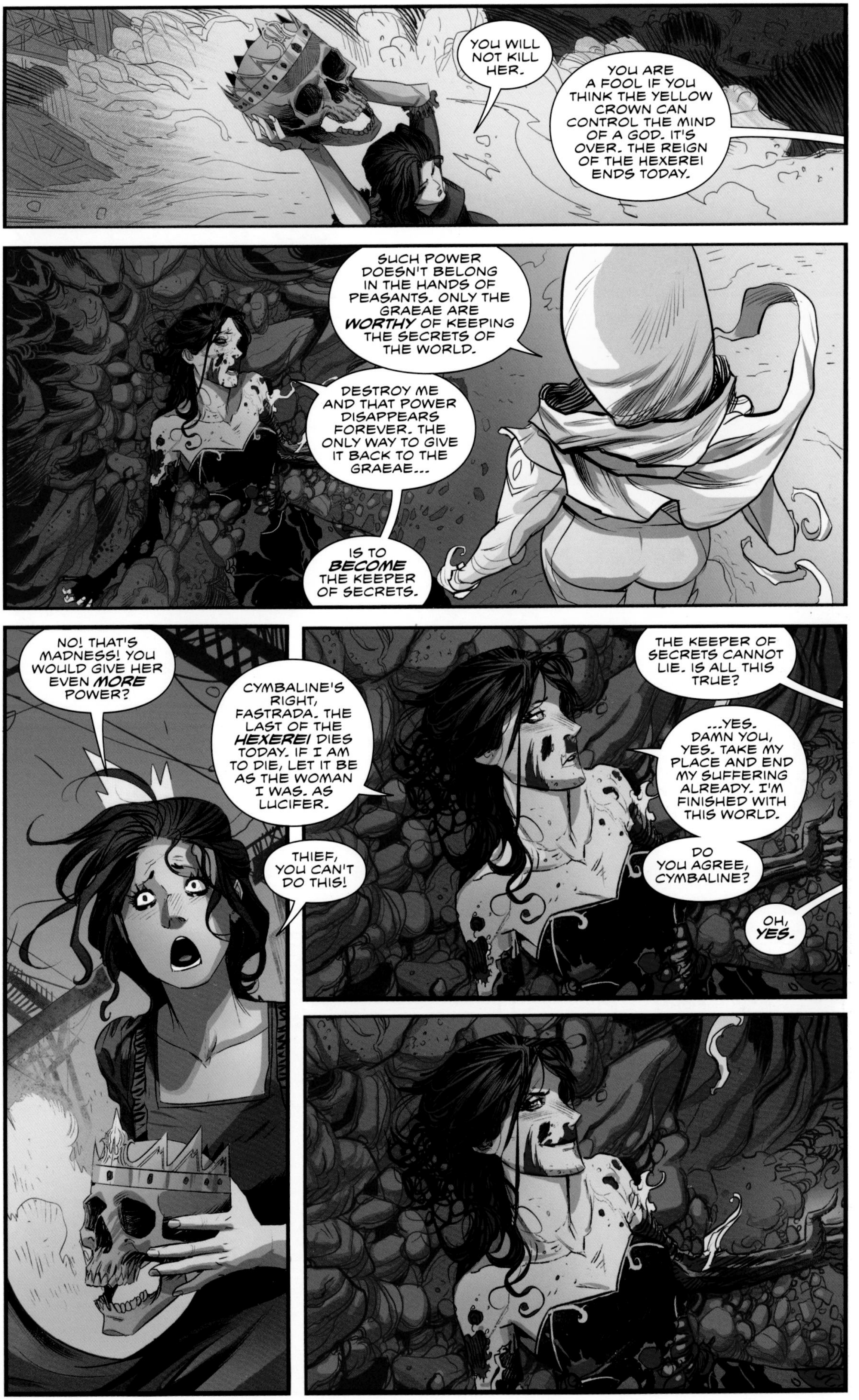
YOU WILL NOT KILL HER.
YOU ARE A FOOL IF YOU THINK THE YELLOW CROWN CAN CONTROL THE MIND OF A GOD. IT'S OVER. THE REIGN OF THE HEXEREI ENDS TODAY.
SUCH POWER DOESN'T BELONG IN THE HANDS OF PEASANTS. ONLY THE GRAEAE ARE WORTHY OF KEEPING THE SECRETS OF THE WORLD.
DESTROY ME AND THAT POWER DISAPPEARS FOREVER. THE ONLY WAY TO GIVE IT BACK TO THE GRAEAE...
IS TO BECOME THE KEEPER OF SECRETS.
NO! THAT'S MADNESS! YOU WOULD GIVE HER EVEN MORE POWER?
CYMBALINE'S RIGHT, FASTRADA. THE LAST OF THE HEXEREI DIES TODAY. IF I AM TO DIE, LET IT BE AS THE WOMAN I WAS. AS LUCIFER.
THIEF, YOU CAN'T DO THIS!
THE KEEPER OF SECRETS CANNOT LIE. IS ALL THIS TRUE?
...YES. DAMN YOU, YES. TAKE MY PLACE AND END MY SUFFERING ALREADY. I'M FINISHED WITH THIS WORLD.
DO YOU AGREE, CYMBALINE?
OH, YES.

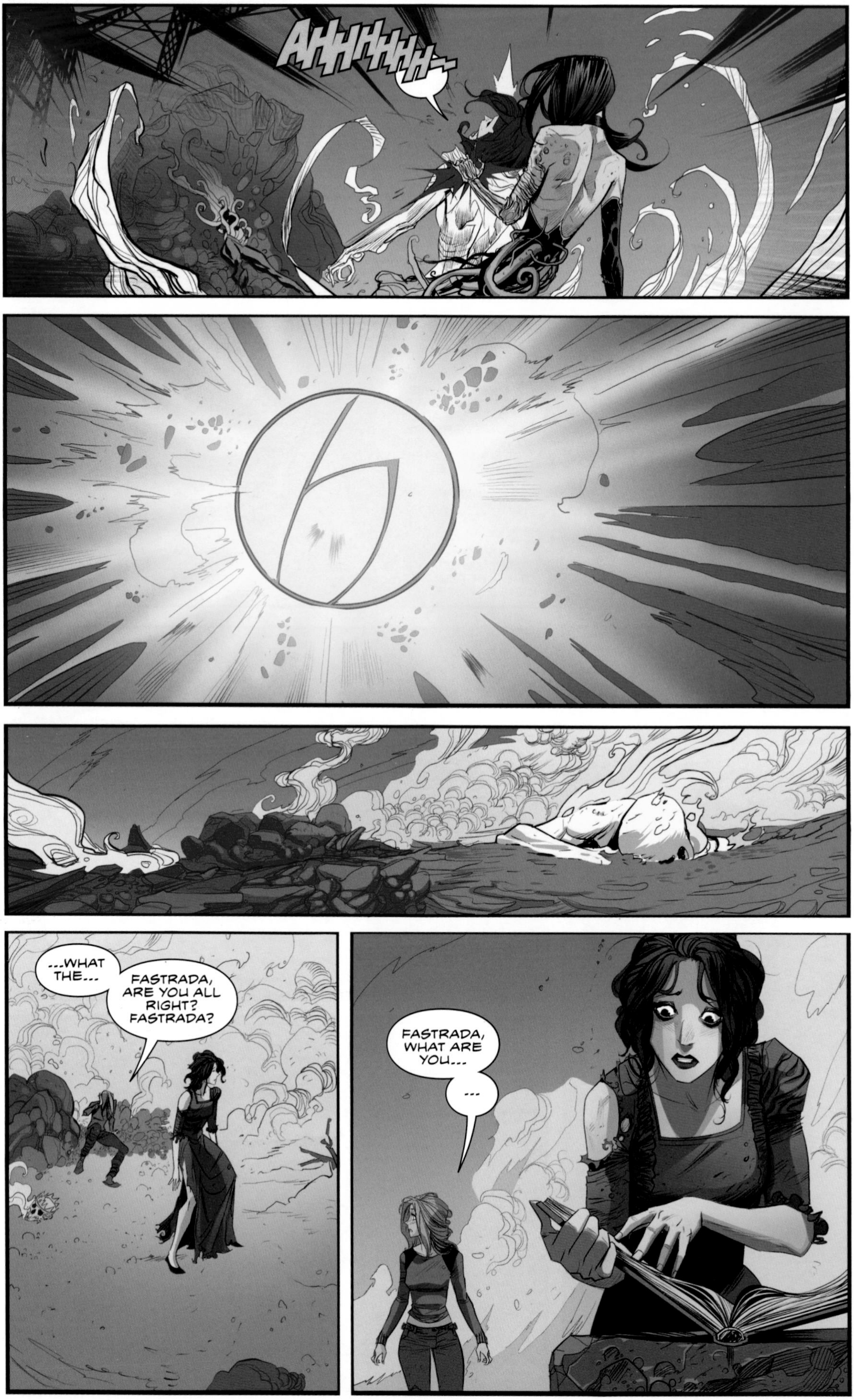
AHHHHHH--
...WHAT THE...
FASTRADA, ARE YOU ALL RIGHT? FASTRADA?
FASTRADA, WHAT ARE YOU...
...

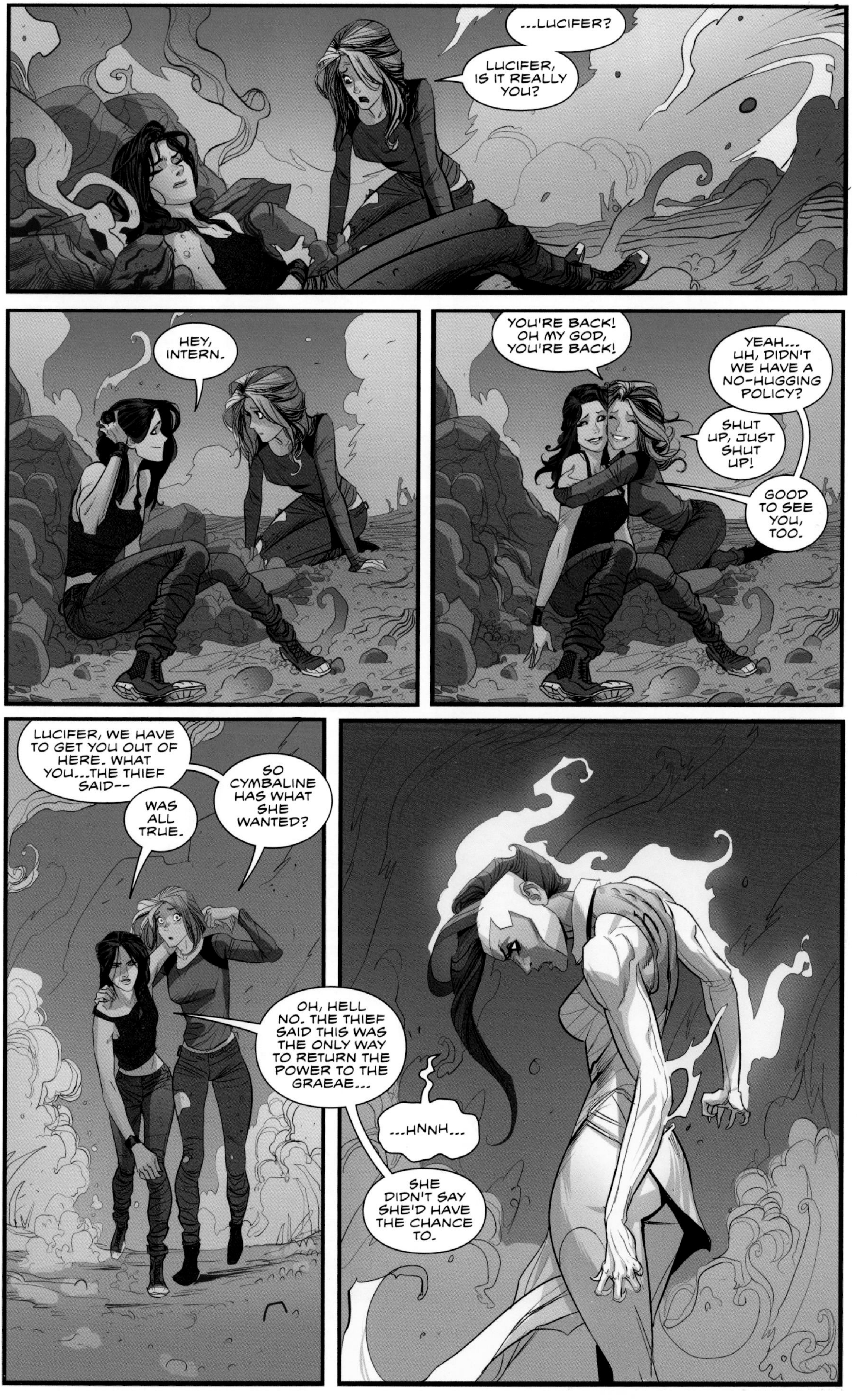
...LUCIFER?
LUCIFER, IS IT REALLY YOU?
HEY, INTERN.
YOU'RE BACK! OH MY GOD, YOU'RE BACK!
YEAH... UH, DIDN'T WE HAVE A NO-HUGGING POLICY?
SHUT UP, JUST SHUT UP!
GOOD TO SEE YOU, TOO.
LUCIFER, WE HAVE TO GET YOU OUT OF HERE. WHAT YOU...THE THIEF SAID--
WAS ALL TRUE.
SO CYMBALINE HAS WHAT SHE WANTED?
OH, HELL NO. THE THIEF SAID THIS WAS THE ONLY WAY TO RETURN THE POWER TO THE GRAEAE...
...HNNH...
SHE DIDN'T SAY SHE'D HAVE THE CHANCE TO.

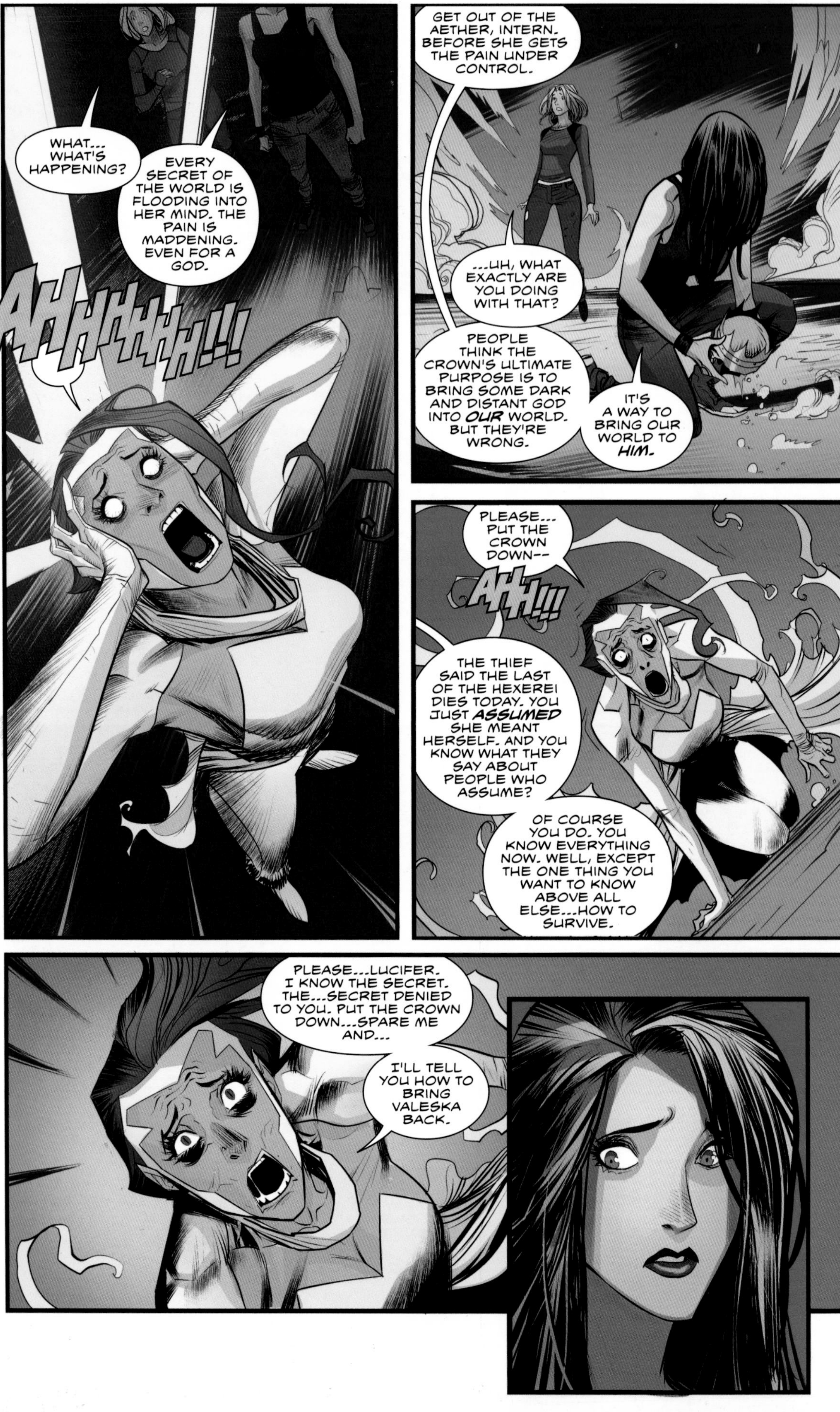
WHAT... WHAT'S HAPPENING?
EVERY SECRET OF THE WORLD IS FLOODING INTO HER MIND. THE PAIN IS MADDENING. EVEN FOR A GOD.
AHHHHHH!!!
GET OUT OF THE AETHER, INTERN. BEFORE SHE GETS THE PAIN UNDER CONTROL.
...UH, WHAT EXACTLY ARE YOU DOING WITH THAT?
PEOPLE THINK THE CROWN'S ULTIMATE PURPOSE IS TO BRING SOME DARK AND DISTANT GOD INTO OUR WORLD. BUT THEY'RE WRONG.
IT'S A WAY TO BRING OUR WORLD TO HIM.
PLEASE... PUT THE CROWN DOWN--
AHH!!!
THE THIEF SAID THE LAST OF THE HEXEREI DIES TODAY. YOU JUST ASSUMED SHE MEANT HERSELF. AND YOU KNOW WHAT THEY SAY ABOUT PEOPLE WHO ASSUME?
OF COURSE YOU DO. YOU KNOW EVERYTHING NOW. WELL, EXCEPT THE ONE THING YOU WANT TO KNOW ABOVE ALL ELSE...HOW TO SURVIVE.
PLEASE...LUCIFER. I KNOW THE SECRET. THE...SECRET DENIED TO YOU. PUT THE CROWN DOWN...SPARE ME AND...
I'LL TELL YOU HOW TO BRING VALESKA BACK.

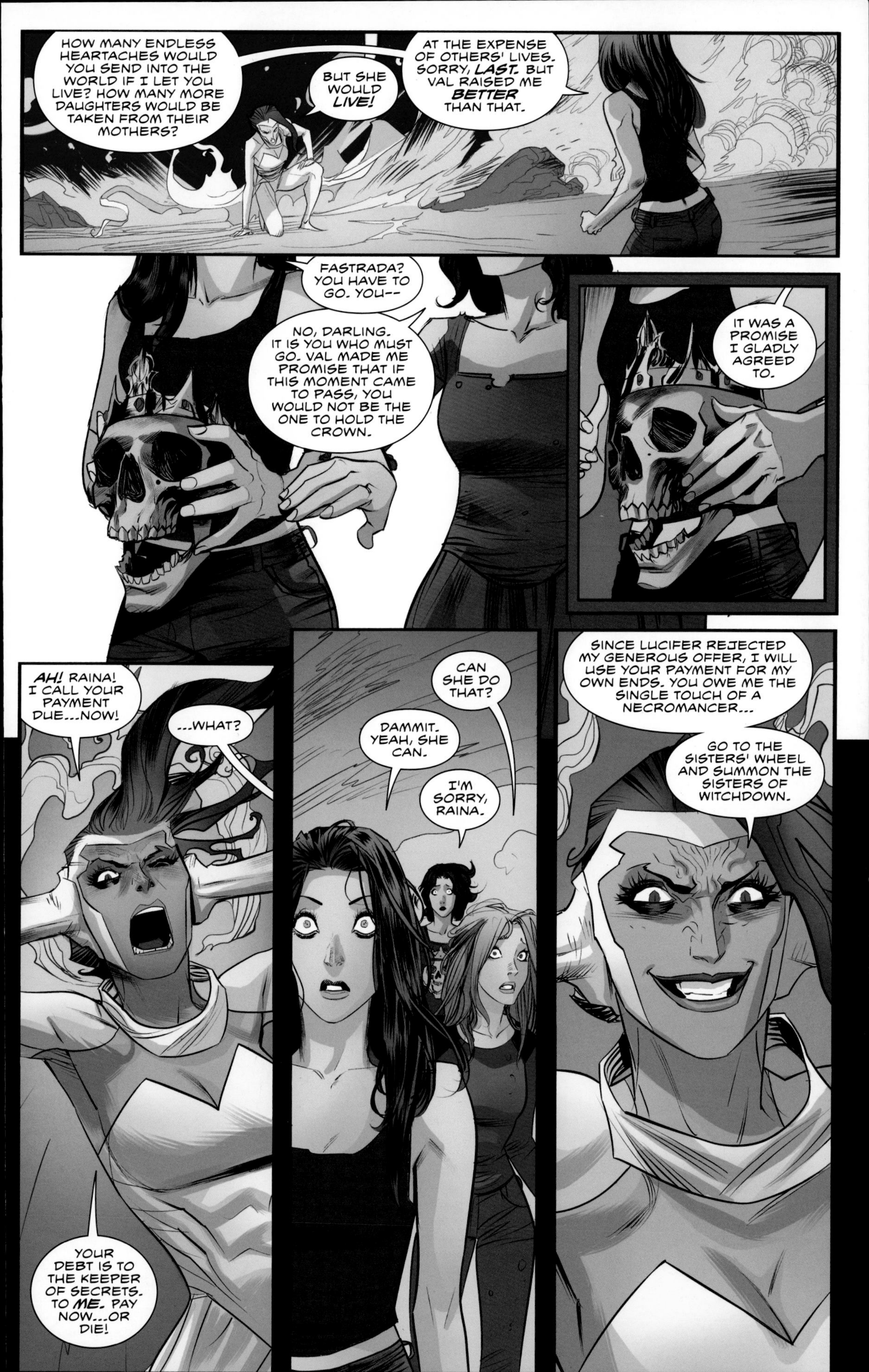
HOW MANY ENDLESS HEARTACHES WOULD YOU SEND INTO THE WORLD IF I LET YOU LIVE? HOW MANY MORE DAUGHTERS WOULD BE TAKEN FROM THEIR MOTHERS?
BUT SHE WOULD LIVE!
AT THE EXPENSE OF OTHERS' LIVES. SORRY, LAST. BUT VAL RAISED ME BETTER THAN THAT.
FASTRADA? YOU HAVE TO GO. YOU--
NO, DARLING. IT IS YOU WHO MUST GO. VAL MADE ME PROMISE THAT IF THIS MOMENT CAME TO PASS, YOU WOULD NOT BE THE ONE TO HOLD THE CROWN.
IT WAS A PROMISE I GLADLY AGREED TO.
AH! RAINA! I CALL YOUR PAYMENT DUE...NOW!
...WHAT?
YOUR DEBT IS TO THE KEEPER OF SECRETS. TO ME. PAY NOW...OR DIE!
CAN SHE DO THAT?
DAMMIT. YEAH, SHE CAN.
I'M SORRY, RAINA.
SINCE LUCIFER REJECTED MY GENEROUS OFFER, I WILL USE YOUR PAYMENT FOR MY OWN ENDS. YOU OWE ME THE SINGLE TOUCH OF A NECROMANCER...
GO TO THE SISTERS' WHEEL AND SUMMON THE SISTERS OF WITCHDOWN.

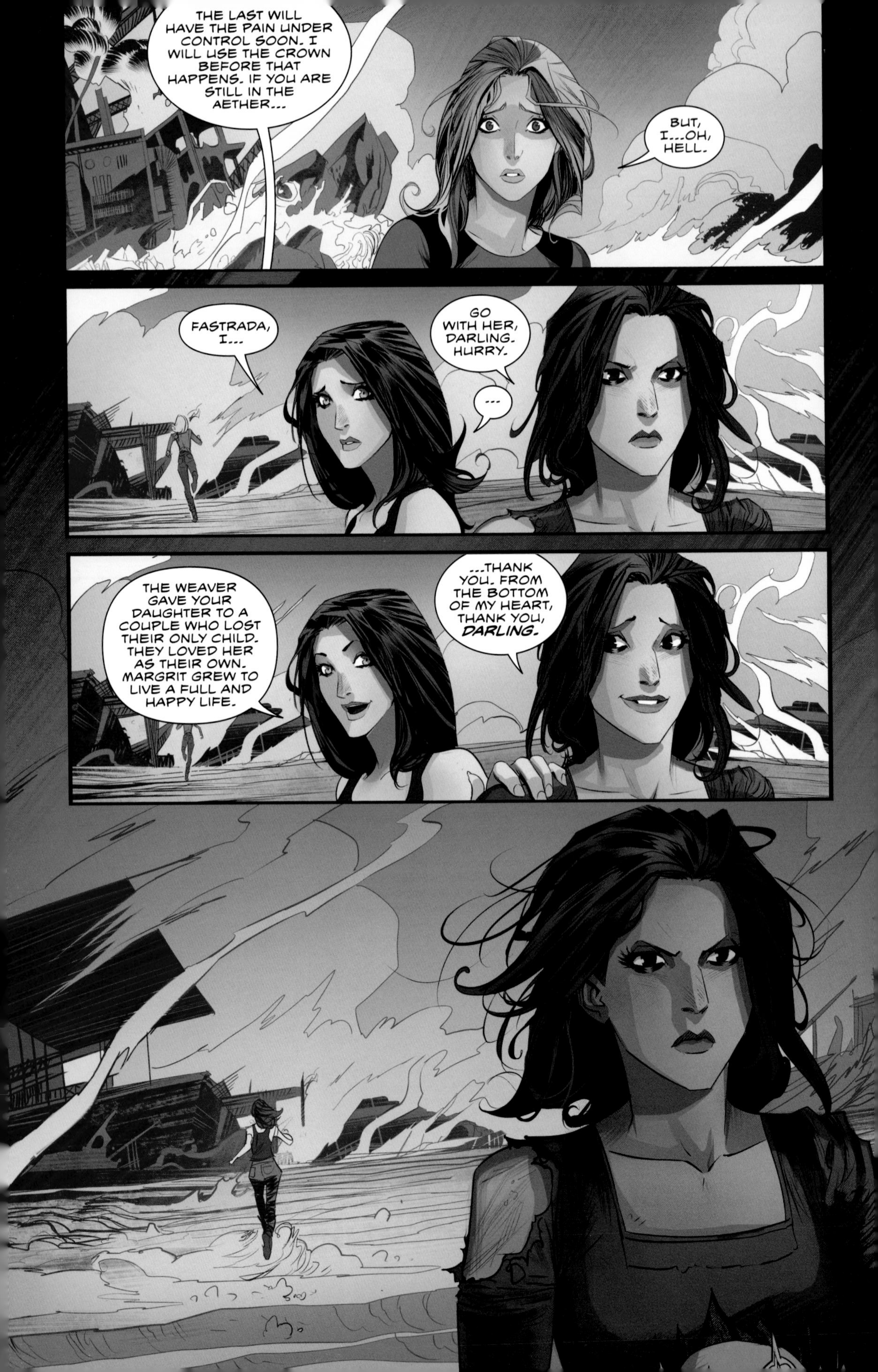

THE LAST WILL HAVE THE PAIN UNDER CONTROL SOON. I WILL USE THE CROWN BEFORE THAT HAPPENS. IF YOU ARE STILL IN THE AETHER...
BUT, I...OH, HELL.
FASTRADA, I...
GO WITH HER, DARLING. HURRY.
...
THE WEAVER GAVE YOUR DAUGHTER TO A COUPLE WHO LOST THEIR ONLY CHILD. THEY LOVED HER AS THEIR OWN. MARGRIT GREW TO LIVE A FULL AND HAPPY LIFE.
...THANK YOU. FROM THE BOTTOM OF MY HEART, THANK YOU, ***DARLING.***

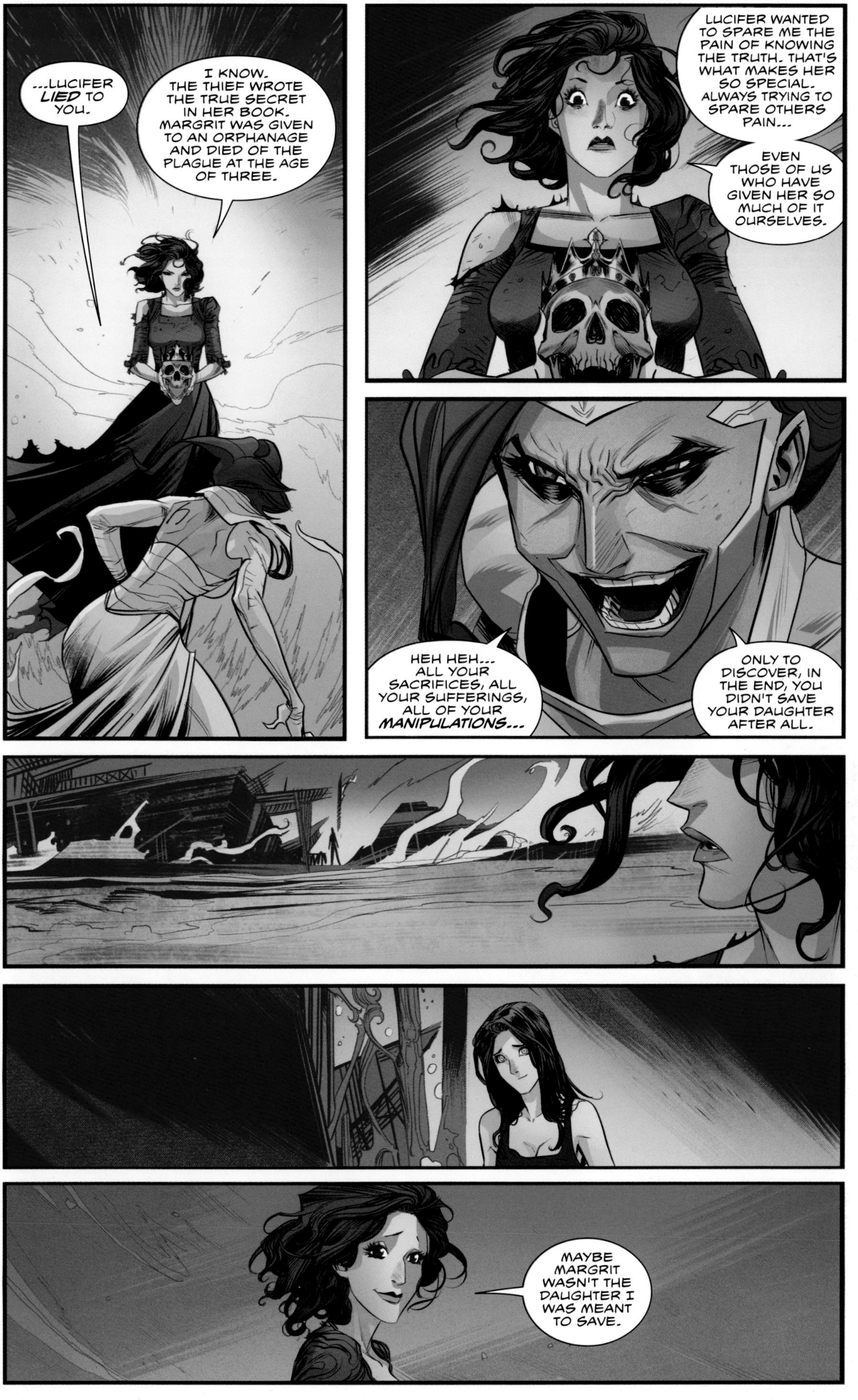
...LUCIFER LIED TO YOU.
I KNOW. THE THIEF WROTE THE TRUE SECRET IN HER BOOK. MARGRIT WAS GIVEN TO AN ORPHANAGE AND DIED OF THE PLAGUE AT THE AGE OF THREE.
LUCIFER WANTED TO SPARE ME THE PAIN OF KNOWING THE TRUTH. THAT'S WHAT MAKES HER SO SPECIAL. ALWAYS TRYING TO SPARE OTHERS PAIN...
EVEN THOSE OF US WHO HAVE GIVEN HER SO MUCH OF IT OURSELVES.
HEH HEH... ALL YOUR SACRIFICES, ALL YOUR SUFFERINGS, ALL OF YOUR MANIPULATIONS...
ONLY TO DISCOVER, IN THE END, YOU DIDN'T SAVE YOUR DAUGHTER AFTER ALL.
MAYBE MARGRIT WASN'T THE DAUGHTER I WAS MEANT TO SAVE.

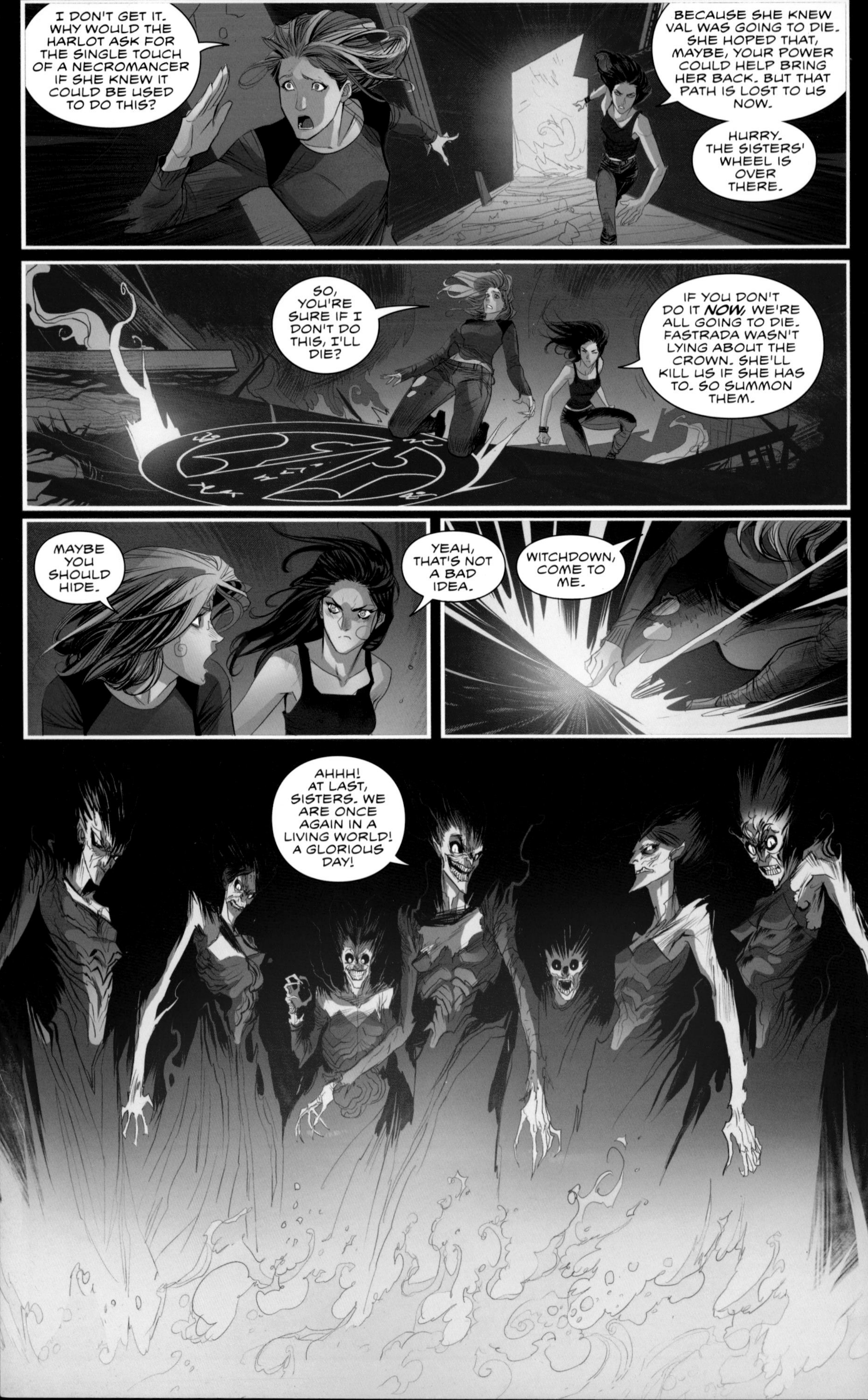
I DON'T GET IT. WHY WOULD THE HARLOT ASK FOR THE SINGLE TOUCH OF A NECROMANCER IF SHE KNEW IT COULD BE USED TO DO THIS?
BECAUSE SHE KNEW VAL WAS GOING TO DIE. SHE HOPED THAT, MAYBE, YOUR POWER COULD HELP BRING HER BACK. BUT THAT PATH IS LOST TO US NOW.
HURRY. THE SISTERS' WHEEL IS OVER THERE.
SO, YOU'RE SURE IF I DON'T DO THIS, I'LL DIE?
IF YOU DON'T DO IT NOW, WE'RE ALL GOING TO DIE. FASTRADA WASN'T LYING ABOUT THE CROWN. SHE'LL KILL US IF SHE HAS TO. SO SUMMON THEM.
MAYBE YOU SHOULD HIDE.
YEAH, THAT'S NOT A BAD IDEA.
WITCHDOWN, COME TO ME.
AHHH! AT LAST, SISTERS. WE ARE ONCE AGAIN IN A LIVING WORLD! A GLORIOUS DAY!

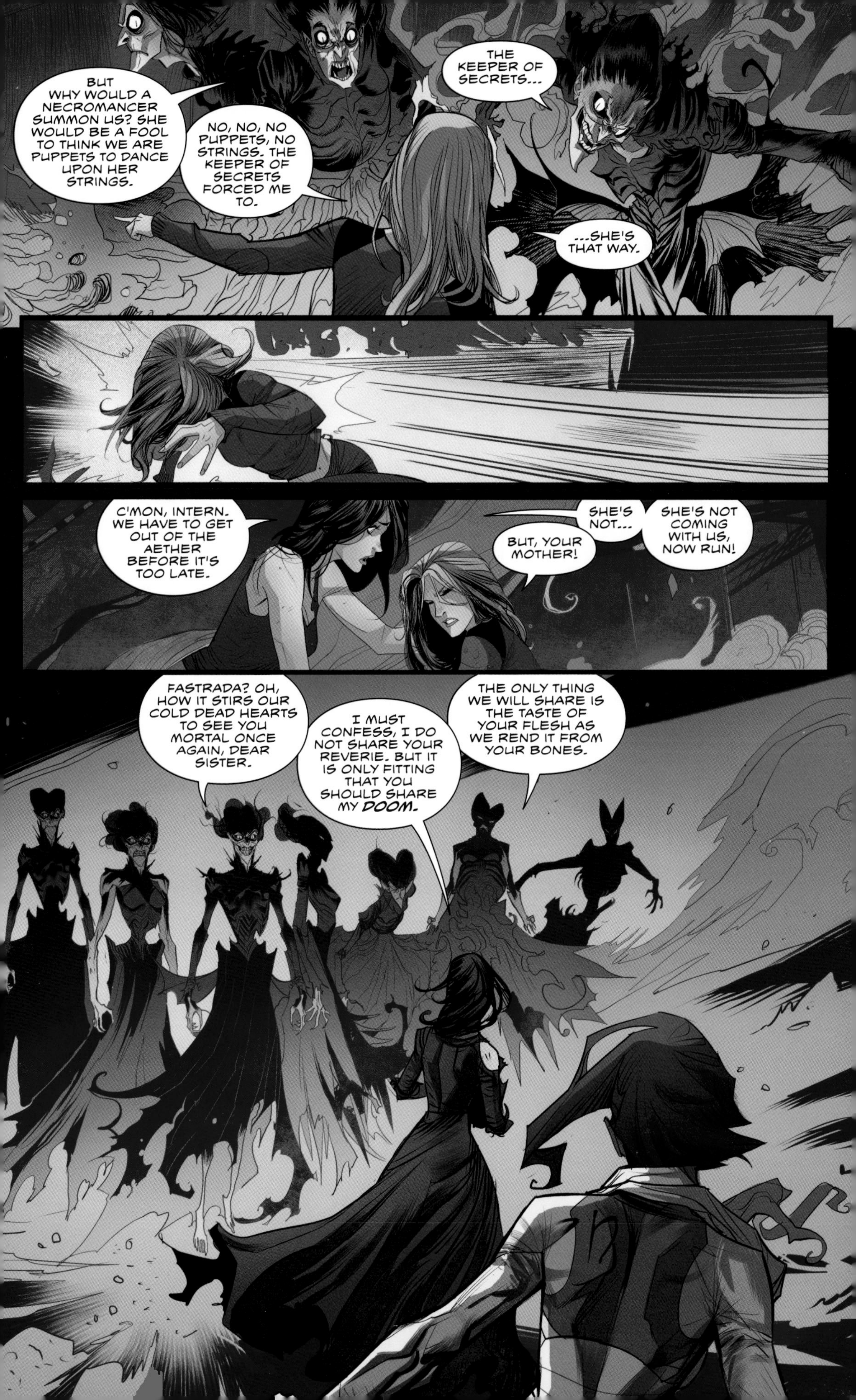
BUT WHY WOULD A NECROMANCER SUMMON US? SHE WOULD BE A FOOL TO THINK WE ARE PUPPETS TO DANCE UPON HER STRINGS.
NO, NO, NO PUPPETS, NO STRINGS. THE KEEPER OF SECRETS FORCED ME TO.
THE KEEPER OF SECRETS...
...SHE'S THAT WAY.
C'MON, INTERN. WE HAVE TO GET OUT OF THE AETHER BEFORE IT'S TOO LATE.
BUT, YOUR MOTHER!
SHE'S NOT...
SHE'S NOT COMING WITH US, NOW RUN!
FASTRADA? OH, HOW IT STIRS OUR COLD DEAD HEARTS TO SEE YOU MORTAL ONCE AGAIN, DEAR SISTER.
I MUST CONFESS, I DO NOT SHARE YOUR REVERIE. BUT IT IS ONLY FITTING THAT YOU SHOULD SHARE MY ***DOOM.***
THE ONLY THING WE WILL SHARE IS THE TASTE OF YOUR FLESH AS WE REND IT FROM YOUR BONES.

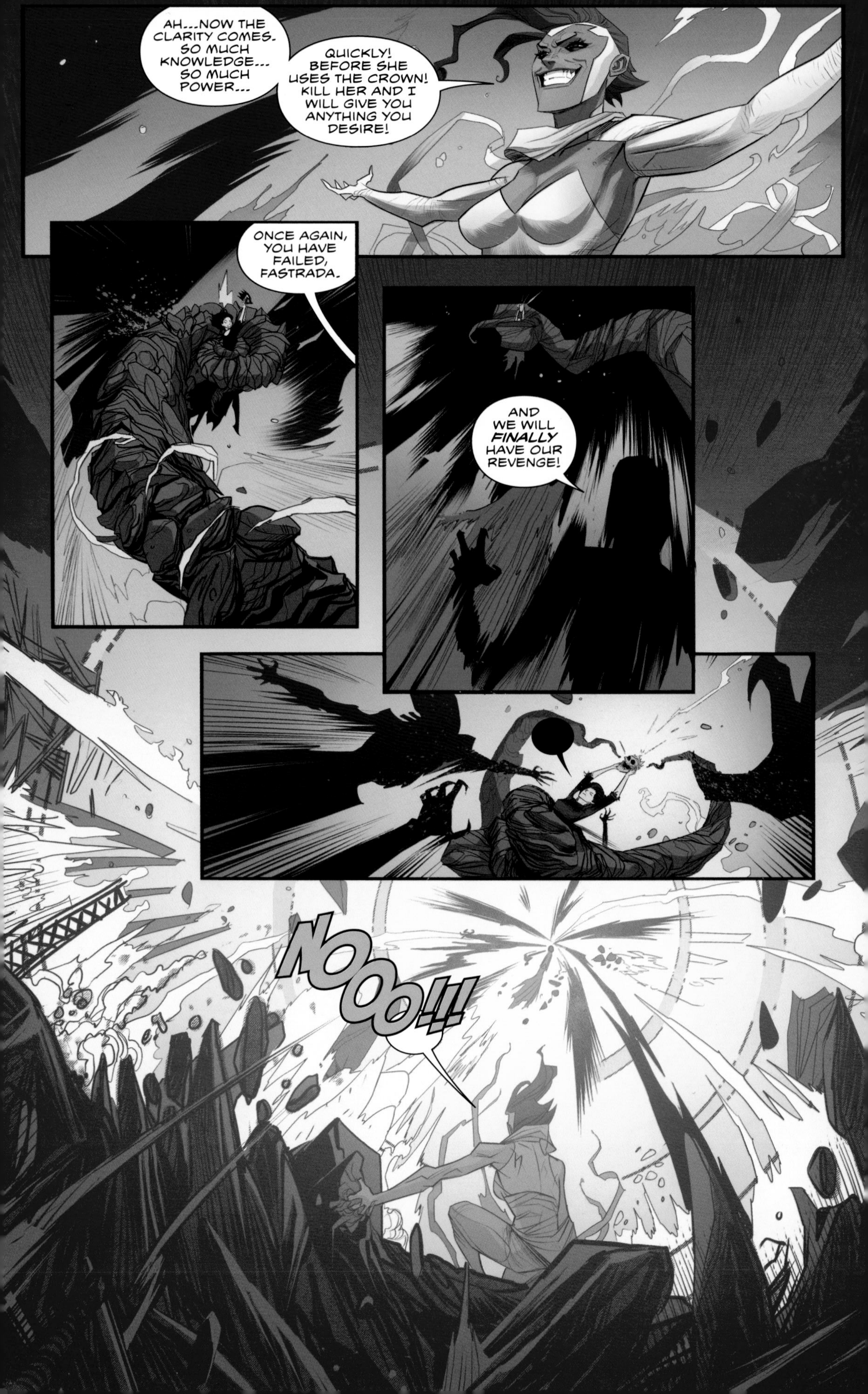
AH...NOW THE CLARITY COMES. SO MUCH KNOWLEDGE... SO MUCH POWER...
QUICKLY! BEFORE SHE USES THE CROWN! KILL HER AND I WILL GIVE YOU ANYTHING YOU DESIRE!
ONCE AGAIN, YOU HAVE FAILED, FASTRADA.
AND WE WILL FINALLY HAVE OUR REVENGE!
NOOO!!!

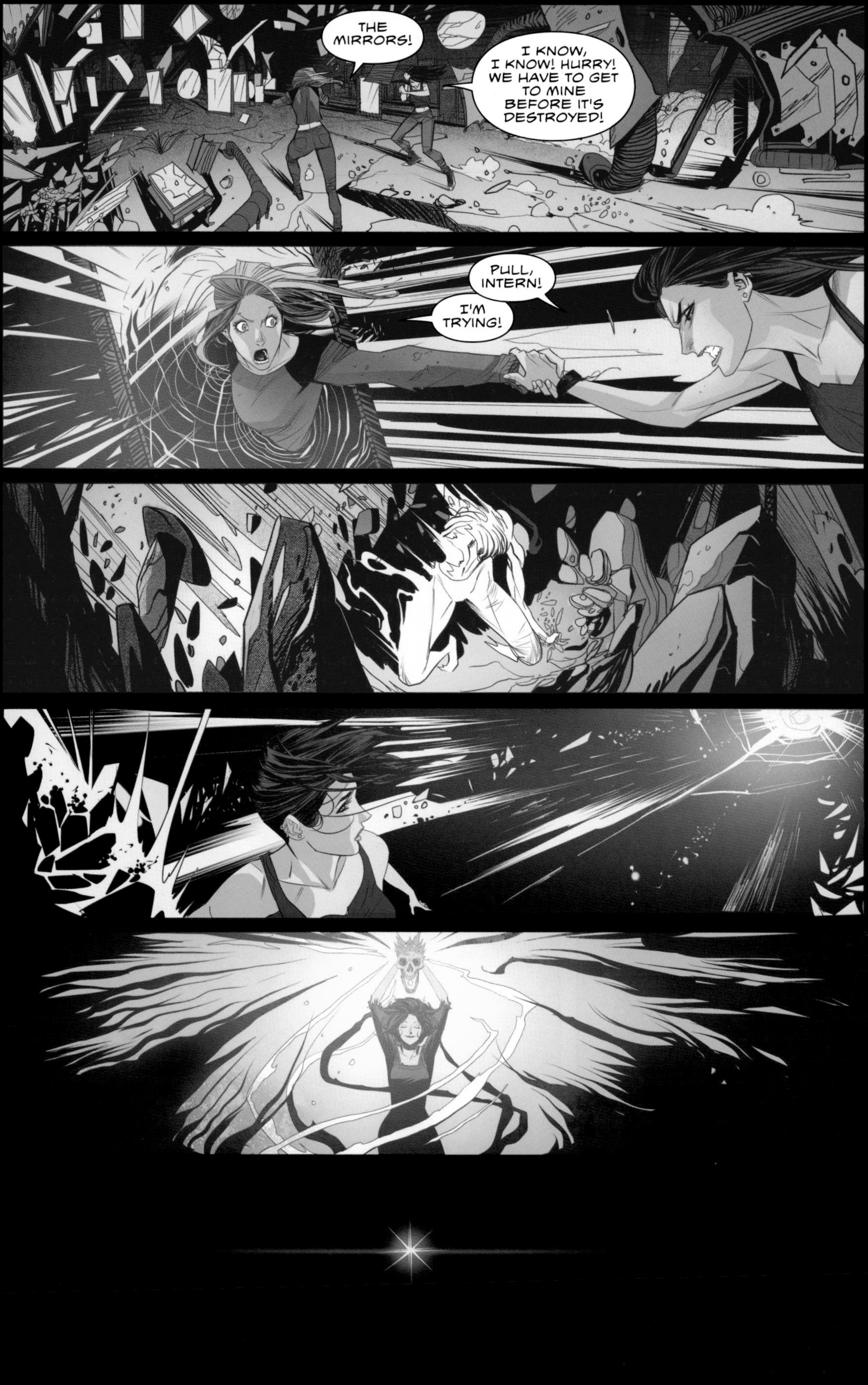
THE MIRRORS!
I KNOW, I KNOW! HURRY! WE HAVE TO GET TO MINE BEFORE IT'S DESTROYED!
PULL, INTERN!
I'M TRYING!

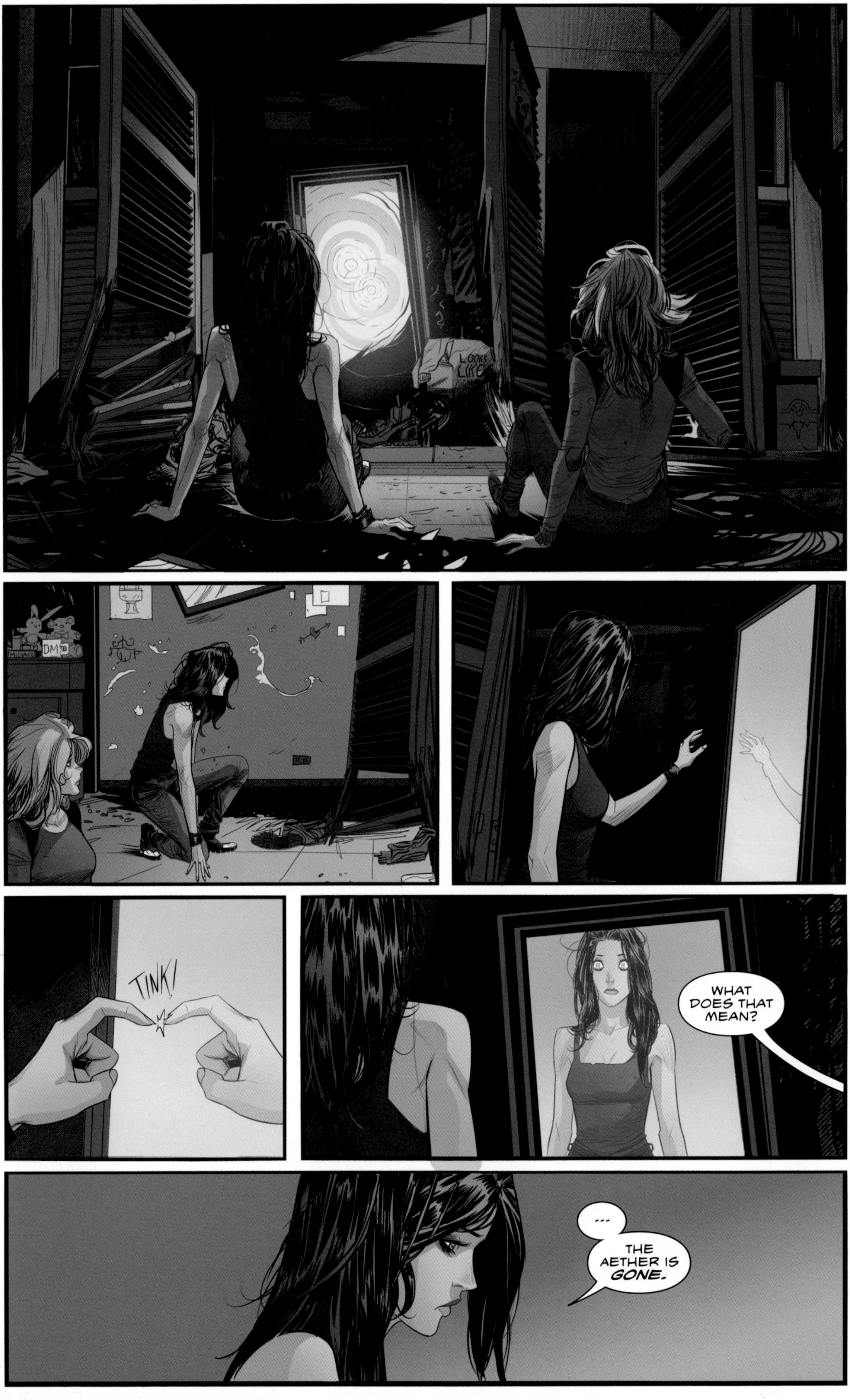
LOOKS LIKE
DM
TINK!
WHAT DOES THAT MEAN?
...
THE AETHER IS *GONE.*

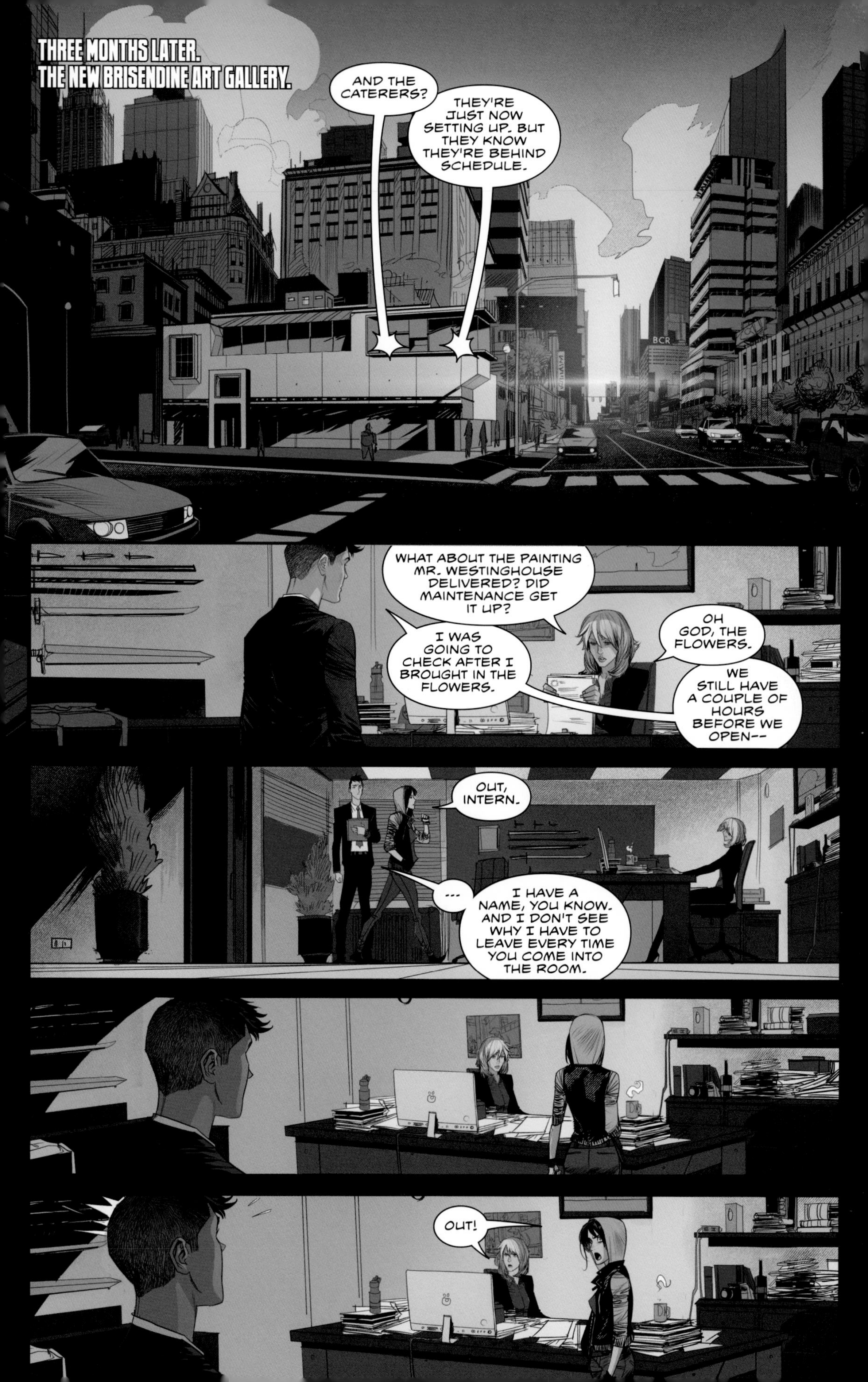
THREE MONTHS LATER.
THE NEW BRISENDINE ART GALLERY.
AND THE CATERERS?
THEY'RE JUST NOW SETTING UP. BUT THEY KNOW THEY'RE BEHIND SCHEDULE.
BCR
WHAT ABOUT THE PAINTING MR. WESTINGHOUSE DELIVERED? DID MAINTENANCE GET IT UP?
I WAS GOING TO CHECK AFTER I BROUGHT IN THE FLOWERS.
OH GOD, THE FLOWERS.
WE STILL HAVE A COUPLE OF HOURS BEFORE WE OPEN--
OUT, INTERN.
...
I HAVE A NAME, YOU KNOW. AND I DON'T SEE WHY I HAVE TO LEAVE EVERY TIME YOU COME INTO THE ROOM.
OUT!

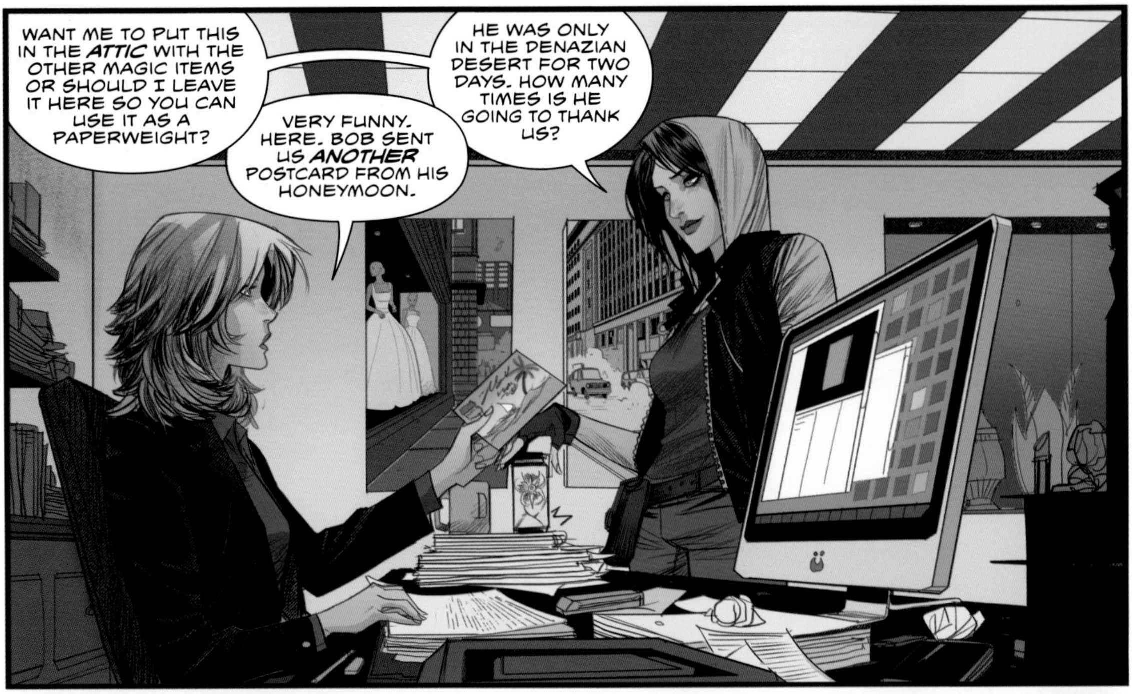
WANT ME TO PUT THIS IN THE ATTIC WITH THE OTHER MAGIC ITEMS OR SHOULD I LEAVE IT HERE SO YOU CAN USE IT AS A PAPERWEIGHT?
VERY FUNNY. HERE. BOB SENT US ANOTHER POSTCARD FROM HIS HONEYMOON.
HE WAS ONLY IN THE DENAZIAN DESERT FOR TWO DAYS. HOW MANY TIMES IS HE GOING TO THANK US?

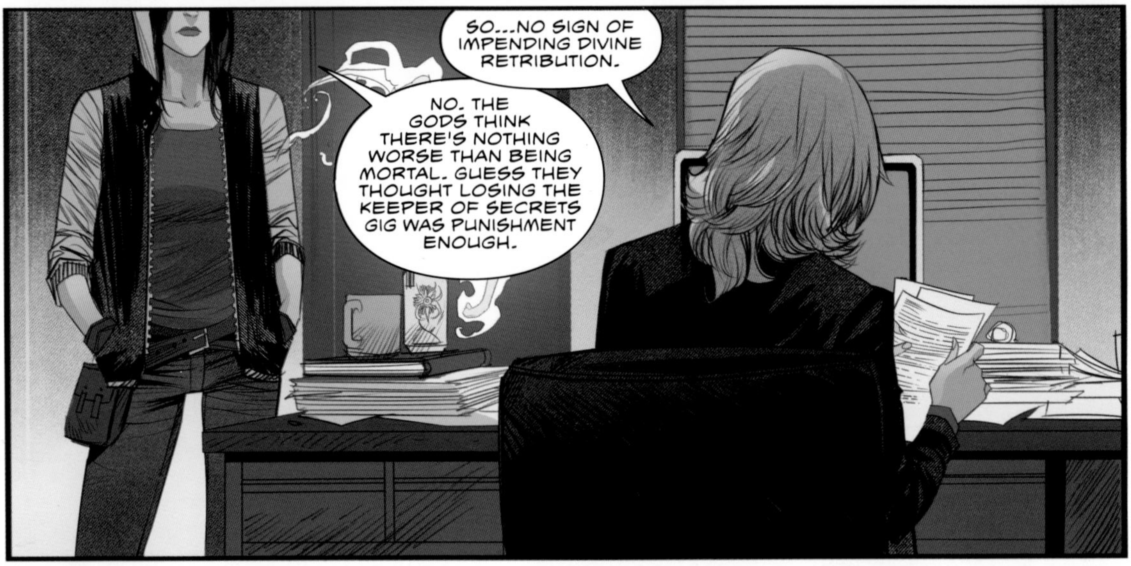
SO...NO SIGN OF IMPENDING DIVINE RETRIBUTION.
NO. THE GODS THINK THERE'S NOTHING WORSE THAN BEING MORTAL. GUESS THEY THOUGHT LOSING THE KEEPER OF SECRETS GIG WAS PUNISHMENT ENOUGH.

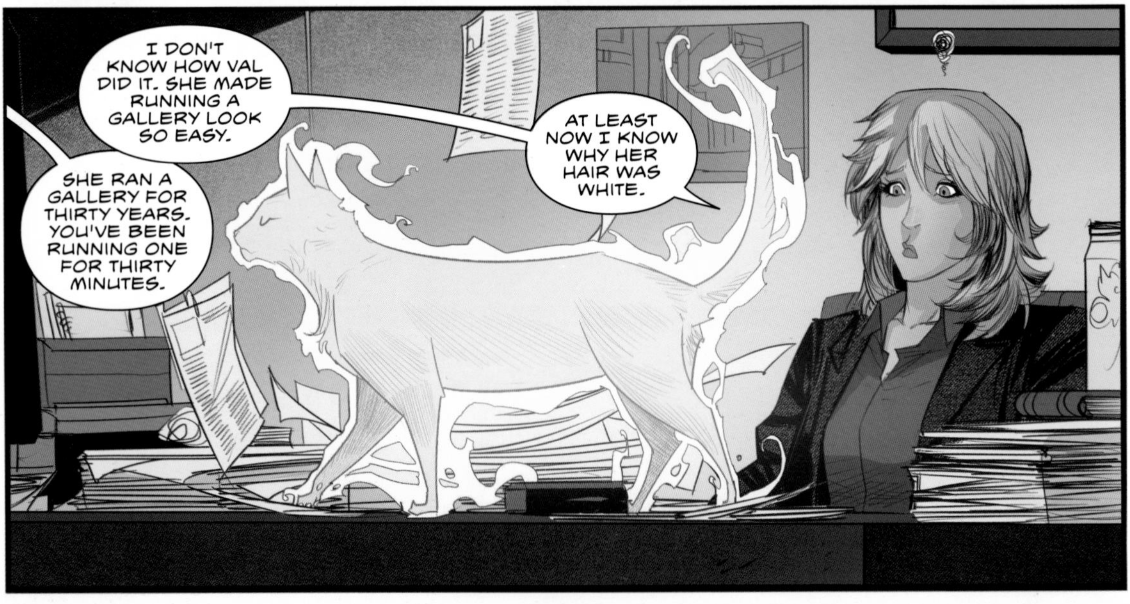
I DON'T KNOW HOW VAL DID IT. SHE MADE RUNNING A GALLERY LOOK SO EASY.
AT LEAST NOW I KNOW WHY HER HAIR WAS WHITE.
SHE RAN A GALLERY FOR THIRTY YEARS. YOU'VE BEEN RUNNING ONE FOR THIRTY MINUTES.

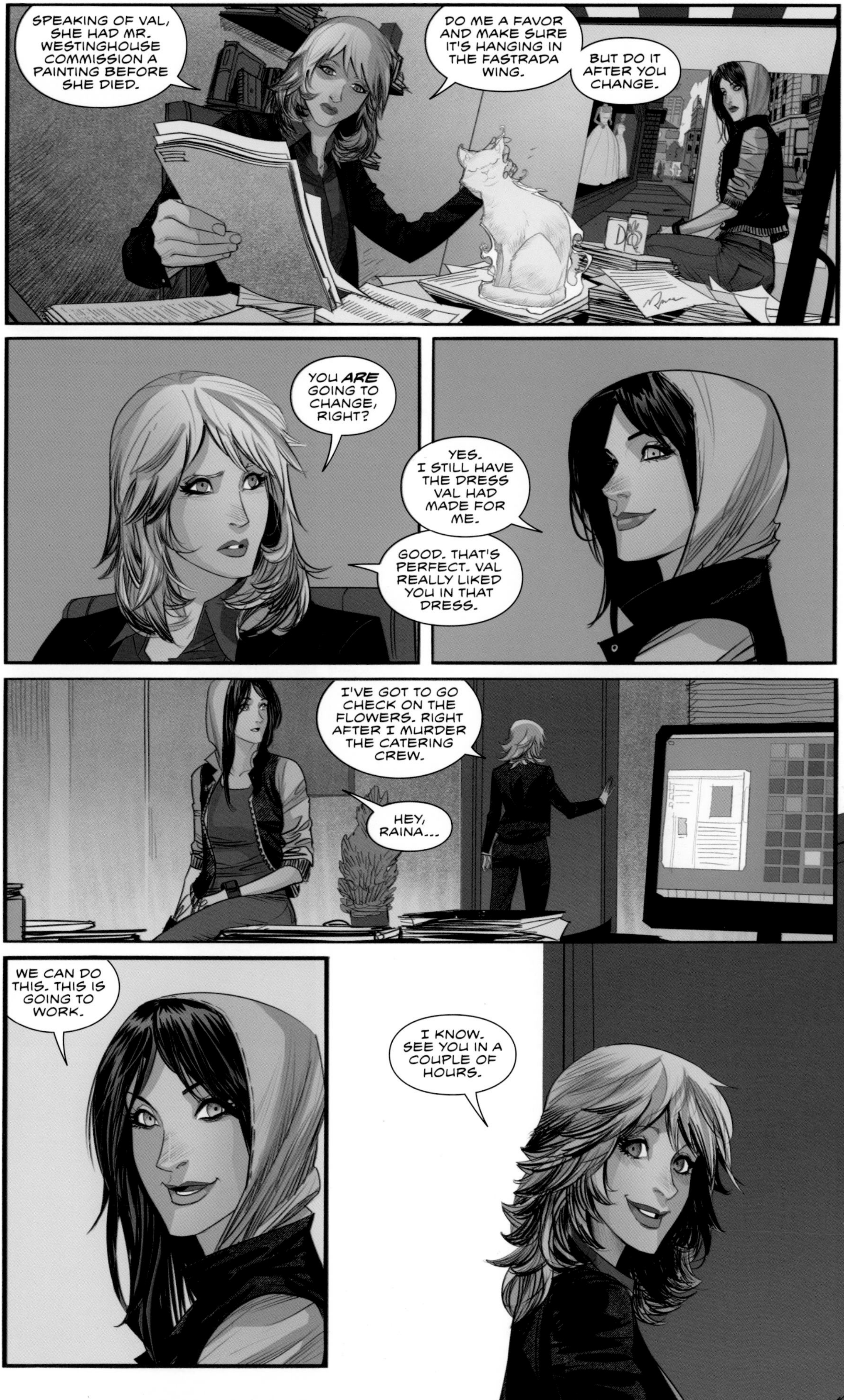
SPEAKING OF VAL, SHE HAD MR. WESTINGHOUSE COMMISSION A PAINTING BEFORE SHE DIED.
DO ME A FAVOR AND MAKE SURE IT'S HANGING IN THE FASTRADA WING.
BUT DO IT AFTER YOU CHANGE.
YOU *ARE* GOING TO CHANGE, RIGHT?
YES. I STILL HAVE THE DRESS VAL HAD MADE FOR ME.
GOOD. THAT'S PERFECT. VAL REALLY LIKED YOU IN THAT DRESS.
I'VE GOT TO GO CHECK ON THE FLOWERS. RIGHT AFTER I MURDER THE CATERING CREW.
HEY, RAINA...
WE CAN DO THIS. THIS IS GOING TO WORK.
I KNOW. SEE YOU IN A COUPLE OF HOURS.

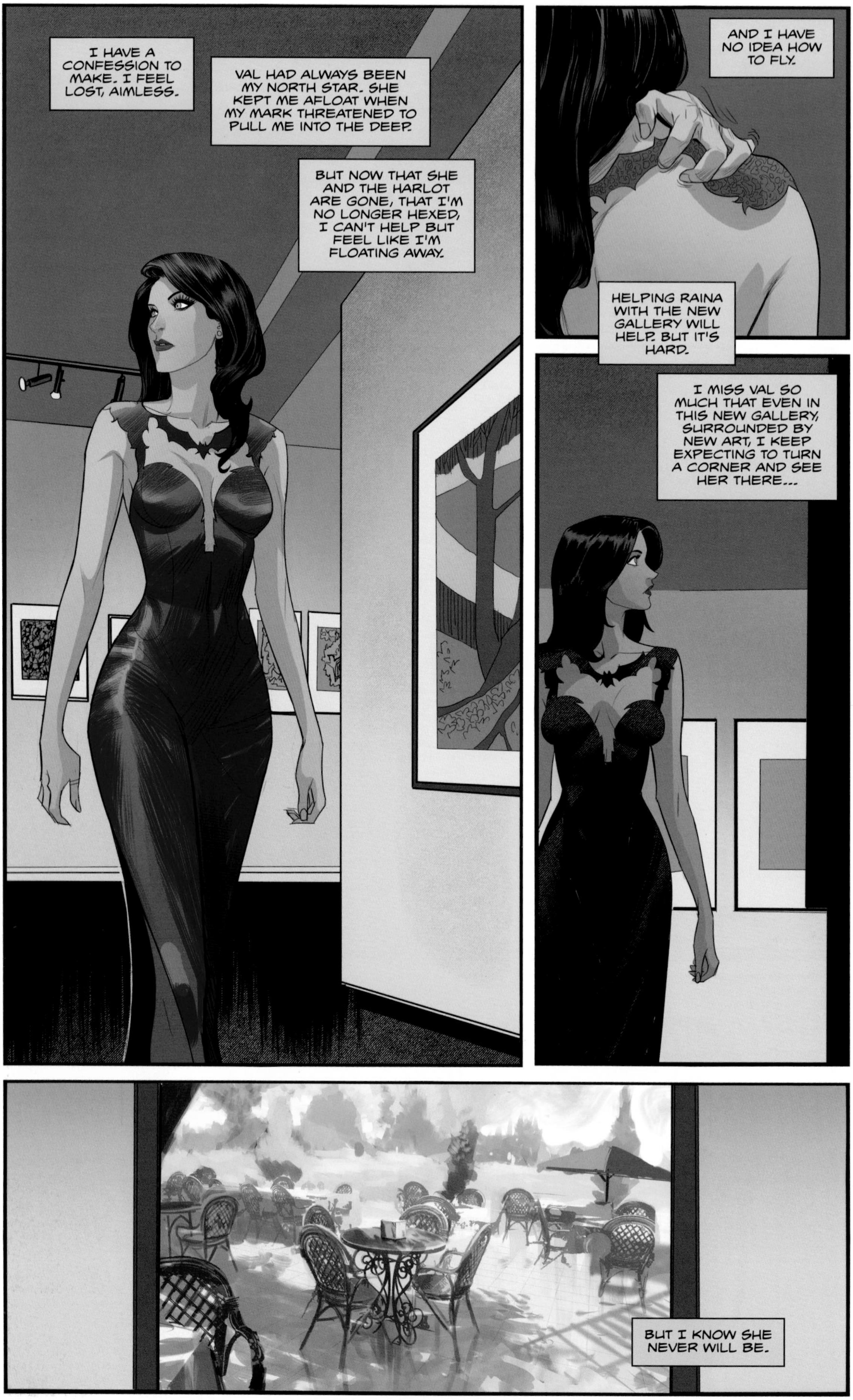
I HAVE A CONFESSION TO MAKE. I FEEL LOST, AIMLESS.
VAL HAD ALWAYS BEEN MY NORTH STAR. SHE KEPT ME AFLOAT WHEN MY MARK THREATENED TO PULL ME INTO THE DEEP.
BUT NOW THAT SHE AND THE HARLOT ARE GONE, THAT I'M NO LONGER HEXED, I CAN'T HELP BUT FEEL LIKE I'M FLOATING AWAY.
AND I HAVE NO IDEA HOW TO FLY.
HELPING RAINA WITH THE NEW GALLERY WILL HELP. BUT IT'S HARD.
I MISS VAL SO MUCH THAT EVEN IN THIS NEW GALLERY, SURROUNDED BY NEW ART, I KEEP EXPECTING TO TURN A CORNER AND SEE HER THERE...
BUT I KNOW SHE NEVER WILL BE.

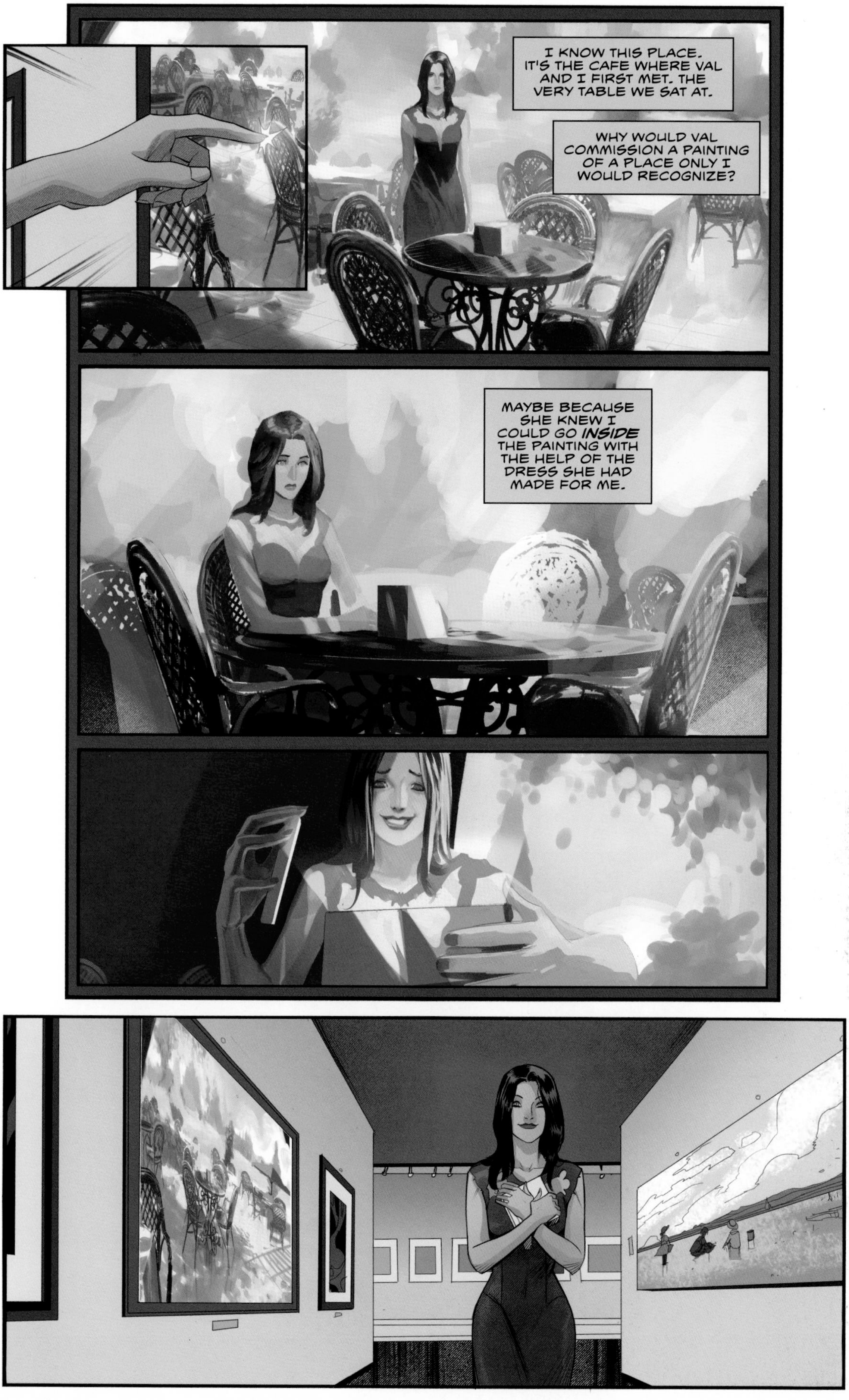
I KNOW THIS PLACE. IT'S THE CAFE WHERE VAL AND I FIRST MET. THE VERY TABLE WE SAT AT.
WHY WOULD VAL COMMISSION A PAINTING OF A PLACE ONLY I WOULD RECOGNIZE?
MAYBE BECAUSE SHE KNEW I COULD GO *INSIDE* THE PAINTING WITH THE HELP OF THE DRESS SHE HAD MADE FOR ME.

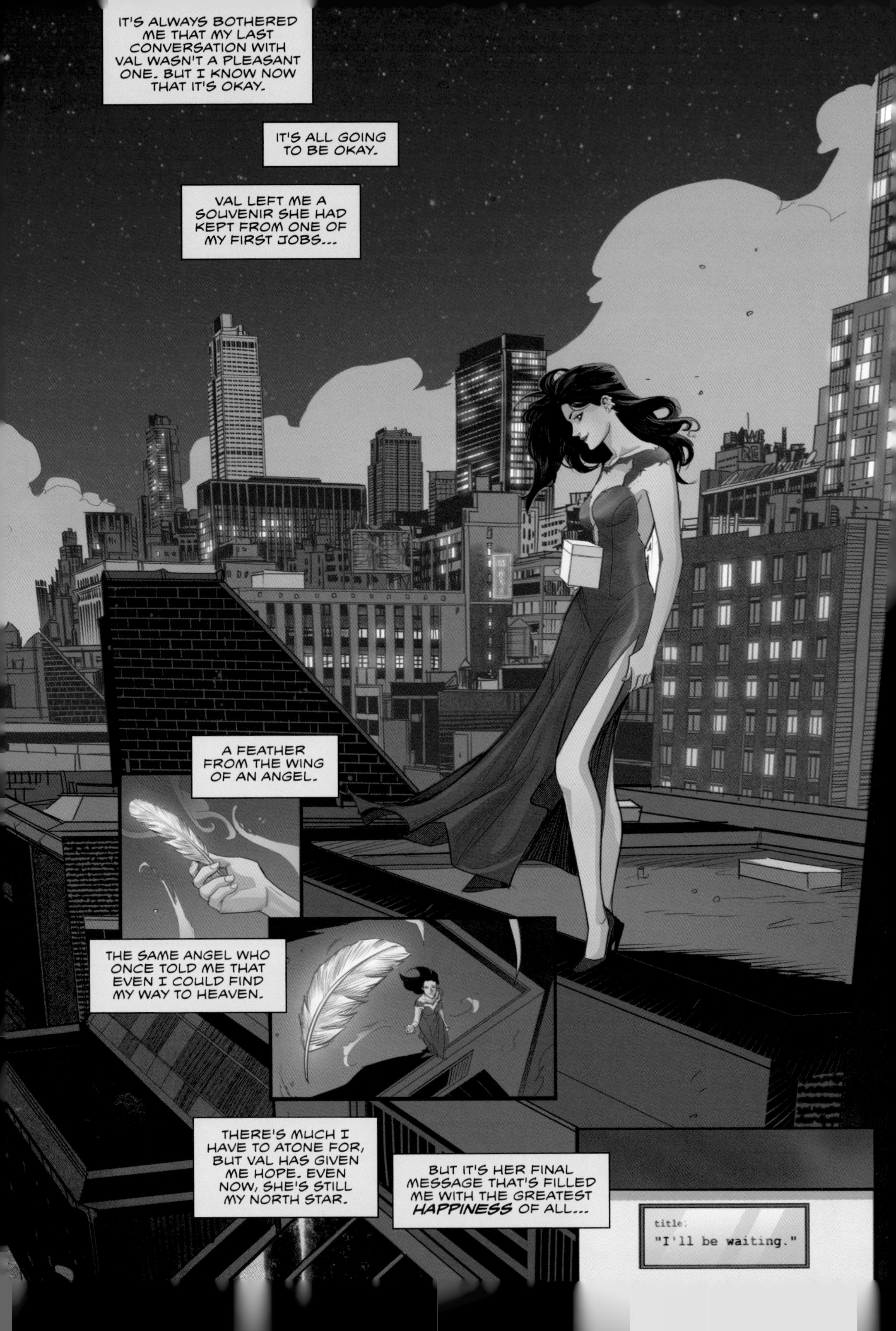
IT'S ALWAYS BOTHERED ME THAT MY LAST CONVERSATION WITH VAL WASN'T A PLEASANT ONE. BUT I KNOW NOW THAT IT'S OKAY.
IT'S ALL GOING TO BE OKAY.
VAL LEFT ME A SOUVENIR SHE HAD KEPT FROM ONE OF MY FIRST JOBS...
A FEATHER FROM THE WING OF AN ANGEL.
THE SAME ANGEL WHO ONCE TOLD ME THAT EVEN I COULD FIND MY WAY TO HEAVEN.
THERE'S MUCH I HAVE TO ATONE FOR, BUT VAL HAS GIVEN ME HOPE. EVEN NOW, SHE'S STILL MY NORTH STAR.
BUT IT'S HER FINAL MESSAGE THAT'S FILLED ME WITH THE GREATEST *HAPPINESS* OF ALL...
title:
"I'll be waiting."

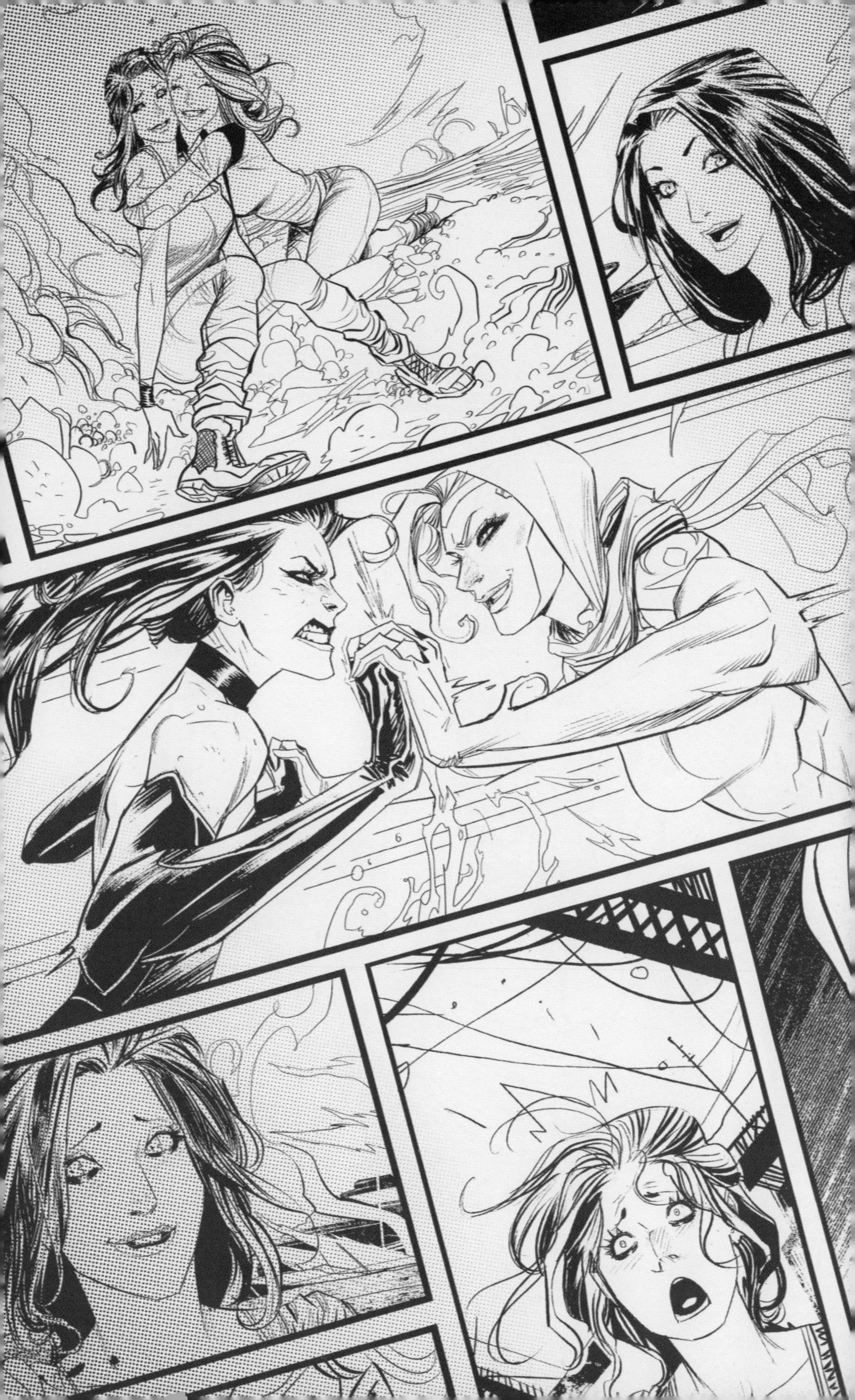

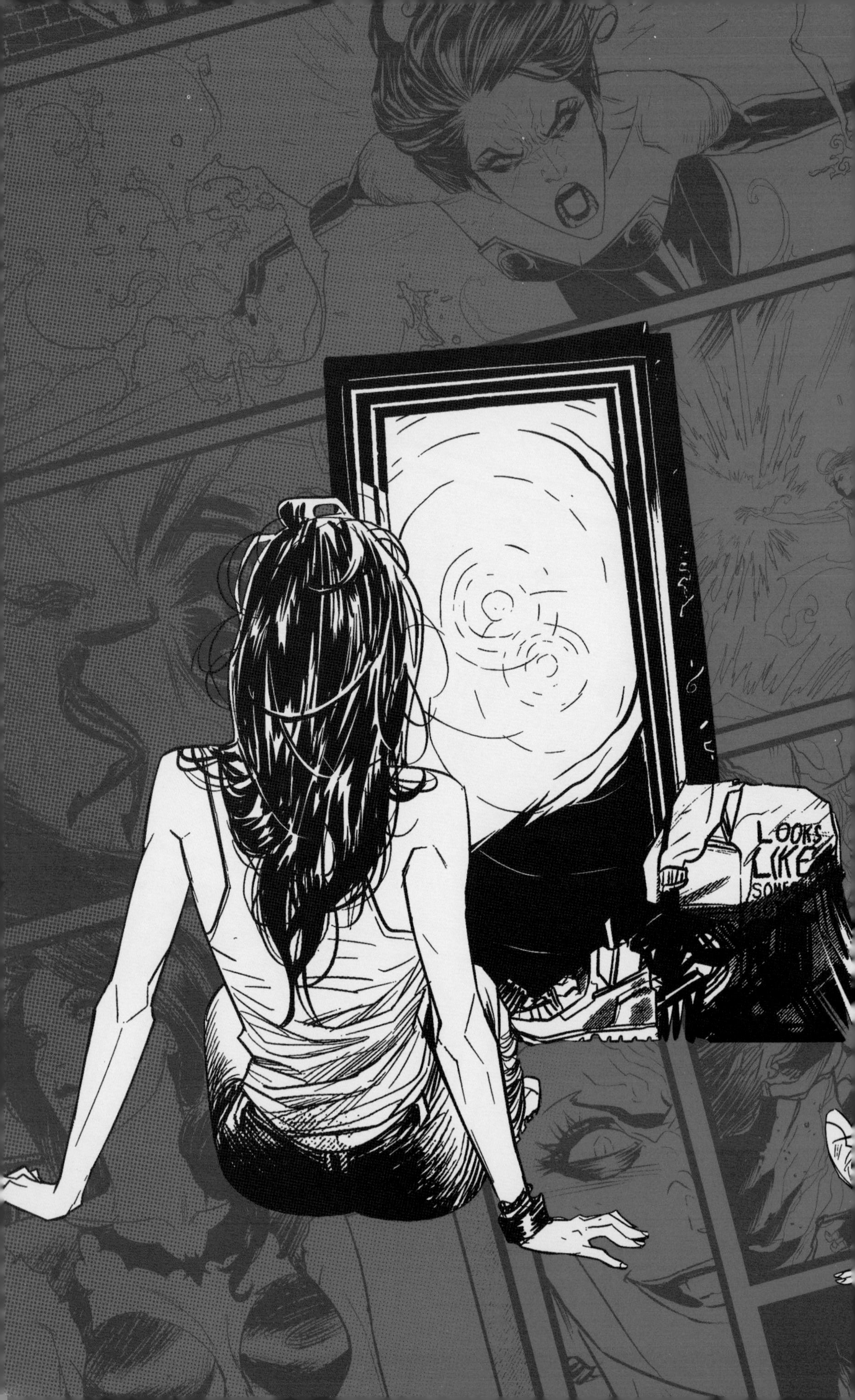
LOOKS LIKE

COVER GALLERY

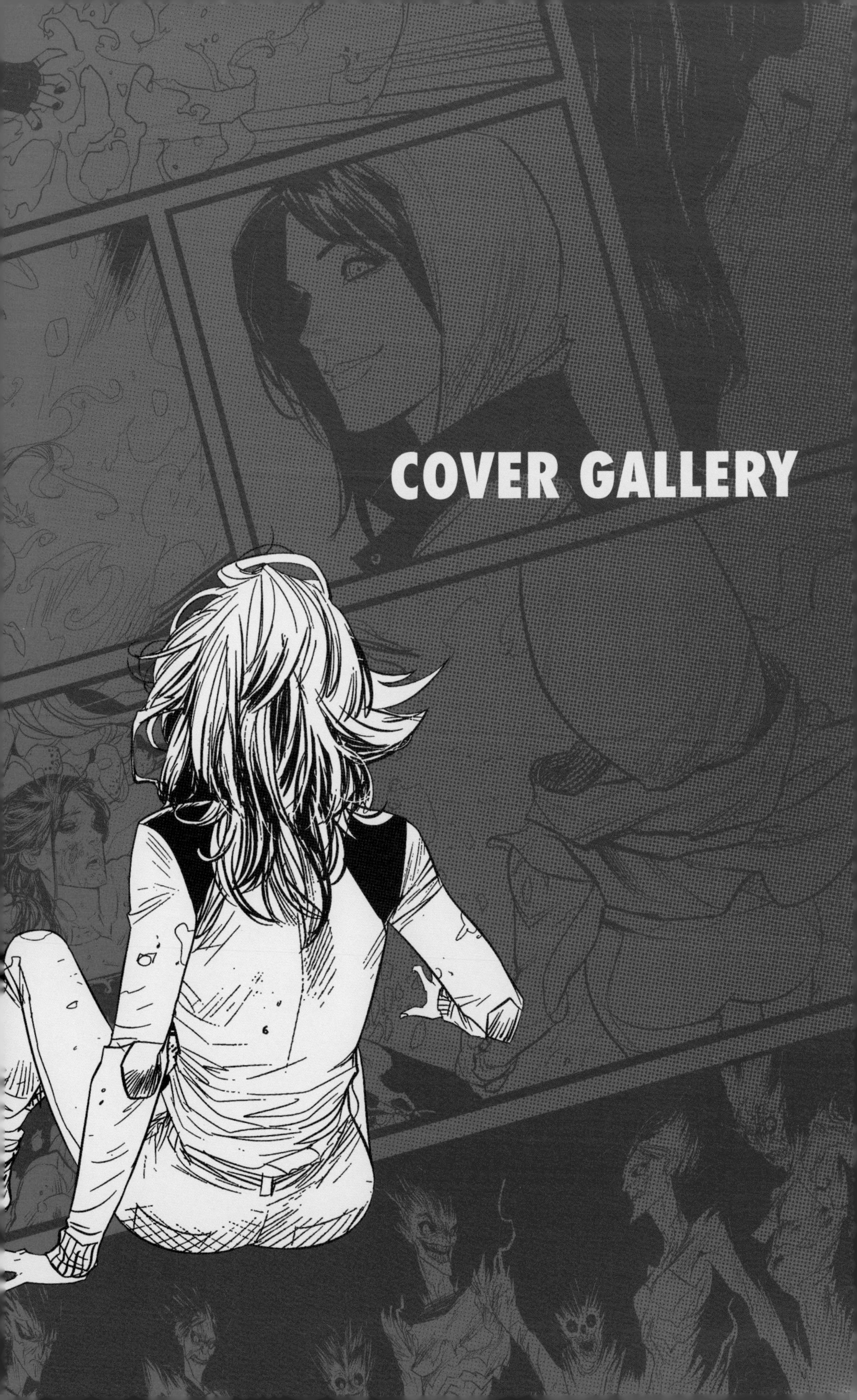

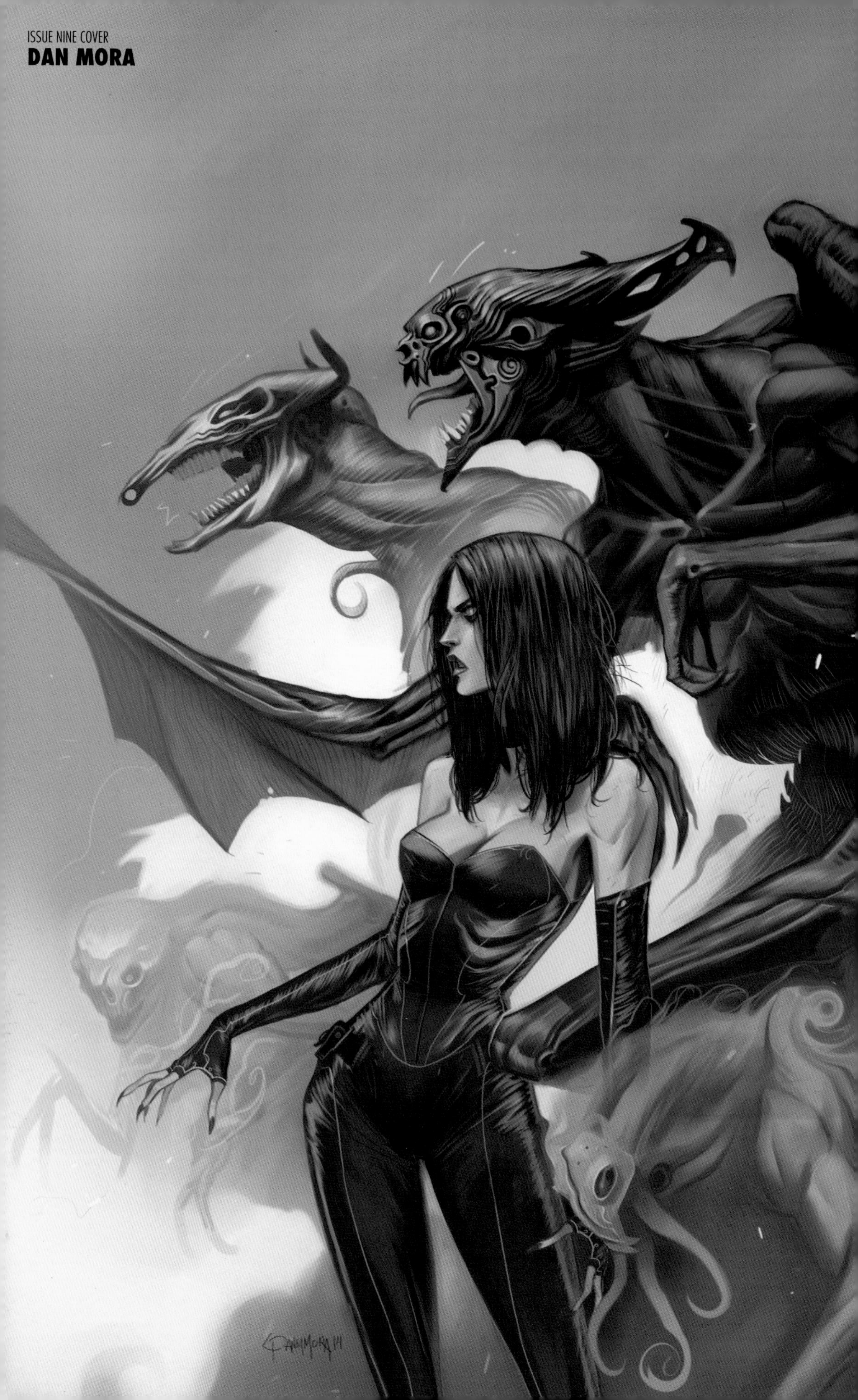

ISSUE NINE COVER
DAN MORA

ISSUE TEN COVER
DAN MORA

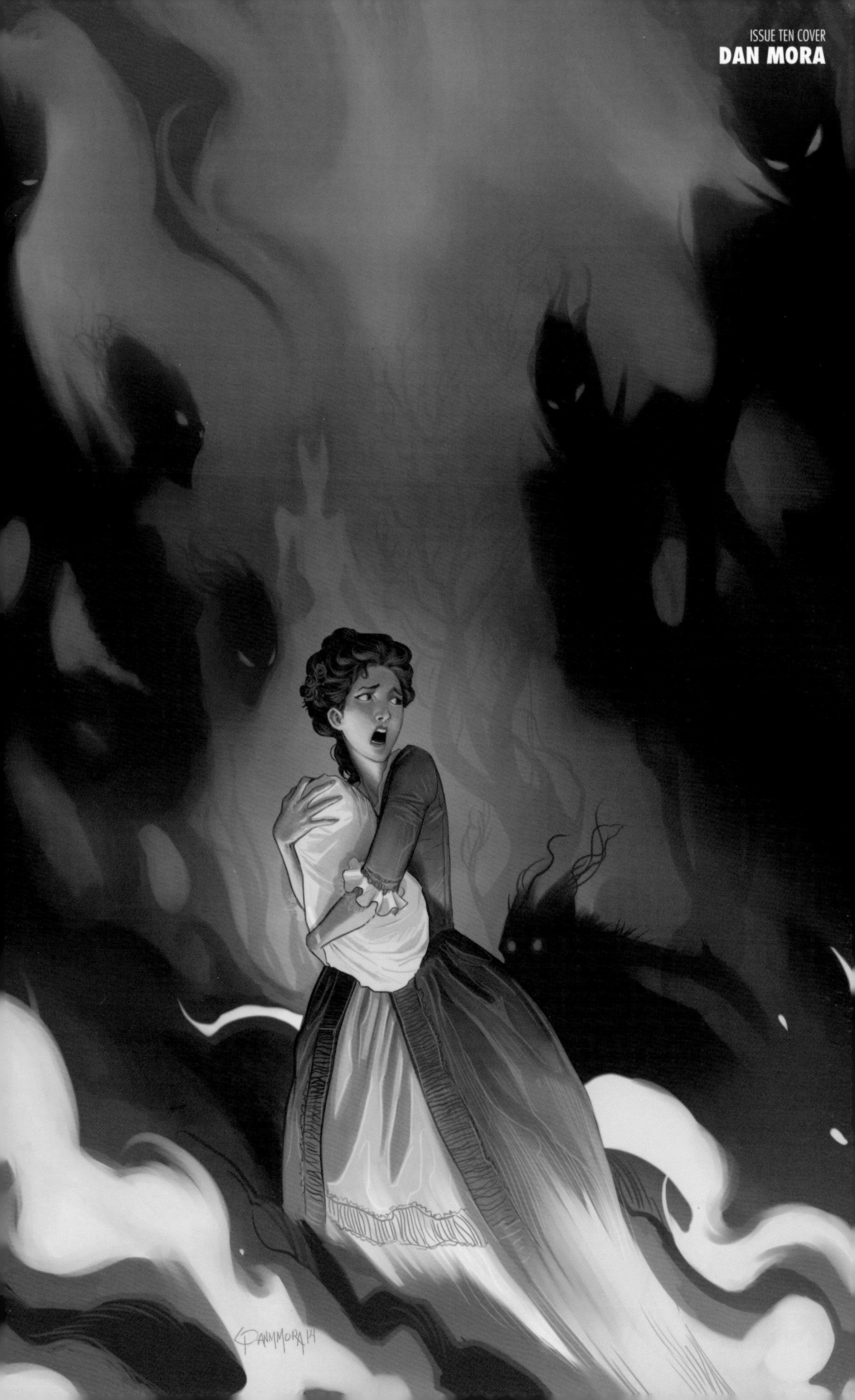

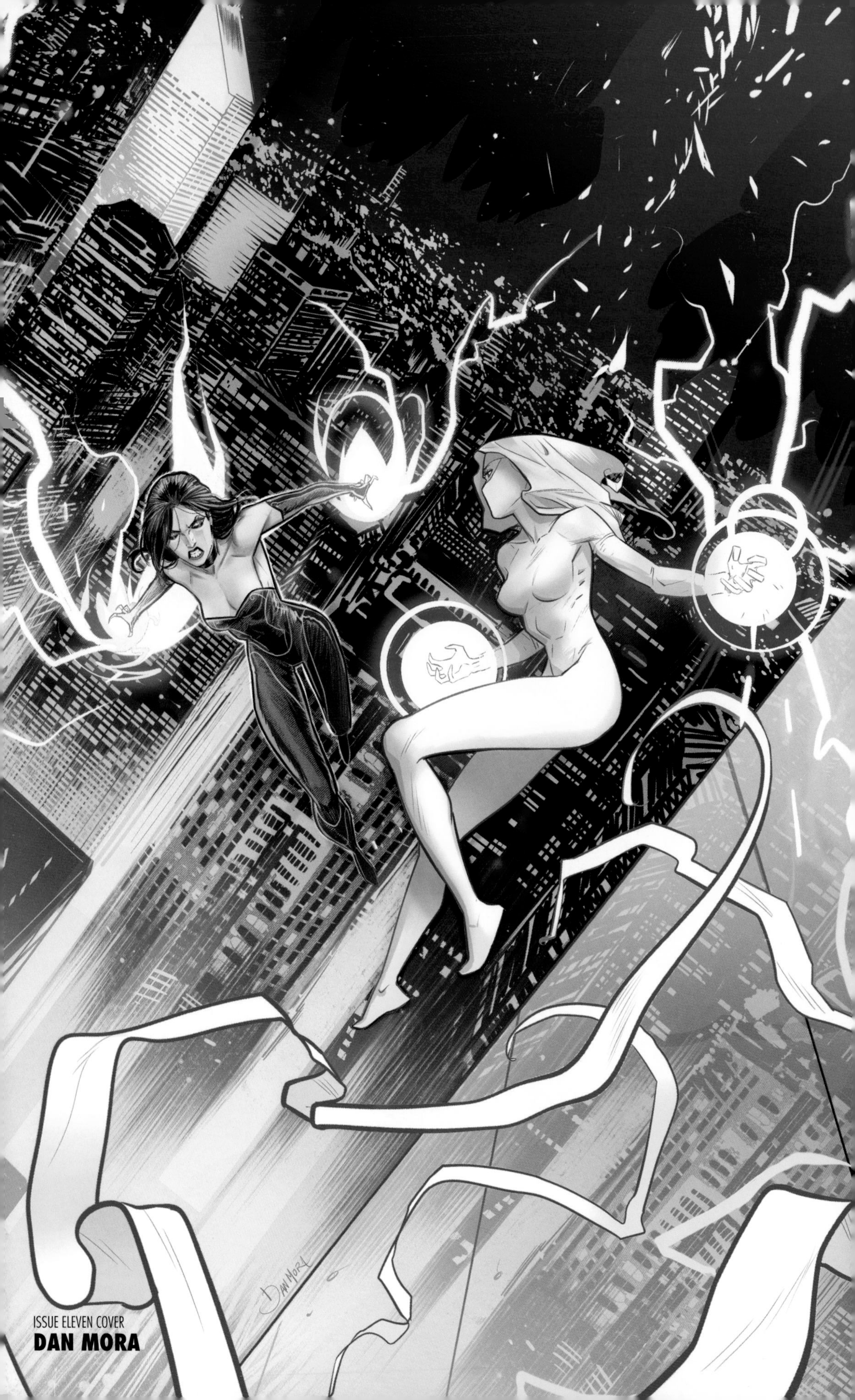

ISSUE ELEVEN COVER
DAN MORA

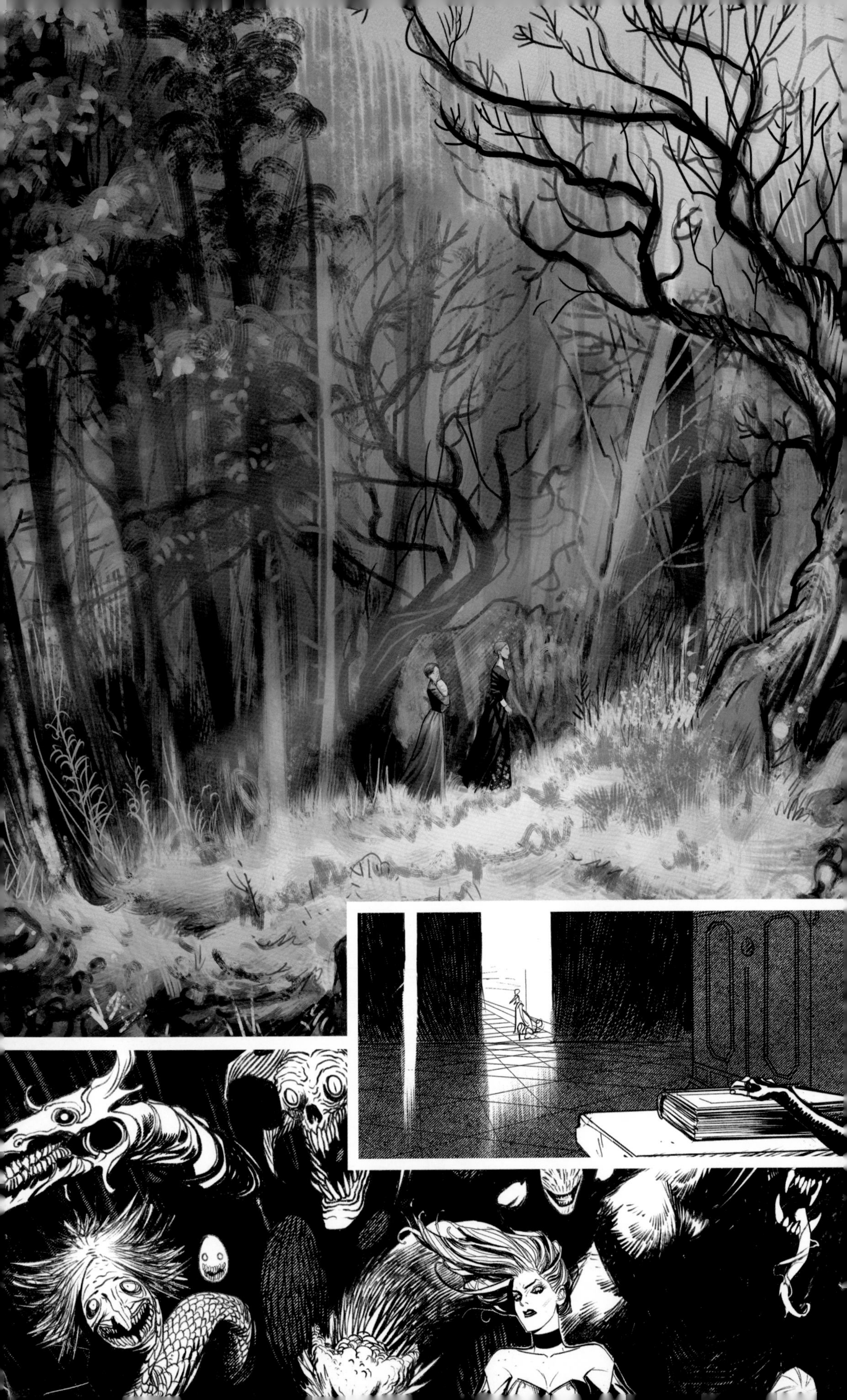

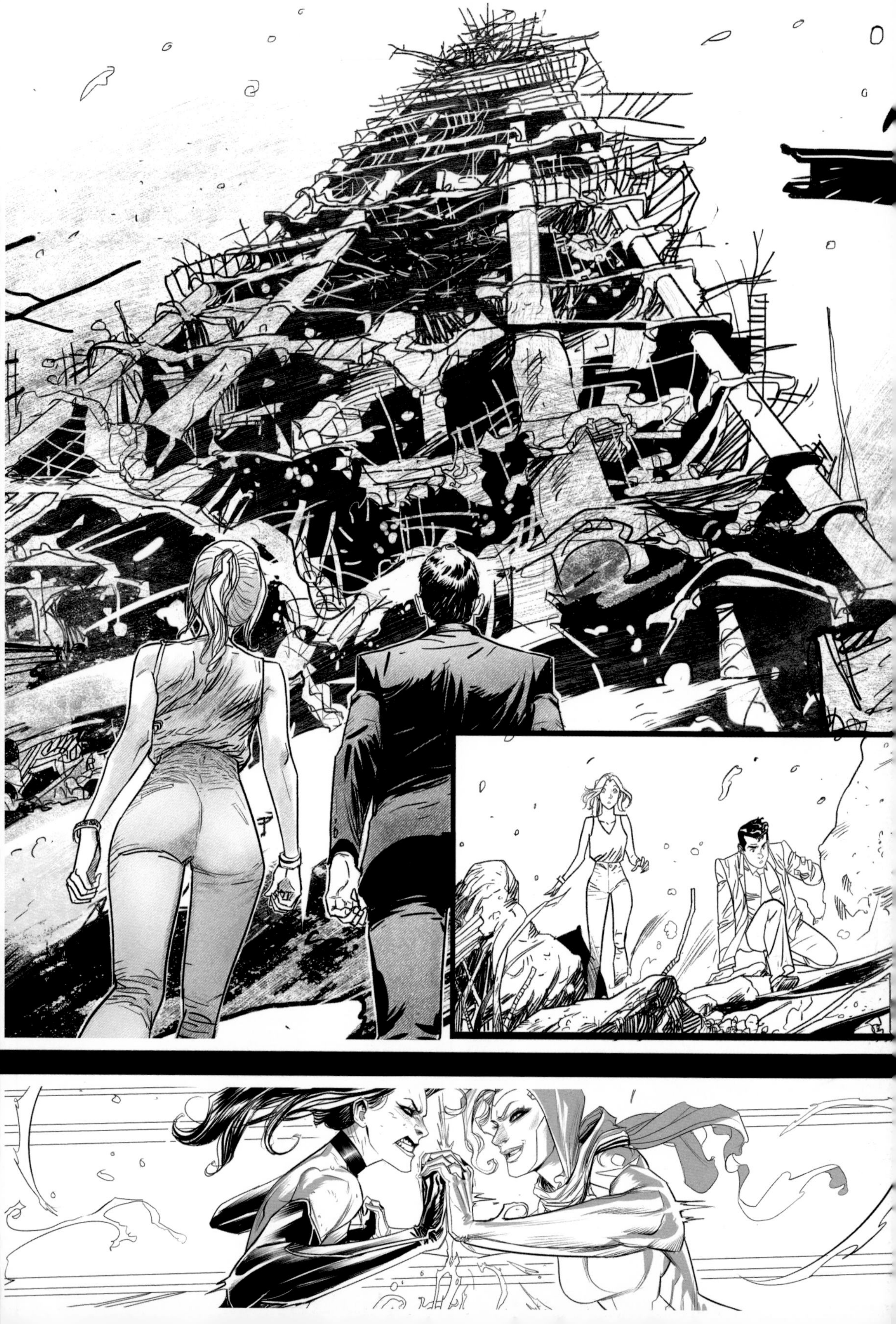

DAN MORA **INK GALLERY**

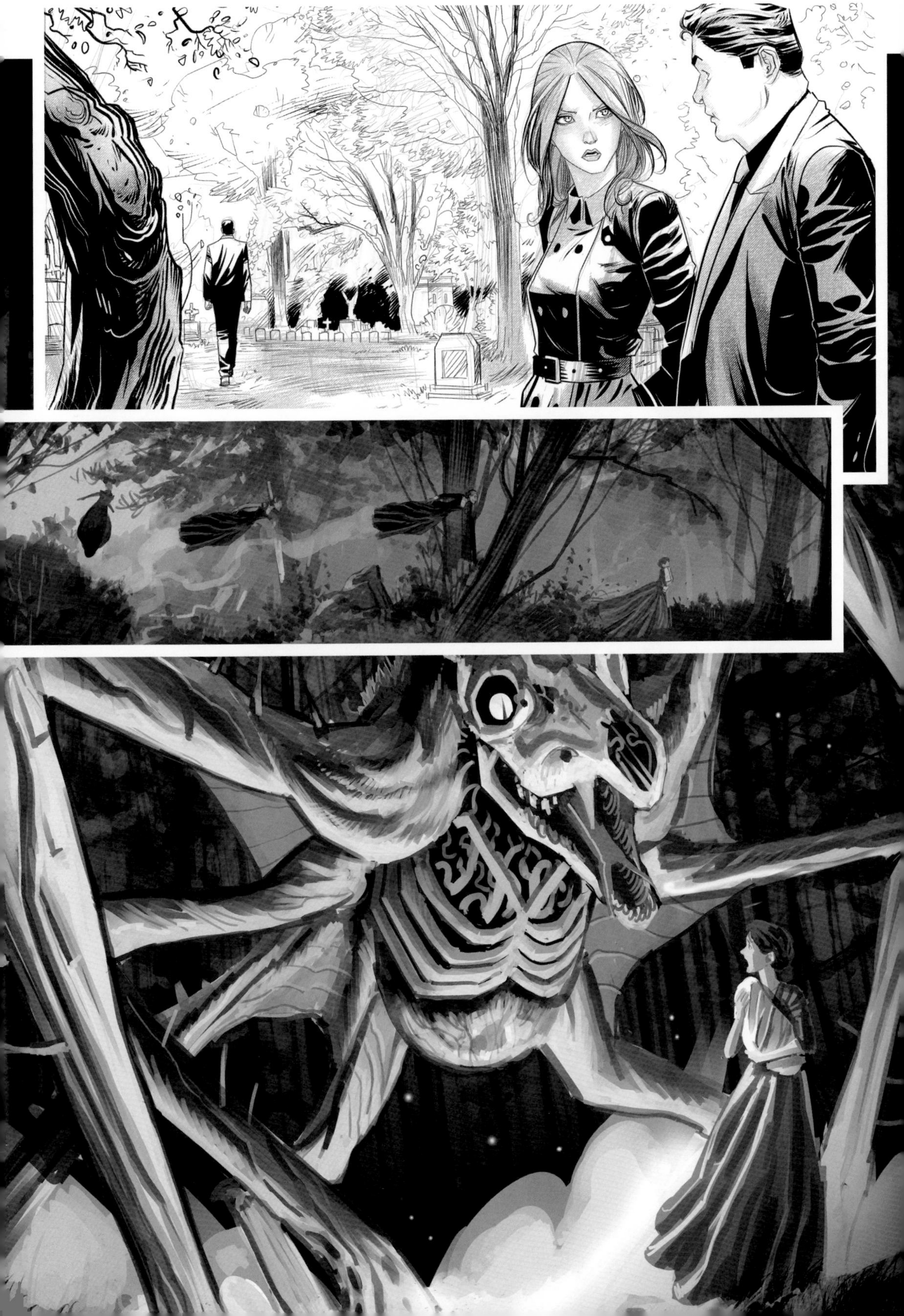

ISSUE TWELVE COVER
DAN MORA

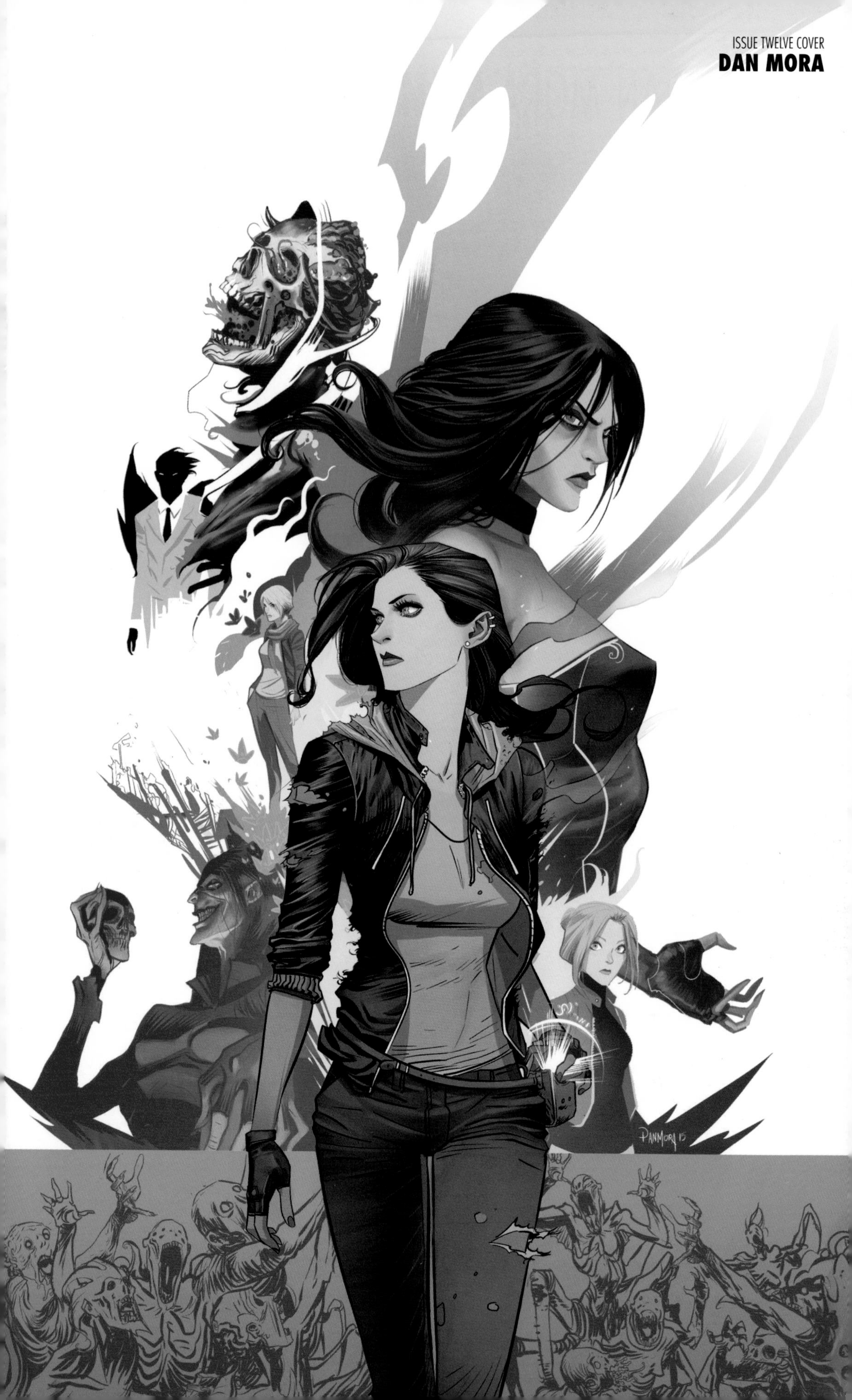

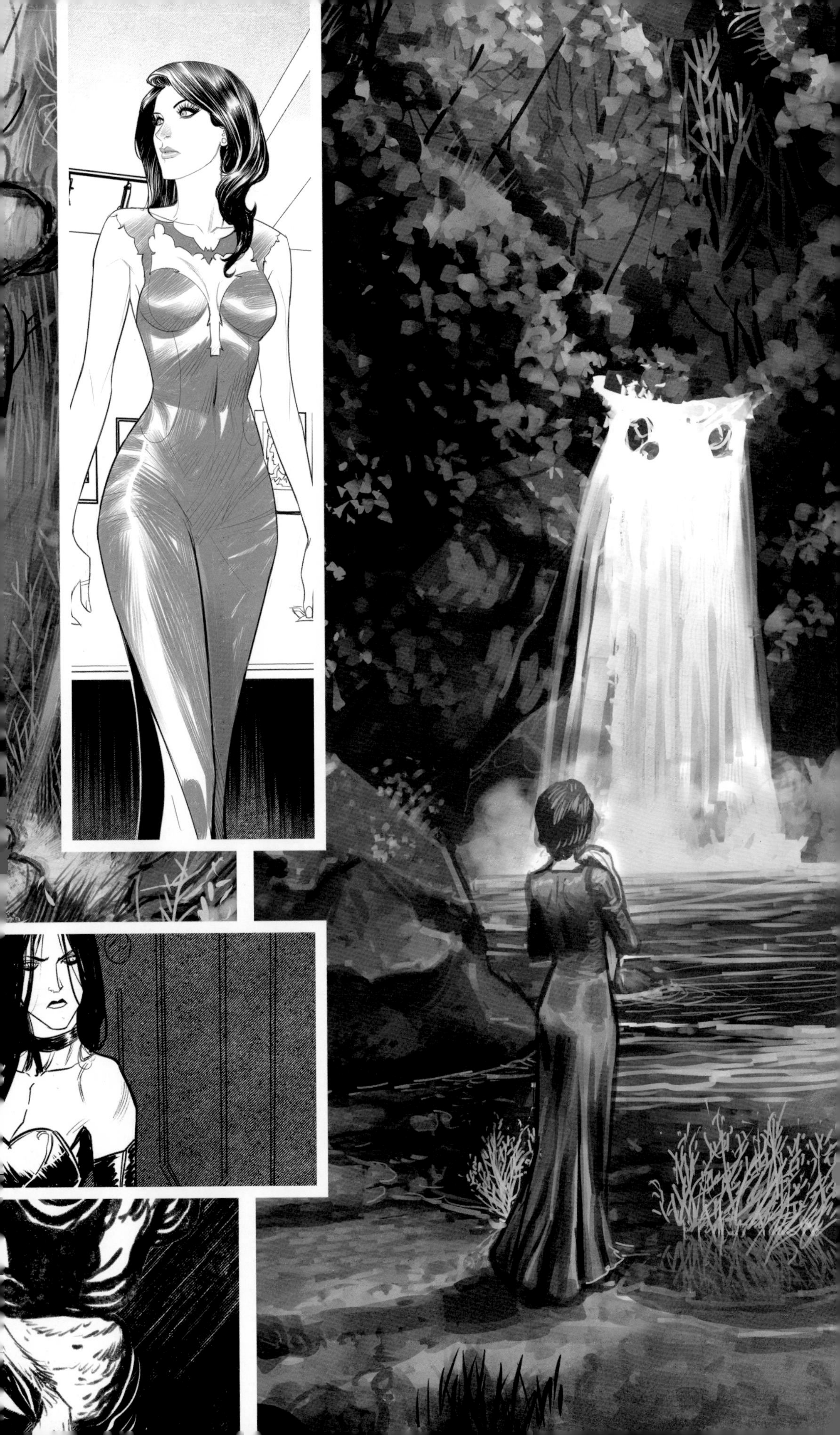